Public Policy and Politics

Series Editors: Colin Fudge and Robin

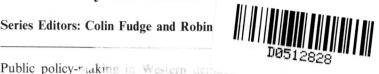

Public policy-making in Western dem...
pressures. Central values relating to the role of the state, ...
markets and the role of citizenship are now all contested and the
consensus built up around the Keynesian welfare state is under
challenge. New social movements are entering the political arena;
electronic technologies are transforming the nature of employment;
changes in demographic structure are creating heightened demands for
public services; unforeseen social and health problems are emerging;
and, most disturbing, social and economic inequalities are increasing in
many countries.

How governments – at international, national and local levels –
respond to this developing agenda is the central focus of the *Public
Policy and Politics* series. Aimed at a student, professional, practitioner
and academic readership, it aims to provide up-to-date, comprehensive
and authoritative analyses of public policy-making in practice.

The series is international and interdisciplinary in scope and bridges
theory and practice by relating the substance of policy to the politics of
the policy-making process.

Public Policy and Politics

Series Editors: Colin Fudge and Robin Hambleton

PUBLISHED

Kate Ascher, *The Politics of Privatisation: Contracting Out Public Services*

Rob Atkinson and Graham Moon, *Urban Policy in Britain: The City, the State and the Market*

Jacqueline Barron, Gerald Crawley and Tony Wood, *Councillors in Crisis: The Public and Private Worlds of Local Councillors*

Danny Burns, Robin Hambleton and Paul Hoggett, *The Politics of Decentralisation: Revitalising Local Democracy*

Aram Eisenschitz and Jamie Gough, *The Politics of Local Economic Policy: The Problems and Possibilities of Local Initiative*

Stephen Glaister, June Burnham, Handley Stevens and Tony Travers, *Transport Policy in Britain*

Christopher Ham, *Health Policy in Britain: The Politics and Organisation of the National Health Service* (third edition)

Ian Henry, *The Politics of Leisure Policy*

Peter Malpass and Alan Murie, *Housing Policy and Practice* (fifth edition)

Robin Means and Randall Smith, *Community Care: Policy and Practice* (second edition)

Gerry Stoker, *The Politics of Local Government* (second edition)

Kieron Walsh, *Public Services and Market Mechanisms: Competition, Contracting and the New Public Management*

FORTHCOMING

Tony Green and Geoff Whitty, *The Changing Politics of Education: Education Policy in Contemporary Britain*

John Solomos, *Racial Inequality and Public Policy*

Public Policy and Politics
Series Standing Order
ISBN 0–333–71705–8 hardcover
ISBN 0–333–69349–3 paperback
(outside North America only)

You can receive future titles in this series as they are published. To place a standing order please contact your bookseller or, in the case of difficulty, write to us at the address below with your name and address, the title of the series and the ISBN quoted above.

Customer Services Department, Macmillan Distribution Ltd
Houndmills, Basingstoke, Hampshire RG21 6XS, England

Community Care

Policy and Practice

Second Edition

Robin Means and Randall Smith

First edition 1994
Reprinted three times
Second edition 1998

Published by
MACMILLAN PRESS LTD
Houndmills, Basingstoke, Hampshire RG21 6XS
and London
Companies and representatives
throughout the world

ISBN 0–333–73194–8 hardcover
ISBN 0–333–73195–6 paperback

A catalogue record for this book is available
from the British Library.

This book is printed on paper suitable for recycling and made from
fully managed and sustained forest sources

10 9 8 7 6 5 4 3 2
07 06 05 04 03 02 01 00 99

Copy-edited and typeset by Povey–Edmondson
Tavistock and Rochdale, England

Printed and bound in Great Britain by
Antony Rowe Ltd, Chippenham, Wiltshire

To Joanna and Kate

Contents

List of Tables and Figures	xi
Acknowledgements	xiii
Guide to Reading the Book	xv

1 Introducing Community Care — 1
What is community care? — 2
Who are the users? Who are the carers? — 7
Introducing the community care 'players' — 11
Key issues in community care — 14

2 From Institutions to Care in the Community: The History of Neglect — 16
The long history of neglect – services for elderly people and physically impaired people — 17
Services for people with mental health problems and learning difficulties — 27
Explanations of neglect — 34
Concluding comments — 44

3 Community Care and the Restructuring of Welfare — 47
The run-up to the Griffiths Report — 47
The Griffiths Report — 52
Reactions to the Griffiths Report — 55
The White Paper on community care — 56
Further legislative change — 59
Quasi-markets and the restructuring of welfare in Britain — 61
Post-Fordism and the community care reforms — 64
Conclusion — 68

4 Towards User and Carer Empowerment? — 70
What is empowerment? — 71
Normalisation and ordinary living — 72
The fourth dimension of power — 73
Empowerment and the disability movement — 74
Common needs? Common interests? — 76
Users versus carers? — 78

Strategies of empowerment   82
Empowerment through 'exit'   83
Empowerment through 'voice'   87
Rights and empowerment   94
Empowerment through struggle   98
Conclusion   100

5 **Leaders at Last: The Changing Rôle of Social Services**   **102**
Managing change in a climate of uncertainty   102
Establishing the new funding regime   106
Establishing care management   110
Establishing purchaser–provider splits   123
Establishing a mixed economy of social care   126
Conclusion   135

6 **The Health Dimension of Community Care: Towards**
   Collaborative Working?   **137**
The health care and community care reforms   137
Collaborative working: the theory   141
Who should lead? Historical perspectives   144
What is health care? What is social care?   147
Hospital discharge and the changing rôle of the NHS   150
Continuing care and the changing health and social care
  divide   152
The lead rôle in the provision of mental health services   155
Community care planning and joint commissioning   160
Collaboration: an assessment of progress   165

7 **Housing and Community Care**   **168**
The meaning of home   168
Resettlement and the meaning of home   173
Supported housing: institution or home?   175
Mainstream housing and community care   179
Housing conditions   184
Towards an integrated response?   191
Conclusion   198

8 **European Perspectives on Community Care**   **199**
The rôle of the family in caring   200
The place of institutional care   204
The mixed economy of welfare   208
Collaboration   209
User empowerment   212

The institutions of the European Union and policy   214
The impact of EU policies on community care   217
Concluding comments   227

**9 Community Care: Achievements, Failures and Challenges
   for the Future**   **229**
The impact of the community care reforms: a stakeholder
   perspective   230
New Labour? New vision?   238
Towards a new vision after all?   241
Conclusion   245

Guide to Further Reading   247

Bibliography   250

Index   274

List of Tables and Figures

Tables

1.1 Estimate of numbers of disabled adults in Great Britain
with different types of disability (thousands)   9
4.1 Degrees of empowerment   82
5.1 Local authority social services department funding of
non-statutory organisations as percentage of total
expenditure, 1988–9   129
5.2 Potential alternative modes of provision of community
care   131
7.1 The key characteristics of institutions and home   169
7.2 Dwellings in poor condition by tenure, England and
Wales (1991/93)   184
7.3 Repair and renovation   186
7.4 Home adaptation   192
8.1 'Families are less willing to care for older relatives than
they used to be' (older people only)   202

Figures

1.1 Pressures upon social services committees   13
4.1 Job advertisement   70
4.2 Dimensions of empowerment through voice   89
4.3 Views of user and carer groups on their involvement in
community care planning in four local authorities   92
4.4 Checklist for responsive, flexible, accessible services   101
5.1 The cascade of change   115
5.2 Benchmarks for assessment practice   119
5.3 Order of priority for people living in the community:
example of a priority matrix   121
5.4 Tendering and the mixed economy of care   127
6.1 Services to be arranged and funded by health authorities
and GP fundholders   155
6.2 Relationships between the care programme approach
and other key processes and provisions   158

6.3   Making joint commissioning happen in practice   164
7.1   The lifetime homes standards   190
7.2   Housing and social services staff: key knowledge and
      skills   197
9.1   Conditions of market success   234
9.2   Examples of services available from Bradford LETS   246

Acknowledgements

Like most authors, our ability to produce a book has been dependent upon the support, advice, stimulation and criticism of a wide range of people. We have been particularly fortunate to work in an organisation, the School for Policy Studies (SPS) at the University of Bristol, which is involved in research, consultancy and teaching not only in community care, but also in health, housing and public service management. More specifically, we would like to thank Lyn Harrison (SPS), Jill Manthorpe (University of Hull) and Louise Russell (Age Concern, England) for their comments on redrafted chapters in this second edition. This has been backed up by support and feedback from our publisher Steven Kennedy. We found all their comments to be of enormous help.

The authors have been fortunate in being able to draw upon ongoing community care research at SPS, and in this respect we would like to thank the Joseph Rowntree Foundation for its funding of research on community care reform implementation, Anchor for grants to study personal finance issues for elderly people with dementia and the Department of Health for funding a workbook on housing and community care issues.

Even in such a positive environment, the production of a book is a long and arduous business. In this respect, we would like to thank family and friends for not only offering encouragement, but also for putting up with bouts of weekend and evening working. Finally, our ability to pull the book together has owed much to secretarial support from Carol Marks and Linda Price.

The authors and publishers wish to thank the following who have kindly given permission for the use of copyright material: The Office of Population Censuses and Surveys for the table from J. Martin, H. Meltzer and D. Elliot, *The Prevalence of Disability Among Adults*, 1988; the Policy Press for a table from M. Taylor, L. Hoyes, R. Lart and R. Means, *User Empowerment in Community Care: Unravelling the Issues*, 1992, an illustration from P. Hoggett, 'The Politics of Empowerment' in *Going Local*, no.19, 1992, and for the table from P. Leather and T. Morrison, *The State of UK Housing*, 1997; the Audit Commission for an illustration from *Community Care: Managing the Cascade of Change*, 1992; Personal Social Services Research Unit for a table from M. Knapp, G. Wistow, J. Forder and B. Hardy, *Markets for Social Care: Opportunities, Barriers and Implications*, 1993; Basil Blackwell Ltd for a table from G. Wistow, M. Knapp, B. Hardy and C. Allen, 'From Providing to Enabling: Local Authorities and the Mixed Economy of Social Care' in *Public Administration*, vol.70, no.1, 1992, for a table from J. Higgins, 'Defining Community Care: Realities and Myths' in *Social Policy and Administration*, vol.23, no.1, 1989, and for the table from M. Nolan and K. Caldock, 'Assessment: Identifying the Barriers to Good Practice' in *Health and Social Care in the Community*, vol.4 no.2; Professor Alan Walker and the Commission of the European Communities for a table from Eurobarometer Survey, *Age and Attitudes: Main Results from a Eurobarometer Survey*, 1993; King's Fund for a table from J. Morris, *The Power to Change: Commissioning Health and Social Services with Disabled People*, 1995; Crown Copyright for permission to use tables from Department of Health, *Building Bridges*, 1995, and R. Means, M. Brenton, L. Harrison and F. Heywood, *Making Partnerships Work in Community Care*, 1997; the Joseph Rowntree Foundation for the table from C. Cobbold, *A Cost Benefit Analysis of Lifetime Homes*, 1997.

Guide to Reading the Book

The aim of this book is to provide a context for and an overview of recent developments in community care in England and Wales. The examination of changes and continuities at national level is linked to specific local studies and to particular concerns about the rôle of the service user and carer in a mixed economy of welfare. Social services authorities were officially designated as the lead agency for community care under the National Health Service and Community Care Act 1990, though it is arguable whether adequate resources have been made available to carry out their responsibilities effectively. It is also the case that a range of agencies is involved in the delivery of community care, and the restructuring of the welfare system widened that range. Collaboration between agencies such as health and local authorities has never been easy, and their increasing number has made working together even more difficult.

These are among the themes of this book, which is aimed at students on courses for the caring professions, social policy students and the reflective practitioner. The story is still unfolding, but the authors argue that the continuities may be as important for understanding what is happening as the changes brought about by the reforms in the policy and practice of community care in the early 1990s.

Chapter 1 introduces the notion of community care and locates it in the politics of health and social care and in the legislative framework. The extent of need for community-based services is examined and the chapter ends with a scrutiny of the key issues addressed in the book. Chapter 2 offers a perspective of community care over time and suggests that there has been a long history of neglect in the development of non-institutional services. Differing explanations for this neglect are outlined. Chapter 3 places community care in the contemporary context of the restructuring of welfare in the UK, starting in the mid-1980s with the run-up to the 1988 Griffiths Report, which offered an agenda for action, and following developments through the 1989 White Paper and the 1990 legislation and its associated policy guidance. The notions of post-Fordism and quasi-markets are introduced as plausible explanations for the direction in which policy change has gone. These notions also underlie the theme of Chapter 4, which reflects on whether the reforms are likely to lead to increased involvement and participation on the part of the consumers of services – users and carers. The first part of the chapter examines ideas about normalisation and ordinary living and also focuses on the contribution to the empowerment debate of the disability movement. The second half outlines various strategies of empowerment, covering 'exit', 'voice', 'rights' and 'struggle'.

Chapter 5 looks at the problems faced by the local authority social services department as lead agency in implementing the community care reforms. The uncertain political and financial climate provides a backcloth to a commentary on the progress so far made by social services in implementing care management, developing a mixed economy of welfare, introducing the purchaser–provider split and in developing community care planning. Chapter 6 wrestles with the decades-old problem of collaboration between care agencies, particularly health and social care. It summarises theoretical approaches to collaborative working and the arguments about the differences between health and social care. Key issues are addressed such as the co-ordination of mental health services, the provision of continuing care and joint commissioning. Chapter 7 looks at the part to be played by housing in the community care context, both supported and mainstream housing. In relation to the latter, issues of availability, affordability, repair and adaptations are examined in some detail, as this has traditionally been a neglected aspect of community care. The chapter ends with a comment on the prospects for an integrated service.

Chapter 8 outlines some of the community care issues faced by some other member states of the European Union, particularly Greece, Germany, Italy and Denmark. A number of themes are pursued, including the rôle of the family in caring, the part played by institutional care, working together, user empowerment and the salience of the mixed economy of welfare arguments. In the second part of the chapter, the institutions of the European Union are described briefly, together with an outline of the EU policy process. The impact of particular EC policies on community care are followed through in relation to older and disabled people and in terms of the agencies, such as local authorities, which are providers of community care. Finally Chapter 9 takes an overview on achievements so far, problems to be faced and the likelihood of policy failure in the context of an election of a Labour government. It concludes with a plea for local authorities to develop a broader vision of community care.

1 Introducing Community Care

The NHS and Community Care Act 1990 introduced far-reaching changes into community care policy and practice in England and Wales. It gave the lead agency role to social services authorities for all the main 'core' groups of service users. This lead agency role was to take the form of stimulating a mixed economy of care through encouraging independent providers. At a strategic level, this was to be achieved through the publication of community care plans on the basis of wide consultation with key agencies and groups, including service users and carers. At an operational level, care management was to be used to ensure service users were offered flexible packages of care which drew upon the independent sector. *Caring for People*, the White Paper on community care, justified these changes by reference to the need to develop choice and user-driven services (Department of Health, 1989a) while subsequent guidance went much further in arguing that 'the rationale for this reorganisation is the empowerment of users and carers' (Department of Health/Social Service Inspectorate, 1991, p. 7).

However, these community care changes find themselves under extensive attack in the late 1990s from academics, practitioners and service users. In *Care in Chaos*, Hadley and Clough (1996) lament 'the widespread malaise which seems currently to exist in the community care services' (p. 194) and express concern that 'the new system may be ill conceived in theory and defective in practice' (p. 206). Dominelli and Hoogvelt (1996, p. 52) claim the 1990 Act brought the market and the contract culture into social work and they comment how 'social workers are increasingly drawn into becoming managers and accountants, with their time spent pushing paper and pen, or should we say exercising their fingers on the keyboards of their computers, rather than in direct work with users'. The community care reforms are seen by many as having undermined a rights-based and free system of care which placed a high emphasis upon counselling. This has been replaced by a community care approach driven by the need to ration and to charge, and controlled by managers whose central concern is to stay within budget rather than to meet need.

The central concern of *Community Care: Policy and Practice* is to explore this bleak scenario 'head on'. How truthful is this rosy picture of past provision? What concerns of central government really lay behind the 1990 Act? Has the impact of the reforms been universally bad for service users and carers? What are the prospects for the future and the implications of the election of a Labour government in May 1997? However, before these questions can begin to be tackled we need to say a little more about what we understand by the term 'community care', and how this relates to the present organisational and legislative framework.

What is community care?

Over the past thirty-five years community care has come to be almost universally espoused as a desirable objective for service users and a central pillar of policy for governments and politicians of all persuasions. An obvious starting point is for the authors to offer a clear statement about what they understand by the term 'community care'. Which groups will be covered? Will the book cover unpaid care as well as paid care? Does it include institutional care as well as domiciliary services? Which health care services are included? What does 'community' mean in the context of the term 'community care'? These are simple questions but do not necessarily have simple answers. 'Community care' has long been a contested term used by different people in different ways at different points in time.

The starting point in this definitional quest has to be the loaded power of the word 'community' within the term 'community care'. Titmuss described community care as 'the everlasting cottage-garden trailer' and went on to remark:

> Does it not conjure up a sense of warmth and human kindness, essentially personal and comforting, as loving as the wild flowers so enchantingly described by Lawrence in *Lady Chatterley's Lover*? (1968, p. 104)

Some twenty-five years later, in more prosaic language, Baron and Haldane (1992) complained that 'today we are in a period of striking certainties about the value of community care, still strangely combined with silences and absences about the details of what care in the community means, and how it is to operate for the benefit of those with special needs' (p. 3).

But where does the positive power of the term 'community care' come from? Baron and Haldane argue that it flows from the fact that 'community' is what Raymond Williams (1976) called a keyword in the development of culture and society. From the ninth century BC through to the twentieth century AD, Williams traced the use of the term 'community' to grieve for the recent passing of a series of mythical Golden Ages; each generation perceiving the past as organic and whole compared to the present. As Baron and Haldane point out, the term 'community' thus enables 'the continuous construction of an idyllic past of plenty and social harmony which acts as a critique of contemporary social relations' (p. 4). Thus the call by politicians and policy-makers to replace present systems of provision with community care feeds into this myth by implying that it is possible to recreate what many believe were the harmonious, caring and integrated communities of the past.

This perspective helps to explain the popularity of terms such as community care, community schools and community policing with politicians and policy-makers. However, a key objective of our book is to delve behind the rhetoric of community care and caring communities. For example, several authors have pointed out that individuals and not communities carry out caring work, and that unpaid care is primarily carried out by female relatives (see Chapters 2 and 4). Equally, most people, including the users of community care services, have a highly complex notion of community. For some it is a small number of local streets, and for others their sense of community may come from work or leisure networks which are not geographically based. The provision of community care services based on local authority boundaries rarely reflects how service users perceive community. A day centre may not seem like a community service to a user if they have to travel three miles by specialist bus to reach it.

An important starting point for this analytical approach to community care is to trace the emergence of the term and its changing use over time. Yet it is very difficult to pin down the exact source. In a 1961 lecture delivered to the National Association of Mental Health, Titmuss (1968) claimed he had tried and failed to discover in any precise form its social origins, but went on to reflect that

Institutional policies, both before and since the Mental Health Act of 1959, have, and without a doubt, assumed that someone knows what it means. More and more people suffering from schizophrenia, depressive illnesses and other mental handicaps have been discharged from hospitals, not cured but symptom-treated and labelled 'relieved'. More and more of the mentally subnormal have been placed under statutory supervision in the community. (p. 105)

Titmuss's concern was that the reduced reliance on hospitals would not be balanced by a major expansion of community-based services. In the following year, the then Minister of Health, Enoch Powell, took the 'policy' of community care one stage further with his 1962 Hospital Plan which launched an official closure programme for large mental health and mental handicap hospitals and their replacement by a network of services to be provided in the community by local health and welfare services.

Although the origins of the phrase are obscure, it is clear that the term 'community care' was initially used to refer to a policy shift away from hospitals and towards community-based provision for 'mentally handicapped' people and for people with mental health problems. However, it soon began to be used in reference to the provision of services for elderly people and for physically disabled people. For example, the Chief Welfare Officer at the Ministry of Health was claiming in 1964 that with regard to older people:

the true centre of the picture so far as geriatric services are concerned, really has shifted, or is rapidly shifting to care in the community supported by domiciliary services, and the important thing is to remember that residential homes are in fact a vital and most important part of community service. (Aves, 1964, p. 12)

The context of this quotation was government concern about the cost of long-term hospital care for frail elderly people. The Chief Welfare Officer was justifying a move to a cheaper form of institutional care (local authority residential care) by referring to it as a community service.

The Chief Welfare Officer included the residential home in her definition of community care. But this was increasingly challenged in the 1970s. Residential care was seen by many as an expensive form of provision which consumed resources which needed to be used to fund genuine community services such as home care, day care and sheltered housing (Bosanquet, 1978). By this definition, community care policies are about keeping people out of expensive hospital *and* residential home provision. But how was this to be achieved? *A Happier Old Age* was published by the then Labour government as a discussion document (Department of Health and Social Security, 1978) and it asked whether a combination of suitable ordinary housing, high-quality domiciliary services and more support for informal carers could keep the majority of frail elderly people out of expensive local authority residential care.

In the 1980s the definition of community care seemed to have been tightened by central government yet again. The White Paper response, *Growing Older*, to the discussion document was produced by a Conservative rather than Labour government. It argued that

> Whatever level of public expenditure proves practicable and however it is distributed, the primary sources of support and care for elderly people are informal and voluntary. . . It is the rôle of public authorities to sustain and, where necessary, develop – but never to displace – such support and care. Care in the community must increasingly mean by the community. (Department of Health and Social Security, 1981b, p. 3)

The overall message was that community care (that is, informal care) needed to be maximised, partly because it was cheaper than care based on the provision of state-provided domiciliary services. By this definition, community care becomes what Abrams (1977, p. 151) called 'the provision of help, support and protection to others by lay members of societies acting in everyday domestic and occupational settings'.

In the past, therefore, the term 'community care' has been used to argue for changes in service emphasis. The positive virtues of community care have been juxtaposed against expensive, rigid and bureaucratic alternatives, such as hospitals, residential care, and sometimes even domiciliary services. However, the Wagner Committee (1988) review of residential care found it very difficult to distinguish between residential care services and care in the community services because of the growth of sheltered housing schemes, resettlement hostels and 'core and cluster' schemes which offered a combination of support and housing in non-institutional settings. Equally, the boundaries between informal care and paid care have become blurred with the emergence of a variety of payment for caring schemes through tax allowances, social security benefits and social services payments, which are designed to increase the willingness of relatives, neighbours and volunteers to perform caring rôles.

Increasingly, 'community care' is used to refer to the full spectrum of care and services received by certain groups. This was the approach adopted by the 1989 White Paper on community care, *Caring for People*, which stated that

> Community care means providing the right level of intervention and support to enable people to achieve maximum independence and control over their own lives. For this aim to become a reality, the development of a wide range of services provided in a variety of settings is essential. These services form part of a spectrum of care, ranging from domiciliary support provided to people in their own homes, strengthened by the availability of respite care and day care for those with more intensive care needs, through sheltered housing, group homes and hostels where increasing levels of care are available, to residential care and nursing homes and long-stay hospital care for those for whom other forms of care are no longer enough. (Department of Health, 1989a, p. 9)

The White Paper explains that its focus is mainly upon the rôle of the statutory and independent sectors but that 'the reality is that most care is provided by family, friends and neighbours' (ibid.). The statutory and independent sectors are seen as responsible for providing social care (including housing), health care and appropriate social security benefits. This book takes a similarly broad view of what is meant by the term 'community care'. It thus considers not only informal support by unpaid carers but also the provision of the full spectrum of institutional and non-institutional services by the public, private and voluntary sectors.

Having said this, the problematic nature of the 1990 Act as a definitional source needs to be recognised. The Act told social services authorities they were the lead agency in community care and required social services authorities to produce community care plans. However, the encouragement for this lead rôle to involve the development of care management systems, purchaser–provider splits and a mixed economy of social care is to be found mainly in the community care White Paper (Department of Health, 1989a) and subsequent policy guidance (Department of Health, 1990). The development of these tasks required social services to draw upon a patchwork of previous law. Thus, the National Assistance Act 1948 remains the pivotal piece of legislation for residential provision while the legislative underpinning for the provision of domiciliary services is more complex. For example, the Chronically Sick and Disabled Persons Act 1970 made local authorities responsible for finding out the numbers of disabled people within their area and required them to offer a range of services to those persons. The Disabled Persons (Services, Consultation and Representation) Act 1986 increased the rights of disabled people to be assessed for such services.

And the law has continued to mushroom. For example, the Carers (Recognition of Services) Act 1995 gave carers, who are providing substantial and regular care, a right to request a separate assessment of their own needs. The Community Care (Direct Payments) Act 1996 has made it much easier for local authorities to develop personal assistance schemes based on cash payments to enable service users to purchase their own care packages.

Who are the users? Who are the carers?

The White Paper (Department of Health, 1989a) seemed clear at first glance about who are the users of community care services:

> Many people need some extra help and support at some stage in their lives, as a result of illness or temporary disability. Some people, as a result of the effects of old age, of mental illness including dementia, of mental handicap or physical disability or sensory impairment, have a continuing need for care on a longer-term basis. People with drug and alcohol related disorders, people with multiple handicaps and people with progressive illnesses such as AIDS or multiple sclerosis may also need community care at some time. (p. 10)

The emphasis of this book is equally broad although it concentrates most of its comment upon the traditional main client groups, namely older people, physically impaired people, people with mental health problems and people with learning difficulties. However, it does this with a recognition that client groups are really bureaucratic and/or medical labels which rarely reflect how service users and carers perceive their personal assistance needs. Such labels have a number of negative consequences. First, they have the effect of dividing service users against each other in the scramble for resources rather than facilitating a coming together to campaign for the appropriate resourcing of health and welfare systems (see Chapter 4). Second, they fail to recognise that many people cut across these traditional categories. For instance, physically impaired people get old (Zarb, 1993), as do people with learning difficulties (Walker *et al.*, 1996). The danger is that social services will respond to only some aspects of the support needs of such individuals and this will be determined by the client focus of the team their social worker is based in. Thus, Walker *et al.* (1996) in their study of 120 people with learning difficulties in the community found that

> For the most part, the client group-orientated health and social services culture has not begun to address the emergence of this new user group and, as a result, they are falling between services for people with learning difficulties and those for older people. This double jeopardy is resulting in older people with learning difficulties being even more excluded and marginalised than those who fall neatly into the service provision categories. (p. 56)

Third, much service provision, especially in areas such as supported housing, targets narrowly defined groups such as drug abusers, homeless people or people with mental health problems (Means, 1996a). People in need of accommodation and support are thus encouraged to define themselves as drug abusers, homeless people or people with mental health problems rather than as individuals who might face all three challenges. The requirements of many people cut across narrow administrative categories but they still feel obliged to present themselves as having one particular dominant need if they want to get help. Client group categories encourage service-led rather than user-driven community care provision.

Finally, it should be remembered that those 'known' to the community care system are only a small percentage of those with support needs or those providing informal caring services. However, attempts to research prevalence rates and then to estimate from this the numbers in need of additional support through community care provision are fraught with difficulties. The Office of Population Censuses and Surveys (OPCS) research in the mid-1980s is still often quoted as the main evidence on the prevalence, range and severity of 'disability' in Britain. The researchers distinguished thirteen different types of 'disability' based on the international classification of impairments, disabilities and handicaps used by the World Health Organisation (see Table 1.1). They also developed a classification system for severity of 'disability' which could be used to classify people with different numbers and types of 'disabilities'. The severity of 'disability' in each of the thirteen areas was established for each individual and the three highest scores were then combined so that people could be allocated to an overall severity category. Category one was for the least severe and category ten was for the most severe.

TABLE 1.1 Estimate of numbers of disabled adults in Great Britain with different types of disability (thousands)

Type of disability	In private households	In establishments	Total population
Locomotion	4,005	327	4,332
Reaching and stretching	1,083	147	1,230
Dexterity	1,572	165	1,737
Seeing	1,384	284	1,668
Hearing	2,365	223	2,588
Personal care	2,129	354	2,483
Continence	957	185	1,142
Communication	989	213	1,202
Behaviour	1,172	175	1,347
Intellectual functioning	1,182	293	1,475
Consciousness	188	41	229
Eating, drinking, digesting	210	66	276
Disfigurement	391	*	*

* Data not provided.
Source: Martin, Meltzer and Elliot (1988) p. 25.

With regard to adults, it was estimated that six million people in Great Britain have one or more impairments, of whom 400,000 are living in some kind of communal establishment. One million adults are assigned to the lowest severity category. Smaller numbers are identified in each successive category, with 200,000 in category ten. Elderly people dominated the two highest degrees of severity:

> The rate of disability at this level of severity did not rise steeply until age 70, and rose very steeply after 80. Altogether 64% of adults with this degree of severity were aged 70 or over; 41% were aged 80 or over. (Martin, Meltzer and Elliot, 1988, p. xii)

In terms of types of impairment, problems of locomotion were found to dominate (over four million adults) followed by difficulties with hearing and personal care (see Table 1.1). A separate report was published on disability amongst children (Bone and Meltzer, 1989) and this concluded that 360,000 children in Great Britain have some degree of 'disability', of which 2 per cent live in some kind of communal establishment. The most common difficulties are to do with behaviour, followed by impairments in the areas of communication, locomotion and continence.

However, great care needs to be taken with this type of approach to defining disability, for a number of reasons. First, the overall figures are open to challenge as over- or under-estimates because they are very dependent on the assumptions made by the researchers. For example, the Mental Health Foundation (1993) has estimated that three million Britons have severe mental health problems and twelve million adults approach general practitioners every year with a mental health problem, but only seven million are correctly diagnosed as needing help. Second, the OPCS approach is driven by medical rather than social assessments of the meaning and implications of disability. Hence, the focus is on personal inadequacy or functional limitation, rather than on the disabling impact of many physical and social environments (Abberley, 1991). For example, many people defined as having major locomotion difficulties in the OPCS survey may be suffering from a societal failure to build housing to mobility or wheelchair standard rather than from their own 'limitations'. The OPCS approach can also be criticised for trying to draw strict lines on the types and severity of disabilities experienced by individuals where the situation is in reality much more blurred and perhaps constantly changing. The episodic nature of some mental health problems is but one example of this.

The OPCS surveys also confirmed the extent to which disabled people receive help and support from informal carers. The 1985 General Household Survey indicated that there were 3.5 million female carers and 2.5 million male carers, but that women were far more likely than men to be full-time carers. Only 6 per cent of those carers were in contact with social workers while only 23 per cent were receiving back-up from the home help service and 7 per cent from meals-on-wheels services (Green, 1988). Since then the research on caring has become extensive and Finch (1989) has argued that this indicates a 'hierarchy of obligations', based around four principles:

1. The marriage relationship takes primacy, so that one's spouse becomes the first support for married people.
2. The parent–child relationship is the second source of obligation, with children being a major source of support for elderly parents and parents being the principal supporters of adult handicapped children.
3. People who are members of a household are major providers of care, so that a child who shares a home with his/her parents is much more likely to be giving them personal care than any siblings living away from the family home.

4. Gender is a crucial factor, so that women are much more likely to become the carers when there is an apparent choice between male and female relatives.

For feminist social scientists, the gendered nature of this caring activity has long been a major issue within their more general critique of the impact of the welfare state on women (Wilson, 1977; Land, 1978). Their central complaint is that women are carrying out unpaid domestic labour to the advantage of both central government and of men. The consequence of this for women is stress, poverty and a financial reliance on men and the state (Finch and Groves, 1983; Dalley, 1996).

Introducing the community care 'players'

The last section looked at the most important stakeholders in any community care system, namely service users and informal carers. However, there is also a need to profile the professional stakeholders at both the national and local levels.

It is thus necessary to say something about the policy and organisational context which is responsible for generating legislation and for ensuring its implementation. Since our central concern is the community care reforms which have allocated a lead agency role to social services, our mapping focus will be on social services departments and the various local actors and organisations which influence their attempts to fund, co-ordinate and deliver community care provision.

Our starting point is to stress the need to grasp the complexity and variety of social services departments (SSDs) in England and Wales. Challis (1990, p. 2) has argued that 'the claim which SSDs can make to being something special in the world of organisation does not rest on any one unique feature but upon the dazzling array of problematic characteristics which they exhibit'. These include the accountability of officers to members, the wide range of responsibilities, the variety of employed staff and high media interest. One consequence of this situation, and in particular the location of social services in local government, has been a history of organisational variation. Individual departments can split their activities by such categories as client age (for example, child care services and adult services), geography (for example, north and south of the authority) and function (for example, field services and residential care services) and these dimensions can be combined in a variety of complex ways. Increasingly, this picture is further complicated by the growth of combined housing and social services departments.

Variations in organisational form have long been matched by variations in the range and depth of services provided by different social services authorities. A mid-1980s study by the Audit Commission (1985) on services for elderly people in seven different authorities found wide differences, both in terms of residential places per thousand elderly people and in terms of expenditure on domiciliary services. The following chapters will show how the 1990 Act has encouraged further organisational variation in terms of such issues as approaches to care management and purchaser–provider splits.

Such organisational and service variation is partly a reflection of the fact that social services are part of local government, where councillors from different political parties may have opposing views about what kinds of services should be provided and how best they should be delivered. Clough (1990) provides one of the few detailed considerations of social services departments as a part of local government. He describes both the formal policy-making system of the full social services committee and also the more informal meetings and contacts which ensure that most decisions are made prior to full committee meetings. In deciding on priorities for future service developments, local authorities vary in the extent to which they are officer or councillor-driven. Tensions between the two are common, partly because of the external pressures they face (see Figure 1.1). Many of these are top-down pressures from central government, flowing from such factors as the strengths and weaknesses of the legislation, Treasury-driven financial restrictions as well as the guidance issued by the Department of Health on good practice. Against this, councillors are struggling with a range of professional opinions from social services managers, health managers and others about the direction that community care policy should take in their authority. Both the local professionals and those responsible for central government guidance also make reference to research-based evidence to justify their views. Finally, members see themselves as the conduit for the views of local people in terms of public consultation. However, professional staff are also increasingly taking responsibility for organising consultation meetings with specific groups of service users and carers, so as to increase the ability of such groups to influence service developments, while the disability movement is calling for fundamental changes to the way professionals engage with the consumers of their services.

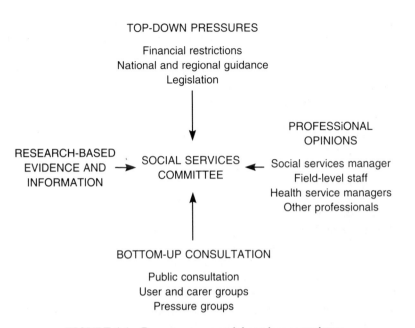

TOP-DOWN PRESSURES

Financial restrictions
National and regional guidance
Legislation

PROFESSiONAL
OPINIONS

RESEARCH-BASED
EVIDENCE AND
INFORMATION

SOCIAL SERVICES
COMMITTEE

Social services manager
Field-level staff
Health service managers
Other professionals

BOTTOM-UP CONSULTATION

Public consultation
User and carer groups
Pressure groups

FIGURE 1.1   Pressures upon social services committees

Working out these conflicting pressures in respect of the community care reforms is a central focus of this book. This section concludes by examining the top-down pressures from central government. What are the mechanisms by which guidance is issued by central government to local authorities on how they should develop services? In terms of the legislation, much of it is permissive and discretionary in nature rather than mandatory and authoritative. In the past, various attempts have been made by central government to establish service norms for provision such as residential care and the home help service, and these have usually been expressed as the number of places required per thousand of the care group. However, more recently such norms have been seen as idiosyncratic in that the origins and justification for the norms are difficult to pin down. Equally, they are seen by central government as problematic because they can be used by local authorities and pressure groups to lobby for more resources in order to fund service expansion to meet those norms.

This move away from service norms has not stopped central government sending local authorities a mass of guidance on how best to implement legislation and on how they might improve the quality of the services they deliver or commission. Much of this is issued through the Social Services Inspectorate of the Department of Health. Social services authorities are also subjected to various other kinds of inspection and guidance. The Audit Commission is a quango with a remit to improve the economy, efficiency and effectiveness of the work of local authorities and health authorities. It has published some of the most influential reviews of local authority performance in the provision of community care services (see Chapter 3). Since July 1996 the Social Services Inspectorate and the Audit Commission have been carrying out a rolling programme of joint reviews of 20 social services authorities per year.

Key issues in community care

Many of the key issues and dilemmas in community care which form the central concerns of this book have already been touched upon in this chapter, which concludes by drawing out five of the most important debates. The first debate concerns the most appropriate rôle, if any, for institutions such as hospitals, residential homes and nursing homes in the provision of health and social care to the main community care groups. The next two chapters examine in some detail the emergence of institutions as the main form of provision and subsequent attempts to shift service delivery towards approaches which enable people to remain within their own homes. Later chapters consider whether the early implementation of the community care reforms was driven by the new funding regime for residential and nursing homes to the detriment of the development of innovative and non-institutional services. In addition, policies of institutional closure will not necessarily lead to the improved well-being of service users unless good-quality care services are backed up by housing policies which deliver affordable and appropriate housing to those with personal assistance and care needs, an issue which is explored in Chapter 7.

The second key issue concerns the respective rôles and responsibilities of the individual, the family and the state. Again this is a debate which our book will trace from the late Victorian period. A continuity in emphasis upon the responsibilities of female relatives is found, although in the context of the state showing an increased willingness to support such carers through the provision of publicly funded services. A key question is whether the community care reforms represent an incremental development of such an approach, or a more radical change of policy, signalling the beginning of a state withdrawal from this arena apart from the provision of service funding for the least well off and those most 'at risk'.

The third key issue is more clear-cut in that Conservative governments have been unambiguous about their desire to stimulate a mixed economy of social care in which the primary rôle of local authorities as the lead agency is to act as enablers rather than as service providers. But this raises fundamental questions about the willingness and ability of local authorities to stimulate and then manage such markets, and it also makes essential an analysis of the likely impact of such a mixed economy upon users and carers. What are the main dangers in strengthening the rôle of markets in community care and what can the experience of other countries tell us about this? The reforms are very much about developing markets, but this does not resolve the need to establish effective systems of collaboration and co-ordination between a wide range of different agencies at both strategic and operational levels. The challenge of effective working together is thus our fourth key issue. The whole history of community care provision in this country is characterised by disputes about the respective rôles of social services, health and housing agencies. Have the community care reforms proved helpful in reducing such tensions, or do major areas of argument still remain?

One final key issue, and the most important one in the opinion of the authors, concerns user and carer empowerment. The justification for the community care reforms came from the critique of past practice which argued that community care systems were being driven by the interests of the producers (the professionals) rather than the consumers (the clients and carers). As a result, service users and carers are offered little choice or flexibility, and in general they lack power compared with the professionals. A key test of the community care reforms is whether or not they have had a positive or negative impact upon the empowerment of service users.

In addressing such fundamental issues about an important and rapidly changing area of public policy, the tendency is to focus down upon the main changes and their likely impact without any detailed consideration of the earlier development of provision. There is also a temptation to become so fascinated by the change elements that the continued relevance of certain basic assumptions and ongoing debates becomes forgotten. Chapter 2 will therefore consider, outline and discuss the long history of neglect of service provision for elderly disabled people and other 'Cinderella' groups.

2 From Institutions to Care in the Community: The History of Neglect

This chapter discusses the historical development of social care and health provision for elderly people and for people with physical impairments, learning difficulties and mental health problems. The response to the perceived needs of all these groups was overwhelmingly institutional in the nineteenth century and early twentieth century. Current services for these groups carry this institutional legacy, and present community care policies are, at least in part, an attempt to shake off that legacy. Thus the inclusion of this chapter is based on the strong belief that a knowledge and understanding of community care history is of practical value to busy social care managers, field-level staff and students as well as of interest to the community care academic. Those struggling with contemporary policy issues can be supported through a grasp of the way the current situation came about. Undertaking contemporary social history certainly has its own intellectual justification, but it also offers to the practitioner a perspective on the basis of which she or he can understand the dilemmas and the problems of today's agenda. As Parker (1988, p. 3) has argued in the context of residential care, no informed conclusions about the future can be reached without an understanding of key external factors and 'that, in turn, cannot be done satisfactorily without some understanding and appreciation of those forces that have shaped its history'.

The history of community care services is highly complex. Therefore tackling this theme in one chapter of a textbook risks the danger of oversimplifying events and issues. No attempt will be made to provide a detailed history for all services since such accounts exist elsewhere for most of the main care groups. Rather the focus will be on the extent of service neglect in terms of priority for resources and in terms of the quality of what has been provided from the resources made available. In the 1950s and 1960s, critics of this neglect often referred to the 'Cinderella services' or the 'Cinderella groups'. In terms of priority for resources, they were always waiting for a fairy godmother to arrive and get them to the ball. The second half of the chapter goes on to explore the main explanations which have been put forward to account for this neglect.

The long history of neglect – services for elderly people and physically impaired people

Through much of the Victorian period, there was little recognition of a social group, definable as elderly people, who needed special provision because of their age. Elderly people, and especially elderly men, were expected to work until they died. Those elderly people who were unable to support themselves in the community through the labour market or with the help of relatives were often forced to enter the workhouse, where no distinction was made between them and other paupers. The stereotype of the workhouse is one of brutality, although research suggests that regimes were often more neglectful in terms of boredom and regimentation rather than anything else (Crowther, 1981) and that there was also considerable local variation in practice (Digby, 1978).

However, a variety of pressures began to change the rôle of the Poor Law in meeting the needs of older people from the late Victorian period onwards. Technological changes were seen as forcing older workers out of the labour market through no fault of their own and into dependence upon Poor Law indoor and outdoor relief. Social researchers such as Booth were chronicling the extent of poverty in old age and calling for the establishment of a national system of old age pensions (Martin, 1990). Major pension legislation was passed in 1908, 1925, 1940 and 1948. However, it would be wrong to believe that this was solely a reflection of societal concern about older people. Increasingly, pension developments were driven by concerns about younger workers. As Roebuck (1979) explains:

> In the 1920s the demand for the reduction of the pension age was supported less by a concern for old age poverty than for the working age poverty caused by unemployment. After a brief post-war boom, England entered a period of chronic depression and unemployment and there was a growing feeling that the pension age should be reduced, partly in the interests of the elderly, but mainly in the interest of unemployed younger people. All political parties made the lowering of the pension age a major election issue in the mid-1920s in the hope that this lowering of the pension age would reduce unemployment. (p. 423)

The complex system of contributory and non-contributory pension arrangements which emerged resulted in the gradual removal of older people from the labour market and the social construction of the concept of retirement (Phillipson, 1982). Nevertheless, large numbers of elderly people continued to enter the workhouse, where they became an increasingly dominant group (Martin, 1990). Meanwhile, workhouse provision for older people was itself undergoing change with separate medical provision for the 'chronic sick' gradually emerging as well as a more general segregation of older people from other inmates in some institutions. Major organisational change of the Poor Law system was introduced by the Local Government Act 1929, through which the best Poor Law hospitals were retitled public health hospitals and became the responsibility of local authority health committees, and hence no longer part of the Poor Law system. However, these hospitals were almost entirely focused on the acute sick, rather than medical provision for older people, who were usually seen as chronic cases.

The remaining medical provision together with other workhouse provision also ceased to be the responsibility of the 62 Poor Law boards, and was transferred to 145 counties and county boroughs, each of which was required to establish a public assistance committee. The workhouse was retitled the public assistance institution (PAI). However, the 1929 Act made little attempt to abolish the taint of pauperism. For example, entry to a PAI meant that the new elderly 'inmate' was disqualified from receiving a pension unless he or she was admitted specifically for medical treatment and even then pension rights were lost after three months. Equally, the principle of family responsibility for destitute people was maintained. The Poor Law Act 1930 stated that

> It should be the duty of the father, grandfather, mother, grandmother, husband or child, of a poor, old, blind, lame or impotent person, or other poor person, not able to work, if possessed of sufficient means, to relieve and maintain that person not able to work.

In other words, an application for relief involved an assessment of the means of near relatives, who were also expected to make a contribution to those in institutional care.

Restrictive regulations remained in force about different elements of the institutional regime such as clothing, the retention of personal possessions, visiting rights and the ability to take days out. As Roberts (1970, p. 26) put it, most elderly inmates continued to sleep 'in large dormitories, sat on hard chairs, looked out on cabbage patches diversified by concrete, were separated by sex and, except on one day a week, could not pass the gates without permission'. Disquiet about this situation developed in the late 1930s. For example, Matthews (undated) called for more colour to be brought into the lives of elderly people in institutions 'through contact with visitors from the outside world, by providing occupations as well as entertainments and by introducing more variety into their food, clothing and surroundings' (p. 13). A campaign emerged calling for the introduction of pocket money for inmates. Some public assistance committees developed small homes with more liberal regimes, although they were usually reserved for 'women of the more gentle type' or men of 'the merit class' (quoted in Means and Smith, 1985, p. 22).

A more detailed picture of life in the medical and non-medical parts of public assistance institutions emerged during and just after the Second World War. It was a portrait of extensive neglect (Means and Smith, 1985, chapters 2 and 3; Titmuss, 1976). With regard to the so-called 'elderly chronic sick', there seems to have been a shortage of both beds and high-quality care. Writing in the late 1940s, McEwan and Laverty (1949) argued that the 1929 Act had a disastrous impact upon people with long-term health care needs since 'many of the new and aspiring municipal hospitals got rid of their undesirable chronic sick . . . sending them to Public Assistance Institutions to upgrade their own medical services' (p. 9). This placed added pressure upon the medical wards of public assistance institutions, many of which could not cope with the increased demand for beds, and so elderly patients often had to be 'housed' elsewhere in the institutions. For example, in Bradford:

In the Public Assistance Hospitals (The Park and Thornton View) . . . patients are discharged or returned from the chronic sick wards to the ambulant or 'house' section. . . In The Park, where the chronic sick wards were overcrowded, the most fit (but often frail) patients had to be sent to the ambulant wards to make room for admissions to the hospital section. There was, in consequence, a proportion of sick or disabled people in the ambulant section, where they had to remain, often confined to bed, there being no room for them in hospital. (p. 8)

The overall situation was further worsened by the creation of a 300,000 bed Emergency Medical Service at the outbreak of the Second World

War since this involved the discharge of 140,000 patients in just two days. Many of the reserved beds were in PAIs and one commentator of the time claimed that

> the people who fared worst of all were the chronically sick, the bed-ridden, the paralysed, the aged, people suffering from advanced cancer or from tuberculosis who were discharged in their hundreds from public institutions to their own homes, where they could get little, if any, care, where in all too many cases they were regarded as an intolerable burden on their relatives, and even to houses from which all their relatives had been evacuated to the country. (Morris, 1940, p. 189)

As the war progressed, further problems emerged. Many elderly patients who remained in PAI hospitals were in danger from bombing raids but there was government reluctance to move them. The ability to manage outside the hospital was undermined by the disruptions of war and so 'thousands who had formerly been nursed at home were clamouring for admission to hospitals when families were split up, when homes were damaged or destroyed, and when the nightly trek to the shelter became a part of normal life for Londoners' (Titmuss, 1976, p. 448). Some of these problems eased, but the extent to which such hospitals continued to fail to offer effective treatment to their 'chronic sick' patients was underlined by the government hospital surveys of the 1940s. Ten survey teams were appointed in 1941, some by the Minister of Health and some in conjunction with the Nuffield Provincial Hospitals Trust to cover both voluntary and public hospitals. The aim of the surveys was to gather information about existing hospital facilities as a basis for future planning for a possible National Health Service. The findings were drawn together in *The Domesday Book of the Hospital Services* which stressed how the surveys outlined the haphazard growth and lack of planning within existing hospital services. The Domesday Book showed how care for the 'chronic sick' received the bitterest comments from the investigators:

> All are agreed that 'the reproach of the masses of undiagnosed and untreated cases of chronic type which litter our Public Assistance Institutions must be removed'. Without proper classification and investigation, at present young children and senile dements are 'banded together' in these institutions, along with many elderly patients whom earlier diagnosis and treatment might have enabled

to return to their homes . . . 'The great essential is that every patient should be thoroughly examined and treated with a view to restoration to a maximum degree of activity. Only if treatment is unsuccessful or is clearly useless, should he be regarded as chronically sick', and 'even then (he) should be subject to periodic review'. (Nuffield Provincial Hospitals Trust, 1946, p. 16)

All the investigators called for hospital services and accommodation to be completely divorced from public assistance institutions.

The subsequent establishment of the National Health Service in 1946 did bring the PAI hospitals under the same administrative system as other types of hospital provision. The Domesday Book did generate government awareness of the cost of blocked hospital beds from the failure both to tackle the acute illnesses of elderly patients and to provide them with appropriate rehabilitation services. Elements of the medical profession also began to argue the need to develop the specialism of geriatric medicine so as to transform the quality of medical care available to elderly patients (Martin, 1995). There is not the space in this chapter to trace the development of hospital-based geriatric medicine after the Second World War. However, it remained a low-status route for medical graduates and a low priority for health care expenditure. Some impressive initiatives did emerge but many elderly people were classified as non-curable and placed in long-stay annexes and supervised by visiting GPs. Martin has argued that these annexes were little better than the overcrowded chronic wards of the inter-war years.

The Second World War also had a negative impact on the ability of elderly people to remain in their own homes even when they had no major health problems. Support from children was reduced. Others were made homeless as a result of bombing raids. One consequence was that 'respectable' elderly people were being pushed towards PAIs, as were many elderly people definable as war victims or casualties. Many felt that regimes of PAIs and their continued association with pauperism were inappropriate for such people. A campaign around these issues emerged in spring 1943 as a result of a letter which appeared in the *Manchester Guardian*. The letter was entitled 'A Workhouse Visit' and spoke of 'a frail, sensitive, refined old woman' of 84 who was forced to live in the regime described in the following extract:

But down each side of the ward were ten beds, facing one another. Between each bed and its neighbour was a small locker and a straight-backed, wooden uncushioned chair. On each chair sat an old woman in workhouse dress, upright, unoccupied. No library books or wireless. Central heating, but no open fire. No easy chairs. No pictures on the walls . . . There were three exceptions to the upright old women. None was allowed to lie on her bed at any time throughout the day, although breakfast is at 7 a.m., but these three, unable any longer to endure their physical and mental weariness, had crashed forward, face downwards, on to their immaculate bed-spreads and were asleep. (Quoted in Samson, 1944, p. 47)

The subsequent Nuffield survey committee on the problems of ageing and the care of old people which was chaired by Seebohm Rowntree indicated that poor conditions and restrictive regimes were not unusual:

Day-rooms in such institutions are usually large and cheerless with wooden Windsor armchairs placed around the walls. Floors are mainly bare boards with brick floors in lavatories, bathrooms, kitchens and corridors. In large urban areas such institutions may accommodate as many as 1,500 residents of various types, including more than a thousand aged persons. (Rowntree, 1980, p. 64)

The survey committee confirmed that rules in these large institutions were often harsh or harshly administered, while apathy was widespread among the residents.

The National Assistance Act 1948 was presented to Parliament as the solution to these problems. Section 21 of the Act stated that 'it should be the duty of every local authority . . . to provide residential accommodation for persons who are by reasons of age, infirmity or any other circumstances in need of care and attention which is not otherwise available to them'. Townsend (1964) argued in *The Last Refuge* that changing the names of PAIs to residential homes and transferring responsibility for running them from public assistance committees to health/welfare committees had achieved little. This is perhaps a little unfair. The old system of family responsibility for maintenance was abolished and users were now perceived as residents who contributed to their keep through their pension, although they were allowed to retain five shillings for pocket money (Means and Smith, 1985). However, in many respects, the tradition of neglect continued. For example, Townsend (1964) reported that ex-PAIs 'accounted for just over half the accommodation used by county and county borough councils, for just under half the residents and for probably over three-fifths of the old people actually admitted in the course of a year' (p. 190). With regard to the thirty-nine former PAIs visited by Townsend, 57 per cent of the accommodation was in rooms with at least ten beds. Basic amenities such as handbasins, toilets and baths were not only insufficient, but were often difficult to reach, badly distributed and of poor quality. With regard to staff, Townsend found that many were middle-aged and elderly persons who had given 'a lifetime's service under the old Poor Law as well as the new administration' (p. 39). Townsend felt:

> it would be idle to pretend that many of them were imbued with the more progressive standards of personal care encouraged by the Ministry of Health, geriatricians, social workers and others since the war. . . Some were unsuitable, by any standards, for the tasks they performed, men and women with authoritarian attitudes inherited from Poor Law days who provoked resentment and even terror among infirm people. (p. 39)

In conclusion, Townsend argued that the main shortcoming was not the failure to improve the quality of residential buildings and staff, but rather the failure to develop community-based services so as to reduce the need for people to enter institutional care.

The legislative power to provide social care services in the community was very slow to develop and is a further indication of neglect, especially towards elderly people. Section 29 of the National Assistance Act 1948 did empower local authorities 'to promote the welfare of persons who are blind, deaf or dumb and others, who are substantially and permanently handicapped by illness, injury or congenital deformity'. Nevertheless, it remained *ultra vires* for local authorities to develop preventive services for most frail elderly people, with the exception of home care, where legal empowerment was provided through the National Health Service Act 1946. Under the 1948 Act, local authorities could not develop their own meals-on-wheels services, chiropody facilities, laundry services, visiting schemes or counselling services for elderly people, a situation which led Parker (1965) to remark:

> The concern to maintain and foster family life evident in the Children Act was completely lacking in the National Assistance Act. The latter made no attempt to provide any sort of substitute

family life for old people who could no longer be supported by their own relatives. Institutional provision was accepted without question. (p. 106)

The belief of the legislators behind the 1948 Act was that domiciliary services were an 'extra frill' and so could be left to voluntary organisations, such as old people's welfare committees (now Age Concern), the W(R)VS and the Red Cross to develop. A complex patchwork of visiting services, day centres, meals services and chiropody did emerge but much of this provision was not easily available or was unevenly spread geographically, despite attempts by central government to develop the planning rôle of local authorities (Sumner and Smith, 1969). For example, Harris (1961) carried out a survey of 453 meals-on-wheels schemes and found that 40 per cent had difficulties finding enough volunteers, 40 per cent of recipients received a meal on only one day a week and 162 schemes closed completely for part of the year.

However, legislative change to empower local authorities occurred very slowly despite growing research evidence of the paucity of services being provided through the voluntary sector (Means and Smith, 1985, chapter 6). The National Assistance (Amendment) Act 1962 allowed local authorities to provide meals services directly for the first time, whereas before they could only provide a grant to enable a voluntary organisation to do so. The Health Services and Public Health Act 1968 gave local authorities the general power to promote the welfare of elderly people, while the National Health Service Act 1977 made home care a mandatory responsibility rather than a discretionary power as previously. The implementation of the 1968 Act was delayed until April 1971 to coincide with the creation of unified social services departments. These new departments were soon dominated by child care concerns, especially after the death of Maria Colwell in January 1973 (Parton, 1983). Research studies confirmed that social services departments maintained client group hierarchies with elderly people at the bottom so that elderly clients were usually allocated to unqualified staff on the grounds that intervention was perceived as likely to be routine and unglamorous (Bowl, 1986). Hopes of a major expansion of domiciliary services were further hit by the first tremors on the public expenditure front in the mid-1970s with the oil crisis. Increasingly, debate shifted away from the need for overall increases in social care expenditure towards arguments about the need for a shift of priorities between domiciliary and residential provision (DHSS, 1978).

Less detailed contemporary research has been carried out on the historical development of health and welfare services for physically impaired people. However, several authors have claimed that 'with the Industrial Revolution and the advent of machinery designed to be operated by the able-bodied, disabled people were progressively excluded from the workplace' (Drake, 1996, p. 150). Thus, the combination of new work patterns and the breakdown of traditional community support systems imposed dependency upon many disabled people and made them heavily reliant upon welfare services. This was not very different from the experience of elderly people. Large numbers of physically disabled people were forced to live in institutions.

At first glance, Section 29 of the National Assistance Act 1948 seemed to ensure that people with physical, visual and sensory impairments were not neglected in the post-war period especially when compared with frail elderly people, since this section gave local authorities the power to develop domiciliary services for these groups. However, this was largely illusory, for reasons pointed out by Eyden (1965):

> It is clear . . . that if local authorities implement to the full this legislation in close co-operation with voluntary organisations, all groups of the handicapped or their families should have a comprehensive service to which they can turn to meet any of their specialized needs. Unfortunately, this has not been the case. The duty of providing services was continued under the National Assistance Act only for the blind. Guidance to local authorities on the provision of welfare services for other classes of handicapped persons was issued by the Ministry of Health in Circular 32/51 in August 1951, and local authorities were invited to submit schemes and their subsequent implementation was not made compulsory until 1960. . . As a result, the development of services for the deaf and other categories of handicapped persons over the past sixteen years has been patchy and inadequate. (p. 171)

Even the 1960 deadline had little meaning since local authorities were able to offer minimal provision yet still meet the requirements of the Act. This situation meant that the main community-based service available to physically impaired people and their families was the home care service (Topliss, 1979).

These inadequacies led Alf Morris MP to introduce a private member's bill designed to compel local authorities to develop comprehensive welfare and support services for disabled people and this subsequently became the Chronically Sick and Disabled Persons Act 1970. This Act imposed duties but it was not paralleled by the allocation of sufficient extra resources to local authorities. Topliss claims that 'this has meant that the claims of the disabled have had to compete with the claims on the local authority budget of all other sections of the community' and that 'the sort of massive reallocation of expenditure needed to implement the . . . Act fully, in the absence of special ear-marked funds, has apparently proved politically impossible for local authorities' (p. 114).

On residential care for physically disabled people, the National Assistance Act 1948 did make reference to the specific needs of younger physically impaired people as being different from those of frail elderly people. However, most local authorities continued to place physically impaired people in residential homes for older people. Only a minority of local authorities developed separate homes in the 1950s and 1960s, despite the growing awareness that the overall number of younger disabled people had increased because of a number of factors, including the war, the 1950s polio epidemic and increased life expectancy from medical advances. Detailed figures in the balance of provision are difficult to come by, although Leat (1988, p. 206) shows that in 1972 'there were 8,000 younger people in homes also housing elderly people although more than half of these younger people were in their early sixties'. She also draws upon a survey by Harrison (1986) to show that by the mid-1980s only 54 of the 115 local authorities in England and Wales had set up homes catering specifically for younger physically impaired people, but she points out that many of the others may have been making use of specialist voluntary and private homes. By far the most influential of these independent sector providers of residential care was Cheshire Homes, which was founded in 1948 and developed the concept of a 'family home' which claimed to meet the needs of younger physically impaired people.

The most detailed survey of residential provision in the early post-war period was carried out by Miller and Gwynne (1972) who revealed many of the same inadequacies found by Townsend (1964) for elderly people, but with the added concern that many of those surveyed were being offered residential care as their only accommodation option for the whole of their adult life course and not just for the last part of it. They lamented that 'by the very fact of committing people to institutions of this type, society is defining them as, in effect, socially dead' because 'society has effectively washed its hands of the inmates as significant social beings' (p. 89). By the early 1980s, some of these 'inmates' had decided to organise their own housing and support solutions outside such residential institutions. Integrated living and independent living models began to emerge. However, most commentators point out that this was the response of disabled people to the neglect they had received from able-bodied professionals and policy-makers in terms of developing service responses which enable disabled people to be fully integrated within society (Finkelstein, 1993).

Services for people with mental health problems and learning difficulties

Having looked at the development of provision for elderly and physically impaired people, it is now appropriate to consider the growth of services for people with mental health problems and learning difficulties. Does the same pattern of neglect emerge? Several authors have charted the growth of asylums for 'lunatics' (people with mental health problems) and 'idiots' (people with learning difficulties) from a community care perspective (see, for example, Murphy, 1991; Malin *et al.*, 1980; Jones, 1993) while others have studied asylums from a more general sociological interest in madness (Scull, 1979). Murphy (1991) has argued that asylum growth from the late 1840s onwards was initially a development to be welcomed, since previous workhouse provision was failing to cope. She argues that the social reformers had a vision of a therapeutic community in which 'insanity . . . might be healed by a gentle system of rewards and punishments, amusements, occupation and kindly but firm discipline' (p. 34) although she accepts that the reality proved far inferior to the vision. Others have been far less sanguine. Scull (1979) saw the asylums as a mechanism by which the community and individual families could shed their responsibilities for troublesome and unwanted people. Certainly the legislative frame-work was draconian up to 1930, since admission depended on certifica-tion as 'a lunatic, an idiot or a person of unsound mind', which involved an order to be detained by a judicial authority. As Parker (1988, p. 12) points out:

> Such a requirement imposed a stigma additional to any that was associated with being in an asylum. Not only was admission dependent upon certification, but the order for commitment carried with it the prospect of its irrevocability. De-certification and release were not easily obtained.

The majority of such inmates were also certified as paupers unless they or their relatives could pay privately for their detention.

The numbers of people with mental health problems detained in asylums (renamed mental health hospitals in 1930) grew spectacularly. Gibbins (1988, p. 161) talks of a situation where

> By 1890 there were sixty-six county and borough asylums in England and Wales with an average 802 inmates and 86,067 officially certified cases of insanity in England and Wales, more than four times as many as forty-five years earlier. By 1930 there were nearly 120,000 patients in public asylums and by 1954 at the peak in numbers, there were over 148,000.

Gibbins sums up this situation as being one in which there were 'ever larger numbers of chronic cases in institutions of increasing size, with ever fewer therapeutic pretensions' (p. 160).

Murphy (1991) provides a glimpse of life in the typical Victorian asylum. She claims that

> Life . . . was governed by a rigid timetabled regime of sleep, work, eat. Whitewashed walls; plain brick, stone or wooden floors; deal benches and tables; and two WCs for thirty or forty patients provided a fairly cheerless though roomy environment. Windows were generally barred and many wards were locked, although the better asylums gave considerable internal freedom to the inmates. (p. 38)

Such asylums had few trained doctors, perhaps three or four for every thousand patients. Hence, much of the day-to-day work was performed by low-paid nursing attendants who often worked a 90-hour week.

In many respects, the situation was even more alarming for people with learning difficulties in the pre-war period. The term 'neglect' is probably misleading since services for this group have often been influenced by moral panics about the need to protect the genetic stock of the country by discouraging those of 'low' intelligence from 'breeding'. Gladstone (1996) indicates that the Victorian period was often a period of optimism about the potential for training and educating people with learning difficulties, even if this was often in the context of their removal to an institution under the Idiots Act 1886. However,

Ryan and Thomas (1980) point out that the growth of such institutionalised provision reflected pressures upon families as a result of the
industrial revolution which undermined the capacity of families to care
for those with long-term dependency needs.

In any case, optimism about the potential of institutions to help
those with learning difficulties was undermined by the new science of
genetics with its tendency to perceive 'mental defectives' as less than
human. Most geneticists believed that intelligence was innate. They
were alarmed by high birth rates amongst the poorest, and by
implication the least intelligent members of society, since such a trend
could undermine the overall genetic stock of the nation and hence the
capacity to remain a dominant colonial power. Mental defectiveness
was seen as genetically inherited and hence the segregation of 'mental
defectives' from the rest of society was essential.

Several authors have charted how this led to calls for the establishment of farm and industrial colonies, together with the prohibition of
marriages involving those labelled as 'moral defectives' who were seen
as often on the borderline of 'mental defectiveness' (Abbott and
Sapsford, 1987; Malin *et al.*, 1980, chapter 4). Such views had a major
impact upon the thinking of the 1908 Royal Commission on the Care
and Control of the Feeble-Minded and on the legislative details of the
Mental Deficiency Act 1913. This Act made reference to idiots,
imbeciles and the feeble-minded, categories based on the extent of
the learning difficulty, while the term 'moral imbecile' was introduced
to cover what was seen as a more generalised social problem group
whose low intelligence made them prone to 'loose morals'. Section 2 of
the Act specified the circumstances under which a 'defective' from these
groups might be dealt with by being sent to an institution or placed
under guardianship:

(a) at the insistence of his parent or guardian;
(b) if in addition to being a defective he was a person (i) who was
found neglected, abandoned, or without visible means of support,
or cruelly treated or . . . in need of care or training which could not
be provided in his home; or (ii) who was found guilty of any
criminal offence, or who was ordered to be sent to an approved
school; or (iii) who was undergoing imprisonment, or was in an
approved school; or (iv) who was an habitual drunkard; or (v) who
had been found incapable of receiving education at school, or that
by reason of a disability of mind required supervision after leaving
school. (quoted in Malin *et al.*, 1980, p. 41)

Once a person had been admitted to an institution on these grounds, the Board of Control was in a position to block the discharge of anyone they considered unfit to live in the community. Certain safeguards were built into this draconian system. Parents and guardians needed two medical certificates, one of which had to be approved for such purposes by the local health authority or the Minister of Health. Section 2(b), quoted above, used the phrase 'in addition to being a defective'. However, in practice, it was relatively easy to place any person with learning disability in an institution using this Act, while others experiencing social difficulties such as homelessness were equally vulnerable irrespective of their mental abilities. Once they were committed, the term ' "certification" had a permanence about it, probably enhanced by the prevailing views of invariance of intellectual abilities and certainly compounded by the essentially subjective nature of the definitions of the Act' (Malin *et al.*, 1980, p. 42).

Ryan and Thomas (1980, p. 107) summed up the overall situation in the following way:

> This Act established the basis of a separate and unified service, which would exclude mental defective people from other welfare and social agencies as well as from the general education system.

The total number of 'defectives' under the care and control of the mental deficiency legislation rose rapidly. Figures supplied by Tredgold (1952) and quoted by Malin *et al.* (1980, p. 43) show that numbers rose from 12,000 in 1920 to 90,000 by 1939. Most of them were placed in large isolated 'colonies', whose regime was outlined in the Report of the Mental Deficiency Committee (1929):

> The modern institution is generally a large one, preferably built on a colony plan, takes defectives of all grades of defect and all ages. All, of course, are probably classified according to their mental capacity and age. The Local Mental Deficiency Authority has to provide for all grades of defect, all types of case and all ages, and an institution that cannot, or will not, take this case for one reason and that case for another is of no use to the Authority. An institution which takes all types and ages is economical because the high-grade patients do the work and make everything necessary, not only for themselves, but also for the lower grade. In an institution taking only lower grades, the whole of the work has to be done by paid staff; in one taking only high grades the output of work is greater than is required

for the institution itself and there is difficulty in disposing of it. In the all-grade institution, on the other hand, the high-grade patients are the skilled workmen of the colony, those who do all the higher processes of manufacture, those on whom there is a considerable measure of responsibility; the medium-grade patients are the labourers, who do the more simple routine work in the training shops and about the institution; the rest of the lower-grade patients fetch and carry or do the very simple work. (Quoted in Malin *et al.*, 1980, p. 43)

How was the situation changed for people with learning difficulties and mental health problems by the establishment of a National Health Service and other related reforms? The National Health Service saw provision for those with mental health problems and learning difficulties brought more into mainstream health care provision. Asylums were redesignated as hospitals and became the responsibility of regional hospital boards. Local authorities became responsible for the following range of services under Section 28 of the National Health Service Act 1946:

(a) The initial care and removal to hospital of persons dealt with under the Lunacy and Mental Treatment Acts.
(b) The ascertainment and (where necessary) removal to institutions of mental defectives, and the supervision, guardianship, training and occupation of those in the community, under the Mental Deficiency Acts.
(c) The prevention, care and after-care of all types of patients, so far as this was not otherwise provided for.

However, the first two were statutory responsibilities, while the third represented a permissive power. Local authorities showed little enthusiasm for using their permissive powers and in 1958/59 overall local authority expenditure on people with mental health problems was only £4.1 million (Goodwin, 1990, p. 68).

Expenditure on hospital-based provision was not much more impressive. Drawing upon a number of sources, Goodwin (1990, p. 67) found that in the early 1950s, mental and mental deficiency hospitals contained 40 per cent of inpatient beds in the NHS but received only 20 per cent of the hospital budget. He also pointed out that the average cost of treating a mentally distressed inpatient was £3 15s 11d in 1950/51 compared with £4 13s 11d in 1959/60 (at 1950/51 prices) but that far more dramatic price rises had occurred for other groups in the same period. For example, the cost of inpatient maternity care rose from £6 9s 5d to £16 11s 3d. Goodwin claims 'these figures clearly underline why the mental health services have earned the tag of a "Cinderella" service' (p. 67).

At first glance, the Cinderella tag appears to have been removed as a result of the Royal Commission on Mental Illness and Mental Deficiency which sat from 1954 to 1957, and the subsequent Mental Health Act 1959. The latter reformed the legislative framework of constraint and envisaged the development of a complex infrastructure of local authority-provided services such as hostels, day care, social work support and sheltered employment schemes.

However, not only did these services fail to materialise, but in 1961, Enoch Powell, the then Minister of Health, informed the annual conference of the National Association for Mental Health that

> I have intimated to the hospital authorities who will be producing the constituent elements of the plan that in fifteen years time, there may be needed not more than half as many places in hospitals for mental illness as there are today. (Quoted in K. Jones, 1993, p. 160)

As a result, Murphy (1991, p. 60) describes 1962–90 as 'the disaster years' for people with mental health problems. She points out that 'by 1974 there were 60,000 fewer residents in large mental hospitals than there had been in 1954, but very few services at all existed in the community'. In a similar vein, Atkinson (1988) notes the failure of local authorities to develop services for children and adults with learning difficulties. She indicates that 'a few residential homes, or hostels, appeared here and there' while 'local authorities developed some training facilities in the community and appointed Mental Welfare Officers to make routine visits to the family homes' (p. 128). Provision remained based on hospitals. Institutional and treatment regimes remained controversial. For people with mental health problems, the emphasis was now on treatment not custody. However, the introduction of anti-psychotic drugs and new treatments such as ECT were seen to raise major issues about civil liberties. There were also numerous exposés of physical and mental cruelty by staff over patients. Such practices with regard to psycho-geriatric patients were outlined by Robb (1967) in *Sans Everything: A Case to Answer*, while Morris (1969) in *Put Away* provided evidence of the generally poor conditions in many long-stay mental handicap hospitals. Against this, Jones (1972) lamented how the popular press of the late 1960s began to exaggerate such stories and to imply that the worst abuses were the norm rather than the exception.

Governments continued to take initiatives in the 1970s to promote community-based provision and to reduce hospital provision for both people with learning disabilities (*Better Services for the Mentally Handicapped*, DHSS, 1971) and for people with mental health problems (*Better Services for the Mentally Ill*, DHSS, 1975). Yet the pivotal report of the Audit Commission (1986), *Making a Reality of Community Care*, found limited movement on the hospital front and virtually no progress in terms of developing adequate community services. Both groups continued to be treated as a low priority for service developments.

As a result it is impossible to be certain about the overall standard of provision and how this varied in the forty-year period from the establishment of the National Health Service in 1946 to the publication of *Making a Reality of Community Care* (Audit Commission, 1986). However, Frank Thomas's diary of everyday life in the ward of a large mental handicap hospital in the late 1970s perhaps captures how 'patients' become treated as less than fully human through mundane everyday actions rather than through spectacular examples of abuse. Here are two examples:

1. Tea mixed with milk and sugar to save time, mess and trouble. How many lumps, say when with the milk? You must be joking (Thomas, 1980, p. 35).
2. Bad habit I picked up from the other nurses. Fitting out someone for his trip to the workshop and muttering 'That'll do', as if the guy's appearance meant nothing to him, just a neat reproduction of my own preferences or lack of them. Not asking the guy if he was all right, whether it'll do. If a person is not allowed a say in what he looks like, then what is the point?

   Haircuts en masse – short back and sides, no one is allowed to refuse. Choice of raincoat from a communal pile, communal underwear and socks. Communal combs and brushes. One tube of toothpaste and a couple of tooth mugs for twenty-five patients (p. 43).

Throughout this section on the long history of neglect of community care services for all the main care groups, one cannot but be struck by the continuity of the images of institutional regimes over the last one hundred years, and the persistent failure to develop alternative community-based systems of provision.

Explanations of neglect

How can we explain the long history of neglect of services for these 'Cinderella' groups? This chapter makes no pretence that there is a single simple answer to this question, but rather identifies a number of strands. Five different explanations will be addressed. First, we will look at the political economy approach which explains social policy developments (or lack of them) by reference to the changing needs of the capitalist mode of production. Second, the complex rôle of institutions in social control will be considered, and third, we will outline the central concern of governments to encourage informal care and the knock-on consequences of this for the neglect of community-based services. The fourth explanation looks at cultural stereotypes about ageing and disability, while the final explanation considers the issue of policy implementation failure which can lead to a major gap between the rhetoric of policy and the reality of practice.

The political economy perspective

The main tenets of the political economy approach to disability have been clearly summarised by Oliver (1990):

> Changes in the organisation of work from a rural based, cooperative system where individuals contributed what they could to the production process, to an urban, factory-based one organised around the individual waged labourer, had profound consequences. . . As a result of this, disabled people came to be regarded as a social and educational problem and more and more were segregated in institutions of all kinds including workhouses, asylums, colonies and special schools, and out of the mainstream of social life. (p. 28)

Oliver points out this is a major simplification of some highly complex processes but stresses that the key insight is the need to search for linkages between changes in public policy and changes in the sphere of production.

Perhaps the clearest example of this relationship concerns the emergence of a system of retirement pensions in the early twentieth century as part of a process of removing elderly people from the labour market during a period of high unemployment (Phillipson, 1982). The effect of such initiatives has been to minimise opportunities for elderly and disabled people in the labour market and this has ensured their 'structured dependency' on the state (Townsend, 1981). At the same time, elderly people form a reserve army of labour which can be drawn back into work during periods of labour shortage. Research has provided graphic illustrations of the way retirement from work was painted as encouraging physical decline and death in the labour market shortage years of the 1950s so as to draw older people back into employment (Phillipson, 1982). Against this, in the recession years of the 1980s, older workers were encouraged to make way for younger workers by retiring as early as possible. In a similar way, it could be argued that Conservative governments in the 1980s encouraged disabled people on to invalidity benefit so as to reduce unemployment rates, only to reverse this trend through the introduction of incapacity benefit when their primary concern switched from unemployment to levels of social security expenditure. The effect of the new benefit has been to define many people previously on invalidity benefit as once again available for work.

Structured dependency has taken a number of forms. First, it has involved dependence on state benefits which keep many elderly and disabled people trapped within poverty (Oliver, 1996). Second, it has encouraged an outlook in which health and community care services for disabled people are seen as a low resource priority compared with service developments for children, since the latter have a clear future rôle in production and reproduction. During the Second World War there was early support for the evacuation of children and mothers from areas under threat from bombing raids, but a great reluctance to extend this provision to frail elderly people because they were not, in the government jargon of the day, 'potential effectives' (Means and Smith, 1985, chapter 2). Equally, the overall cost of providing health and social care services for elderly and disabled people can be seen as a public expenditure burden which inhibits economic growth. Such concerns have appeared in official reports. For example, *The Rising Tide* from the Health Advisory Service (1983) explained that the number of people with dementia would rise rapidly because of the growth of the very old and that 'the flood is likely to overwhelm the entire health care system' (p. 1).

There are several criticisms which can be levelled at the political economy approach, although, in fairness to most of its proponents, they recognise that its value lies in providing a very broad grasp of the link between changes in the means of production and changes in public policy. In Chapter 1, it was shown how some people misuse history to manufacture a fictitious golden past based on mythical values. Prior to the industrial revolution, all frail elderly people were *not* supported in the 'bosom' of their extended families, local villages did *not* 'support' every person with a learning difficulty, and appropriate work was *not* found for all those with physical impairments and mental health problems. However, this is recognised by Oliver (1990, p. 28) who indicates that the industrial revolution had a major impact on disabled people but that it is impossible 'to assess whether these changes affected the quality of the experience of disability negatively or positively, largely because history is silent on the experience of disability'.

Another linked criticism is the argument that the emergence of state benefits represented a major 'gain' for elderly and disabled people compared with their previous reliance on the workhouse, Poor Law relief, the family and low-paid employment. Johnson (1987) points out that pensions are provided as a right. They protect elderly people from the vagaries of the labour market and hence provide many of them with the option of a fairly comfortable retirement which they are likely to prefer to continued employment in unattractive work. However, Johnson's views can be challenged on the grounds that they deflect attention away from the extent of benefit-based poverty amongst elderly and disabled people. They can also be challenged on the grounds that many elderly and disabled people wish to work. Indeed, Oliver (1996) quotes from the fundamental principles of disability as laid out by the Union of the Physically Impaired Against Segregation which included the need to fight for jobs rather than improved benefits. This is because 'in the final analysis the particular form of poverty principally associated with physical impairment is caused by our exclusion from the ability to earn an income on a par with our able-bodied peers, due to the way employment is organised' (p. 23).

A third criticism is that the concept of structured dependency can easily drift into an acceptance of structural determinism which treats elderly and disabled people as 'cultural dopes' who lack any autonomy or capacity for self-determination. It is crucial to recognise the frequent imbalance of power between elderly and disabled people and the providers of state services. However, the consequent 'dependency' should not be perceived as a static, determined phenomenon, but rather recognised as a component of social processes in which elderly and disabled people continue to struggle to influence the form of their lives even in situations where they have only limited power (Dant *et al.*, 1987).

Institutions and service neglect

There is a rich and complex literature on institutions and their rôle in social control. A frequent theme in the literature on institutions is that many were designed to impose stigma upon residents, and that one function of the institution was to provide a warning to others. Here are two quotations reflecting this perspective:

> residential homes for the elderly serve functions for the wider society and not only for their inmates. While accommodating only a tiny percentage of the elderly population, they symbolise the dependence of the elderly and legitimate their lack of access to equality of status. (Townsend, 1986, p. 32)

> the workhouse represented the ultimate sanction. The fact that comparatively few people came to be admitted did not detract from the power of its negative image, an image that was sustained by the accounts that circulated about the harsh treatment and separation of families that admission entailed. The success of 'less eligibility' in deterring the able-bodied and others from seeking relief relied heavily on the currency of such images. (Parker, 1988, p. 9)

From this perspective, neglect within institutions can be understood in terms of the need to generate a negative image to those outside their walls. This negative image, in turn, helps to persuade people into accepting the lack of sufficient public expenditure on benefits, health care services and social care services which would enable people to remain in the community with comfort. Instead, the choice is between discomfort in the community, and discomfort and stigma in the institution.

Not everyone has been satisfied with this approach to understanding institutions. Jones and Fowles (1984) argue that the classic literature on 'total institutions', 'institutional neurosis' and 'carceral power' associated with Goffman (1968), Foucault (1967) and others contained 'sweeping statements, massive generalisations, and some fairly shoddy reasoning; but also disturbing insight, sound scholarship and lively argument' (p. 1). Not all institutional regimes are totally oppressive, and this was true of workhouses (Digby, 1978) as well as more recent institutions. Not all institutions have a negative impact upon potential users. Kathleen Jones (1993) has argued that the rundown of mental health hospitals has itself been a form of neglect with negative consequences for many with severe mental health problems. Nevertheless, the critical literature on institutions does provide insights into the neglect of health and social care services for elderly and disabled people.

Finally, it is quite clear that the increasing cost of institutional provision has been a factor in the growing emphasis of governments in both the UK and other countries in arguing for a need to switch resources from institutional provision to the development of care in the community (Pynos and Liebig, 1995; Goodwin, 1990). What had started as a low-cost form of provision had become an increasingly expensive response to the needs of disabled people. However, to understand the slow government response to the growing criticisms of institutions on grounds of both cost and quality of care, it is necessary to consider the politics of informal care.

Informal care and service neglect

Most disabled people have always lived in the community rather than in institutions, and the majority of them have received enormous support from their families and relatives, and in particular from female kin. There is an extensive literature which argues that the reluctance of government to fund the development of domiciliary services springs from a fear that such services will undermine the willingness of families (that is, female kin) to continue their caring rôle. This would have the effect of both increasing public expenditure and undermining the family as an institution (Means, 1986).

Detailed information about the extent of informal care and the pressures that this places upon carers has been available for a long time. For example, Sheldon (1948) studied 600 elderly people from Wolverhampton and found that the management of illness was carried out by wives and daughters, so that 'whereas the wives do most of the nursing of the men, the strain when the mother is ill is yet to fall on the daughter, who may have to stay at home as much to run the household as to nurse her mother' (p. 164). Sheldon felt the burden upon such women needed to be shared with the rest of the community through the establishment of a national home help service. Sheldon's findings were subsequently backed up by a number of other studies, which emphasised not only the willingness of families to care but also the costs this imposed upon them (Townsend, 1963; Shanas *et al.*, 1968).

However, such evidence was being generated at a time of concern that the welfare state reforms of the 1940s might undermine the willingness of families to carry out their traditional obligations, one of which was to provide care and support for disabled members. Thompson (1949) was involved in the surveys of chronic sick patients after the NHS reforms and he argued that

> The power of the group-maintaining instincts will suffer if the provision of a home, the training of children, and the care of disabled members are no longer the ambition of a family but the duty of a local or central authority. (p. 250)

Ten years later, a consultant physician from a geriatric unit was putting forward a similar argument:

> The feeling that the State ought to solve every inconvenient domestic situation is merely another factor in producing a snowball expansion on demands in the National Health (and Welfare) Service. Close observation on domestic strains makes one thing very clear. This is that where an old person has a family who have a sound feeling of moral responsibility, serious problems do not arise, however much difficulty may be met. (Rudd, 1958, p. 348)

From such a perspective it was essential for the state to avoid the development of domiciliary services if families were not, in turn, to avoid their domestic responsibilities towards elderly and disabled people. The failure to expand home care services and the heavy reliance upon the voluntary sector for the provision of other domiciliary services is a consequence of this point of view.

Such views were heavily challenged by those involved in research on caring:

> The health and welfare services for the aged, as presently developing, are a necessary concomitant of social organisation, and therefore, possibly of economic growth. The services do not undermine self-help, because they are concentrated overwhelmingly among those who have neither the capacities nor the resources to undertake the

relevant functions alone. Nor, broadly, do the services conflict with the interest of the family as a social institution, because they tend to reach people who lack a family or whose family resources are slender, or they provide specialised services the family is not equipped or qualified to undertake. (Townsend in Shanas *et al.*, 1968, p. 129)

Rather than being restricted from a fear of undermining the family, domiciliary services needed to be rapidly expanded to support families and help the isolated.

This argument was gradually accepted by central government. However, this was achieved by emphasising the capacity of domiciliary services to persuade family members to continue to care for disabled relatives rather than their capacity to offer such members real choices about whether or not to continue such care. Moroney (1976) put the argument for more services quite bluntly:

By not offering support, existing social policy might actually force many families to give up this function prematurely, given the evidence of the severe strain many families are experiencing. If this were to happen, the family and the state would not be sharing the responsibility through an interdependent relationship and it is conceivable that eventually the social welfare system would be pressured with demands to provide even greater amounts of care, to become the family for more and more elderly persons. (p. 59).

In this respect, service neglect continues to the present day. All governments assume that if you care about someone you should be willing to care for them (Dalley, 1996).

This has always been the assumption about frail elders but it is also now the basis of policy with regard to people with learning difficulties and mental health problems. The family is assumed to exist and expected to cope. Informal carers may be offered more support from the state than was once the case and this is a positive development where both the service user and informal carer wish the latter to take on the primary caring responsibilities. However, there is little sign of policies emerging which enable service users and family members to make choices about who should carry out such personal assistance roles. In this respect, Morris (1993) asserts that disabled people have a right not to be made dependent upon family members and other close relatives in order to have such needs met.

Cultural stereotypes about ageing and disability

Most western societies support negative stereotypes about old age and about disability. Wilson (1991) has argued that most western views of the life course are pyramidal, in which 'ageing is seen as an inevitable or irreversible slide downwards into dependency' (p. 43). Or as Johnson (1990) has put it:

> Dependency is one of the words closely associated in the public mind with old age. The image of older people becoming like children – dependent on able-bodied adults – and the loss of mental faculties, are other stereotypes which have wide currency. Even my children, long schooled in the rejection of ageism, like to remind me of the epigram 'old professors never die, they only lose their faculties'. (p. 209)

Similarly negative images and stereotypes are often associated with the term 'disability'. Morris (1990a, p. 22) for example, bluntly states that 'just as the issue for black people is racism rather than being black so the issue for disabled people is the fear and hostility that our physical difference and limitations raise for non-disabled people'. Barnes (1996) although sympathetic to this view points out that not all societies and cultures are universally hostile to disabled people. However, 'the importance and desirability of bodily perfection is endemic to western culture' (p. 56), resulting in the oppression of disabled people through such mechanisms as genetic engineering, prenatal screening, denial of medical treatments, misrepresentation in the media, and institutional discrimination in education, employment, housing, welfare and leisure.

Such everyday cultural attitudes to elderly and disabled people will be part of the assumptive worlds of many of those who develop community care policies and by many of those who deliver community care services. Certainly, Rowlings (1981) has argued that this helps to explain the oft-remarked reluctance of social workers to develop their careers in community care rather than child care:

> old age confronts us not just with death (which is inevitable) but with decline (which is probable, at least to some degree). . . It is the prospect of loss in old age – impairment in mental and/or physical function, loss of spouse and family and loss of independence – which is more frightening to contemplate than loss of life itself . . . Social

workers may well be faced with clients whose experience of and response to ageing represent those very aspects of old age which they, the social workers, fear most for their future selves. (pp. 25-6)

Although this quotation is from a book on *Social Work with Elderly People*, similar comments could be made about the fear of many professionals about working with physically impaired people, and people with learning difficulties and mental health problems.

Such fear may provide a partial explanation of service neglect, especially if combined with an appreciation of the low status of work with these groups rather than in child care (for social workers) or acute medicine (for doctors). Neglect can also result from pessimism about what can be achieved in terms of improving lives through health and social care intervention. This pessimism has deep roots. Haber (1983), for example, found in her study of medical models of growing old in the late nineteenth century and early twentieth century that

Most European clinicians seemed to imply that illness and old age were inseparably intertwined, if not quite synonymous. At best the division between the two was extremely subjective. A large proportion of the diseases of old age are attributed to natural intractable changes in the organism. (p. 62)

The term 'chronic sick' sums up this attitude of mind within the medical profession. Illness in old age was chronic, inevitable and barely treatable since 'the organic difficulties that increased with age made the hope of corrective treatment illusory' (p. 72).

However, such arguments do have their limitations. To say that older people and disabled people are oppressed by the negative stereotypes generated by the young and non-disabled does little to help us understand how such stereotypes emerge from a complex interplay of cultural, political, economic and social factors. For example, how do such stereotypes relate to the process of removal from the labour force associated with the industrial revolution? Are these stereotypes and their implications the same for disabled men as for disabled women (Morris, 1990a; Shakespeare, 1996)? And are negative attitudes to frail elderly people connected not just to issues of age but also to the fact that the majority of them are women rather than men (Bernard and Meade, 1993; Arber and Ginn, 1995)? These issues are addressed in Chapter 4.

The politics of implementation

The final approach to explaining service neglect focuses on issues of policy implementation. Although it is possible to characterise the history of services as one of policy neglect, it is also true that health and social care provision for elderly and disabled people has often proved highly resistant to policy change and policy reform. An excellent example of this is that even when central governments have been persuaded of the need to switch the policy emphasis away from institutional care and towards community-based services, progress has often been painfully slow. The next chapter considers this issue in some detail with regard to the slowness of the rundown of large mental health and mental handicap hospitals in the 1980s. In earlier decades progress was equally slow in developing non-residential provision for elderly and physically disabled people, a fact which has been explained by reference to the resistance of those with a vested interest in residential care (Townsend, 1981) and concerns about the cost-effectiveness of care at home for the very frail (Means and Smith, 1985).

However, it is important to stand back from the details of the history of community care provision and to recognise the existence of a wider literature on policy implementation which stresses the frequency of a major gap between the stated objectives of legislative change and what continues to happen on the ground across all policy areas. The seminal book on implementation deficit was a study of a job creation scheme in Oakland, USA by Pressman and Wildavsky (1973). The authors argued that such schemes could only be successful if numerous organisations linked up to create a successful implementation chain. Relatively small failures of co-operation between the different organisations can easily multiply to create a major implementation deficit, which is what occurred in the Oakland scheme.

Two main approaches to theorising implementation deficit subsequently emerged, namely the top-down perspective and the bottom-up perspective (Ham and Hill, 1993). The top-down approach tends to offer advice to policy-makers on how to minimise the discretion of actors lower down the implementation chain so as to ensure that implementation is consistent with policy objectives. The bottom-up approach emphasises that implementation is the inevitable product of negotiation and compromise between the formal policy-makers and those with the task of working out how to turn policy into practice. As Barrett and Hill (1984) argue:

(a) many policies represent compromises between conflicting values;
(b) many policies involve compromises within key interests within the implementation structure;
(c) many policies involve compromises with key interests upon whom implementation will have an impact;
(d) many policies are framed without attention being given to the way in which underlying forces (particularly economic ones) will undermine them. (p. 222)

Such tensions mean that some decisions on goals and objectives are left to what is normally seen as the implementation stage. Top-down theorists tend to see this as regrettable and undesirable. Bottom-up theorists see this as inevitable and some would perceive it as desirable on the grounds that field-level implementors are in the best position to assess the local situation and set appropriate objectives. Even where the discretion to make policy is not formally given by the 'policy-maker', lower-level implementors will still perceive themselves as important 'stakeholders' with the right to pursue their own agendas. Smith and Cantley (1985) in their study of a psychiatric day hospital illustrated how this complicates assessment of 'success' or 'failure' for any given policy initiative. The key stakeholders (administrators, doctors, nurses, relatives and patients) may all try to influence the policy and its implementation, and all will have different views about what represents success and failure. At the very least, stakeholders may have the power to block or disrupt innovation in policy areas such as community care.

The gap between policy change towards user-centred services at the top and the continuance of institutional and professionally dominated services on the ground can be explained by reference to the capacity of vested professional and provider interests to disrupt and undermine well-meaning reforms. However, the level of commitment of central government to these policy changes can also be queried since the implementation literature also refers to symbolic policies (Edelman, 1971) which are designed to reassure the public about good intentions but which are never intended to be appropriately resourced in relation to their far-reaching objectives.

Concluding comments

The focus of this chapter has been upon the neglect of services for elderly and disabled people and the different ways in which this can be explained. However, as we warned at the outset, there is a real danger that a compressed chapter on the complex history of services is likely to oversimplify policy developments. More specifically, the thematic focus on neglect risks obscuring the fact that social care and health provision for these groups has achieved a high visibility on political and policy agendas from time to time.

At least three main strands to such periodic increased interest can be identified. First, wars can generate concern about the quality of health and welfare provision for members of the armed forces and/or civilians. For example, the emergence of blind welfare legislation in 1920 was a response to the perceived needs of blind and partially sighted ex-servicemen from the First World War. With regard to civilians, this chapter has illustrated the lack of priority allocated to older people in terms of evacuation places and with regard to access to health care services. However, the second half of the Second World War saw the debate on reconstruction driven by the Beveridge Report (1942). This period saw elderly citizens being increasingly defined as war victims and deserving of state support. This helps to explain the *Manchester Guardian* campaign about workhouse conditions in the 1940s (see earlier discussion) as well as the emergence of home care and meals-on-wheels services for older people in the same period.

Second, the ideology of family and family care means that there are great sensitivities about the 'abandonment' of elderly and disabled people to the state, especially if this is low-quality provision where staff abuse inmates. The history of institutional provision is one of periodic scandals, taken up by pressure groups and the media, and then responded to with campaigning energy by politicians. However, such energy rarely lasts and the Cinderella groups return to being the concern of the committed few at the margins of political and policy influence. Despite this periodic determination to improve and humanise institutional regimes, one is struck by the continuity of the institutional descriptions in this chapter from the Victorian period to the present day. A colleague at the University of Bristol has remarked that the workhouse regime description in the *Manchester Guardian* article of spring 1943 could have been a description of the geriatric ward she worked on in the early 1980s.

This tradition of scandals about individuals in institutions is now in the process of being transformed into media stories of people being abandoned in the community with inadequate support services. For example, the early 1990s saw high-profile coverage of a young man with mental health problems who was mauled by a lion after entering its cage at London zoo (K. Jones, 1993, pp. 228–34). More recently, there has been enormous press interest in the killings of Jonathan Zito and Jonathan Newby by people with severe mental health problems (Timmins, 1996).

Third, policy-makers raise the visibility of community care debates when they become concerned about the cost of existing, usually institutional, provision because of demographic and other trends. This became the case in the mid-1980s when concern grew about both the projected growth in the old old (those over 75 years), the mushrooming cost of social security payments to residential and nursing homes, and the failure to run down expensive mental health and mental handicap hospitals. The development of disquiet about this situation and how this eventually fed into *Caring for People*, the 1989 White Paper on community care, is the initial focus of the next chapter. A central concern of the rest of the book is whether or not the Cinderella tag of service neglect has become outdated.

3 Community Care and the Restructuring of Welfare

The focus of the last chapter was upon the neglect of service provision for elderly people and for people with physical disabilities, mental health problems and learning difficulties. However, it was pointed out that this neglect has never been absolute. At various times, concern about demographic change or the abuse of inmates in institutions has raised the political profile of these services and led to expressions of a commitment to improve or change the overall situation. This chapter begins by describing how the pressure for reform began to build up in the 1980s and ultimately led to the Griffiths Report (1988), *Community Care: An Agenda for Action,* which in turn fed into the White Paper on community care (Department of Health, 1989a) and the National Health Service and Community Care Act 1990. The second half of the chapter argues that it is a mistake to see these changes either as peculiar to community care or as the product of a temporary phenomenon known as Thatcherism. The community care reforms reflect broader debates about how best to manage private and public sector organisations in increasingly diverse western societies. More specifically they provide an illustration of a growing trend to introduce markets into public services.

The run-up to the Griffiths Report

Chapter 2 traced the growing disillusion with hospitals as the main form of provision for people with learning difficulties and mental health problems. This was to lead to the development of a 'care in the community' initiative designed to close most of the larger hospitals after their replacement by a network of community-based services, to be run jointly by social services authorities and health authorities. Patients in hospitals were to be returned to the community as residents.

The origins of this policy shift are complex. There has been a long-standing concern within central government about the high costs of hospital provision (Guillebaud Report, 1956). In the 1970s, pressure groups such as MIND and MENCAP began to argue for a major rethink about the emphasis upon hospital-based provision and they found increasing support from key practitioners and academics. For example, *An Ordinary Life* (King's Fund Centre, 1980) provided a detailed argument for and outline of 'comprehensive locally-based residential services for mentally handicapped people'. The report was based on three fundamental principles:

1. Mentally handicapped people have the same human value as anyone else and so the same human rights.
2. Living like others within the community is both a right and a need.
3. Services must recognise the individuality of mentally handicapped people.

As such, this report drew upon normalisation theory which emphasised that services for people with learning difficulties should attempt to deliver a high quality of life and that this required them to reproduce the lifestyle experienced by non-disabled citizens through such characteristics as the rhythm of the day, progression through the life course, the development of sexual relationships, self-determination and economic standards (Emerson, 1992; Race, 1987).

Hospital services could not meet these criteria. Indeed the main starting point of the care in the community initiative was growing concern about basic standards of care in hospitals for people with learning difficulties and with mental health problems. Chapter 2 showed how the issue of standards was raised initially by Robb (1967) in a book on hospital provision for elderly mentally infirm people in which allegations of ill-treatment were made. Two years later came the official report on Ely Hospital, Cardiff, which confirmed staff cruelty to patients at this mental handicap hospital. The level of media publicity generated by these incidents became so high that a policy response became inevitable.

Action took three main forms. Special money was set aside, a Hospital Advisory Service was established to visit such hospitals, and a major policy review was announced. The White Papers, *Better Services for the Mentally Handicapped* (DHSS, 1971) and *Better Services for the Mentally Ill* (DHSS, 1975) argued strongly for the abandonment of hospitals as the mainstay provision for these two groups. Both papers set targets for the rundown of long-stay hospitals and for the build-up of community-based services to replace them. But how could the DHSS encourage health and local authorities to set about this task? The NHS Reorganisation Act 1973 established new machinery for joint planning between the two authorities, through member-based Joint Consultative Committees, and these new mechanisms were intended to drive forward the de-institutionalisation policies. They were followed in 1976 by the introduction of joint finance arrangements, partly as an incentive to joint planning, which was failing to make progress. Joint finance was a mechanism by which social services departments could obtain health authority money for a timelimited period to fund community care initiatives, which would either make a contribution to the hospital rundown programme or provide support for people to remain in the community rather than to seek hospital entry.

The next major policy development was the production of the consultative document *Care in the Community* (DHSS, 1981a) which contained a wide-ranging analysis of available options for speeding up the transfer of patients into the community, including some quite radical proposals for transferring and managing funds. However, the subsequent circular, *Care in the Community and Joint Finance* (DHSS, 1983) was a disappointment to those frustrated by the slow progress. The circular discarded the more radical proposals in the discussion document and adopted a fairly unimaginative and incremental approach. With regard to joint finance, the main provisions of the circular were a modest increase in money available, longer periods of funding and an extension to include housing and education projects. Voluntary sector representation on Joint Consultative Committees was announced and resource transfer arrangements between health authorities and local authorities were encouraged. A pilot project programme, financed by special DHSS funds, was initiated.

Pressure for radical change intensified rather than lessened in the mid-1980s. Again, it is difficult to be precise about the reason. There was government frustration at the lack of progress achieved by the 1983 circular. There was growing concern about the implications of demographic change, especially because of the projected growth in numbers over 75 (the old old) who were known to be high consumers of health and social care services (DHSS, 1981b). But a new factor had also arrived. The mid-1980s saw the rapid growth of the private residential and nursing-home sectors (Parker, 1990). In the early 1980s, the DHSS amended the supplementary benefit regulations to make it easier for the low-income residents of private and voluntary homes to claim their fees from the social security system. Public subsidy was based on an assessment of financial entitlement only and not on the need for such care. This encouraged a mushrooming of new homes in the private sector. Places rose from 46,900 in 1982 to 161,200 in 1991 (Laing and Buisson, 1992, p. 156). Although the bulk of new provision was for elderly people, some health authorities used the private sector as a source of alternative accommodation for patients from mental handicap hospitals (Hoyes and Harrison, 1987).

There was growing unease within central government about the public expenditure implications of the growth of the private sector, despite various attempts to restrict the level of charges. In 1979, the annual expenditure was only £10 million, but it had reached £459 million by early 1986, the main reason being the rise of those in receipt of social security payments, from 12,000 to 90,000. A joint working party from the DHSS and the local authority associations was set up to review the situation and concluded that the social security system was providing a major incentive to the development of residential care at a time when central government wished to place emphasis on the development of domiciliary services (Firth Report, 1987). However, expenditure on private institutional care continued to rise and had reached a staggering £1,872 million per annum by May 1991 (Laing and Buisson, 1992).

The mid-1980s saw several other official reports which were highly critical of the failure to develop coherent community care policies. For example, the House of Commons Select Committee report on community care focused on adults with mental health problems and learning difficulties (Social Services Committee, 1985), concluding that:

1. There was a bias in policy towards getting people out of hospitals. This bias was reflected in the joint finance rules and in the selection of pilot projects.
2. Most people with special needs were already being cared for in the community (mainly by their families, that is women). This fact needed to be recognised in policies.
3. There was a lack of agreed philosophy and no consensus on what constitutes 'good' community care. The committee argued that community care should be based on ordinary housing.
4. The pace of running down hospitals was far outrunning the provision of alternative community-based services. It described this as 'the cart and the horse' phenomenon.
5. There was a lack of appropriate financial mechanisms. The mental disability service was underfinanced and understaffed. Joint fi-

nance was 'virtually played out' as a means of transferring responsibilities from health to local authorities. It argued that a real
increase in total resources was required and that a Central Bridging
Fund should be set up for the transitional period.
6. Joint planning arrangements needed strengthening and, in particular, the consumer's voice should be listened to in the design of
   services.

Similar concerns about the limitations of existing joint planning
systems were expressed by the Local Authority Associations, the
National Association of Health Authorities and the Department of
Health and Social Security. *Progress in Partnership* (Working Group
on Joint Planning, 1985) called for the establishment of an 'engine to
drive joint planning' rather than relying on the commitment of
individuals, and demanded full joint plans for all client groups covering
all agencies. Such plans needed to be based on the total resources
available to all agencies for the particular client group, including staff
and finance, both capital and revenue.

However, the argument that most influenced central government was
the Audit Commission (1986) report, *Making a Reality of Community
Care*. It focused on the movement of people with mental health
problems, people with learning difficulties and elderly people from
hospitals into community-based provision. The report concluded that
progress towards community care had been slow, especially for people
with mental health problems. It had been geographically uneven and
too many residents had been moved from one institution (the hospital)
to another institution (private residential or nursing homes) rather than
into genuine community-based provision. Five underlying problems
were identified:

1. *Mismatch of resources.* Funds for community care came from
   numerous sources and they were not co-ordinated. The way in
   which resources were determined and allocated to regions did not
   make any provision for the shift of services and responsibility for
   funding them from the NHS to local authority social services
   departments. The system for distributing rate support grant was
   a deterrent to the expansion of community-based services in many
   local authorities, since such an expansion in many local authorities
   could lead to rate-capping.
2. *Bridging fund.* As argued in previous reports, this was needed to
   fund the transition from a hospital to a community-based service.

3. *Perverse effects of social security policy*. The present system had the effect of encouraging health and local authorities to place people in private residential and nursing homes rather than 'ordinary' housing with community care back-up. Access to benefit was not based on any assessment of need.

4. *Organisational fragmentation and confusion*. Large numbers of agencies were involved in community care. The structure of local community-based services was confused, with responsibility fragmented between different tiers of the NHS and within local government.

5. *Inadequate staffing*. Sound staff planning and effective training were largely absent even though large numbers of hospital staff wished to transfer to community-based work.

On a more optimistic note, the report focused on the characteristics of good community care schemes, which were seen as developing despite, rather than because of, existing arrangements. They tended to have five features:

1. Strong and committed local 'champions' of change.
2. A focus on action, not on bureaucratic machinery.
3. Locally integrated services, cutting across agency boundaries.
4. Focus on the local neighbourhood.
5. A multidisciplinary team approach.

But the report did not believe such 'good practice' could become the norm through incremental tinkering with the present system. Strategic change was required, including clarification of which agencies should have responsibility for which care groups. One possibility was to create joint boards which would be separate from the NHS and from local authorities, but which would draw their budgets from these agencies. The Audit Commission called upon central government to set up a high-level review to come to clear decisions on these issues.

The Griffiths Report

It did not take long for the government to respond to the Audit Commission's recommendation for a high-level review. In December 1986, the then Secretary of State for Social Services asked Sir Roy

Griffiths 'to review the way in which public funds are used to support community care policy and to advise me on the options for action that would improve the use of these funds as a contribution to more effective community care'.

Sir Roy produced an eight-page letter to the Secretary of State and a thirty-page main report. Throughout his letter and the main report, certain themes dominated, which reflected the conclusions of earlier reports. These themes were:

1. That central government for thirty years had failed to develop any link between the objectives of community care policy and the resources made available to meet those objectives.
2. That responsibilities at the local level were unclear between health authorities, social services authorities, housing authorities, the voluntary sector and the private sector, and co-ordination was not well developed.
3. That choice and efficiency should be stimulated through a mixed economy approach in which the public, private and voluntary sectors compete to provide services on an equal footing.
4. That the system of subsidising private and voluntary sector residential and nursing home places through the social security system was wasteful because of the lack of assessment of need for residential care.

To the surprise of many, Sir Roy rejected the Audit Commission's idea of a joint board to manage community care provision. He argued that 'major restructuring can be disruptive and time-consuming and before it is contemplated it has to be shown that the existing authorities are incapable of delivering' (Griffiths, 1988, p. 16). Instead, he came up with the following package of proposals:

• *Central government* should appoint a Minister of Community Care who would be responsible for defining the values and objectives of community care as a guide to service development. The minister would be responsible for ensuring the maintenance of a link between objectives and resources as well as monitoring progress towards the achievement of objectives. A system of earmarked funds should be available to social service authorities to ensure the speedier development of community care services on the ground. The payment of such funds by central government would be dependent upon approval of submitted plans. Where possible the community care plan of a health authority should be approved at the same time as that of its corresponding social services authority. The details of this grant system were not specified but it would be about 40–50 per cent of the money to be spent by social services departments on community care.

- *Social services departments* should play the lead rôle for all community care groups in terms of the identification of need, the creation of packages of care and the co-ordination of services. They should regulate private and voluntary residential and nursing homes. Griffiths stressed this was not a remit for local authorities to become a monopoly supplier, but a remit to organise or regulate a mixed economy system. Community care services needed to be responsive to local need. Social services departments were grounded in the community and were accountable to democratically elected councillors. Hence, Griffiths argued that they should have the lead rôle.

- *Housing authorities* should be responsible for providing only the 'bricks and mortar' component of community care. In other words, they should provide sheltered housing but not employ wardens or organise meals-on-wheels services.

- *Health authorities* would continue to be responsible for medically required community health services, including any necessary input into assessing needs and delivering packages of care. They would be responsible for health care, narrowly defined.

- *General medical practitioners* should be responsible for ensuring that their local social services department is systematically informed about the needs of their patients for non-health care.

- *Residential and nursing home residents* in the public, private and voluntary sectors should receive public financial support only following separate assessments of the financial means of the applicant and of the need for care. These assessments should be managed through social services departments. The process should start with an assessment of whether residential care is the most appropriate way of meeting care needs. The social security system should then contribute a financial assessment, but the resultant benefit (the residential allowance) would be set in the light of the average total of income support and housing benefit to which someone living other than in residential care would be entitled. This system would leave the social services authority 'to pay the balance of the costs' (p. 19).

- *Individuals* in the future would be expected to plan well ahead to meet more of their community care needs in old age. This would include making use of private pension plans and the equity tied up in owner-occupied property. Public subsidy would in the future be aimed at those on low incomes.

Reactions to the Griffiths Report

Academic commentators criticised the Griffiths Report on several grounds. It made assumptions about the ability of people to provide for their own social care needs which were not supported by available information on income and resources (Bosanquet and Propper, 1991). The report praised the rôle of informal carers, but failed to address how burdensome that care can often be (Baldwin and Parker, 1989). It marginalised the importance of the housing dimension of community care (Means and Harrison, 1988) and it treated the further development of a major service delivery rôle for the private sector as unproblematic (Walker, 1989).

However, many felt that the Griffiths Report had much to recommend it, despite these ambiguities and weaknesses. It avoided massive organisational disruption and showed a commitment to local government. It specified the responsibilities of central government, including the need for a Minister of Community Care, so that the relationship of resources to objectives could be addressed for the first time. Earmarked funds seemed to offer the guarantee of service development at the local level. A clear way forward was offered in terms of local leadership for social care and in terms of how best publicly to fund private residential care. Writing in 1988, one of us commented that

> All these are major gains and they are worth striving to get implemented especially when we remember the range of reports over the last few years that have continued to identify the same problems. However, the spirit of implementation at both the national and local levels will be crucial. (Means and Harrison, 1988, p. 18)

Unfortunately, a key theme of the rest of this book is the lack of a positive spirit of implementation, especially at central government level.

Social services authorities welcomed the Griffiths Report with some enthusiasm. They had feared their contribution was to be marginalised, whereas the Griffiths Report had offered them the lead agency rôle for all the main community care groups, even if this involved a reduction of their rôle in direct service provision over time. Others were less convinced. Health professionals and the independent residential and nursing-home sectors were unhappy with the main recommendations. Health professionals had lost in the 'battle' for the lead agency rôle. The independent sector feared the report was hostile to institutional care, and were concerned that the new funding regime would undermine the viability of individual homes.

Central government was silent on its views, but many commentators felt it was surprised and dismayed by the report (Baldwin and Parker, 1989; Means and Harrison, 1988). The Treasury were seen as hostile to the concept of earmarked funds for community care since this would make explicit the level of commitment of central government, and identify clearly when cutbacks in such services were being made. Several members of the Cabinet were said to be horrified at the idea of extending the powers of local authorities in community care; they had expected the Griffiths Report to criticise local authorities and to demand a dramatic reduction in their rôle.

The White Paper on community care

The Griffiths Report was published in March 1988 and yet the White Paper on community care did not appear until November 1989. During that period, central government examined several alternatives to the proposals in the Griffiths Report, but in the end decided that none of them was implementable. The White Paper therefore followed the main recommendations of the Griffiths Report, but with some notable exceptions, and stated that all these changes were to be implemented on 1 April 1991.

Social services authorities retained their lead agency rôle and it was stressed that 'the Government also endorses Sir Roy's vision of authorities as arrangers and purchasers of care services rather than as monopolistic providers' (Department of Health, 1989a, p. 17). The White Paper went on to list the main responsibilities of this lead agency rôle:

- carrying out an appropriate assessment of an individual's need for social care (including residential and nursing-home care), in collaboration as necessary with medical, nursing and other caring agencies, before deciding what services should be provided;

- designing packages of services tailored to meet the assessed needs of individuals and their carers. The appointment of a 'case manager' may facilitate this;
- securing the delivery of services, not simply by acting as direct providers, but by developing their purchasing and contracting rôle to become 'enabling authorities' (p. 17).

Thus, at the operational level, social services authorities were to develop case management (later called care management) as a way to deliver needs-led rather than service-led systems of assessment and care delivery. At the strategic level, social services were to be responsible for producing community care plans consistent with the plans of health authorities and other relevant agencies, and these plans were to be submitted on an annual basis to the Social Services Inspectorate of the Department of Health. These plans were intended to show how services were to make maximum use of the independent sector.

Three other important changes were announced in the White Paper. First, a new system of complaints was to be introduced. Second, a new system of inspection was to be developed for residential care in all sectors. The inspection units were to be 'at arm's length' from the management of services and were to be accountable to the Director of Social Services. Third, a new funding structure for those seeking public support for residential and nursing home care was proposed, with local authorities taking over responsibility for financial support of people in private and voluntary homes, over and above their entitlement to general social security benefits. This was to be funded through a transfer of money from the social security budget to local authorities. However, local authorities would have discretion to use this money to fund domiciliary services, which might reduce the need for so many people to enter residential care.

Most of these proposals were very close to those of the Griffiths Report. However, the White Paper did not propose a Minister of Community Care and it did not offer a new system of earmarked funds for social care along the lines advocated by Griffiths. Apart from a limited scheme to fund community services for those with severe mental health problems and another to fund alcohol and drug services, extra funds to meet the increased social care responsibilities of local authorities were to be channelled through the revenue support grant system. Most of this extra finance was to come from a transfer of money away from the social security budget where it was used as payment for residents with low incomes and resources in private and voluntary residential care. In future, local authorities were to have discretion about how much of this money should be used to develop community services rather than to fund residential provision.

The White Paper followed the Griffiths Report in encouraging local authorities to focus their energies on meeting the needs of consumers. This was to be achieved at an individual level by care managers who were to be responsible for client assessment and then for delivering flexible packages of care. At an aggregate level, this would be supported by the new system of local authority community care plans based on an assessment of need within the whole community. These plans were to be the basis for developing a wide spectrum of services, many of them contracted out, which could be drawn on as appropriate by care managers for their individual clients. The White Paper was quite clear that such packages should 'make use wherever possible of services from voluntary, "not for profit" and private providers insofar as this represents a cost-effective care choice' (p. 22). In other words, social services authorities were expected 'to take all reasonable steps to secure diversity of provision' (p. 22) and 'in particular, they should consider how they will encourage diversification into the non-residential care sector' (p. 23).

However, the White Paper did not recommend compulsory competitive tendering as the best way to achieve such a mixed economy of care. Rather it indicated that 'the government . . . favours giving local authorities an opportunity to make greater use of service specifications, agency agreements and contracts in an evolutionary way'. The White Paper suggested that this required local authorities to separate their purchaser functions from their provider functions. Through this mechanism, purchasing staff within social services could be encouraged to assess objectively the contribution of 'in house' service providers, such as the home care service, against what the independent sector might be able to provide.

The NHS and Community Care Act was passed by Parliament in the summer of 1990, only for the government to announce major delays in the implementation timetable. Proposals on the inspection of residential homes, the new complaints procedure and the earmarked mental health grant proceeded on 1 April 1991, but community care plans did not become a statutory requirement until twelve months later and the new funding regime for residential and nursing-home care was not introduced until April 1993. Social services complained about these delays but many senior managers accepted that they needed much longer preparation time (Hoyes and Means, 1993b).

If the verdict on the Griffiths Report was one of 'cautious optimism' (Baldwin and Parker, 1989, p. 151), then reactions to the White Paper seemed to be far less favourable. Hudson (1990, p. 33) claimed 'the primary imperative for the Government has been to find the least bad option for capping social security payments to private residential care', and hence the White Paper owed 'more to political expediency than to a commitment to a vision of "caring for people" '. Langan (1990) attacked the White Paper as being part of a Thatcherite strategy of marketisation of public services, a view she justified by reference to the emphasis on the contracting-out of social care services to the independent sector and the failure to guarantee adequate public resources. She concluded that these 'market-led proposals for community care' would 'guarantee only greater hardship to that section of society that is least capable of bearing it' (p. 69). Biggs (1990/91) was equally critical of the marketisation of community care, which he believed was built upon both a deep hostility to local government and a misplaced faith in the capacity of the market to generate choice for consumers. More specifically, he attacked the emergence of care management and 'arm's-length' inspection systems as part of a process of professionals distancing themselves from users. Both involved a shift from client care-giving to negotiation and networking with other bodies, and Biggs expressed the fear that

> they also include a tendency to replace client feedback from consumers as an indicator of effectiveness, with administrative or technical issues to do with the internal 'efficiency' of the organisation and in so doing obscure judgements of a political and ethical nature. (p. 24)

He lamented that 'a decade of hostility to local government welfare has severely weakened confidence amongst existing providers, so much so, that radical proposals to replace public with private welfare and change the balance of client care-giving in favour of management systems have not, as yet, been significantly resisted' (p. 35).

Further legislative change

The NHS and Community Care Act 1990 did not see an end to legislative change in community care during the 1990s. Subsequent change included the Carers (Recognition of Services) Act 1995, passed as a result of a private members' bill, which received wide political backing. It gave a right to a separate assessment to people providing informal care on a regular basis to ill, elderly or disabled friends or relatives who were seeking help from social services. Social services were required to take their views and the results of their assessment into account when deciding what services to provide to the person being cared for. The White Paper had acknowledged 'that the great bulk of community care is provided by friends, family and neighbours' and 'that carers need help and support if they are to continue to carry out their rôle' (Department of Health, 1989a, p. 4). The proponents of the Carers Act argued that this required a right to a separate assessment so as (i) to recognise the pivotal rôle of carers in many care packages; (ii) to encourage social services to think about their support needs; and (iii) to discourage social services from exploiting carers, especially where they are young.

The Community Care (Direct Payments) Act 1996 gave physically disabled people under 65 and people with learning difficulties under 65 the possibility of receiving a payment to arrange their own care services rather than receiving services arranged for them by the local authority. Previously, such direct payment, personal assistance or independent living schemes were only legal if social services gave a grant for a third party (usually a well-established voluntary organisation) to run such schemes on their behalf. This private members' bill was campaigned for by the British Council of Organisations of Disabled People and the Independent Living Movement because it would enable many more people to arrange their own personal assistance, employ their own workers and manage their own care. It received cautious government support because it was seen as consistent with their self-help/mixed economy philosophy so long as it was not extended to older people who might 'open the floodgates' in terms of public expenditure (House of Lords Library, 1995).

Direct payments were only a possibility for those entitled to community care services. The social services authorities were given only a permissive power to develop this option, and hence there would be no guarantee of local availability. Where such schemes were to be developed, the Act gives clients the right to refuse this option, while social services have a duty to establish that the recipient can manage a direct payment (with support or through an agent if necessary). The money cannot be used to pay for residential care.

Quasi-markets and the restructuring of welfare in Britain

The strength of the critiques by Hudson, Langan and Biggs is that they locate the community care reforms within broader concerns about the restructuring of welfare in Britain. The rest of this chapter is designed to take such insights further by locating these changes within broad debates about (quasi) markets and post-Fordism.

In the nineteenth century, Marx argued that developed capitalist economies could produce a vast range of goods but not distribute them according to any concept of need. Increasing unemployment and poverty was the inevitable consequence of capitalism for large sections of the working class. A just society could only be achieved through the socialisation of the means of production. The speeding-up of welfare reforms in Britain during the 1940s seemed to offer an alternative approach and one capable of attracting a consensus across the political spectrum. The 1942 Beveridge Report notion of insurance against the hazards of the market economy represented the social component of what was frequently called 'the welfare state'; increasingly, both Labour and Conservative governments seemed to believe that social policies should offer a universal minimum standard of housing, income, education and health for all. However, Mishra (1984) has argued that the ideas developed by Keynes were equally influential because they provided the economic component of the argument. Reduced to bare essentials, Keynesian economics argued that governments could and should intervene to manage demand in the market economy. In particular, public spending during a recession could be used to avoid the mass unemployment of the 1930s.

The attraction of such policies was hardly surprising. The Second World War caused enormous social and economic disruption and led to widespread concern for the development of policies which would foster social integration and citizenship. Such policies represented a stimulus to the war effort and a practical programme for economic recovery after the war had been won. Alternatives to the compromise of welfare statism between capital and labour seemed less than appealing. For the right, there was the fear of labour unrest, and, for the left, an appreciation of the exhaustion of the working class from the war, combined with growing gloom about trends in Eastern Europe and especially Stalinist Russia. Commentators on the left, including most mainstream social policy writers such as Titmuss (Abel-Smith and Titmuss, 1987) saw the welfare state as undermining capitalism by bringing out the essential 'goodness' and altruism in human beings. The welfare state might become a peaceful stepping-stone into socialism, the completion of which required a series of Labour Party victories in general elections. For the right, there was the reassurance of a recovering world economy after the Second World War.

Such policy developments were not a purely British phenomenon and similar trends in welfare provision could be traced in many other developed countries (Deakin, 1987). Equally, however, the legitimacy of large-scale state provision came under challenge from the late 1970s onwards in nearly all these countries. Writing in the early 1980s, Mishra listed the following reasons why welfare states in the industrialised West were in disarray. These were:

> First, the onset of 'stagflation' and the end of economic growth – not only has the resource base for social expenditure ceased to grow but, more ominously, the welfare state is being seen as a barrier to economic recovery. Second, the end of full employment in some countries. Third, the 'fiscal crisis' of the state: partly as a result of the economic recession, governments in many countries face a yawning gap between the resources necessary to finance public expenditure and the revenue actually raised. Fourth, a decline in the resources available to the social services, followed, recently, by a deliberate policy of cutback in services in a number of countries. Fifth, a general loss of confidence in the social system of the Welfare State. (1984, p. xiii)

New Right theorists argued that the social policies associated with Beveridge and the economic policies associated with Keynes undermined economic growth and wealth creation. Entrepreneurial energy was being discouraged by excessive taxation and excessive regulation. Jobs were not taken up because the unemployed were happy to live off social security benefits rather than take low-paid employment. Government had spread its tentacles too far and too deeply; many of the resultant complex and expensive interventions, such as higher education, housing and urban regeneration, had been a failure, with little evidence of tangible results. Finally, the welfare state had become a vast vested interest, largely run for the benefit of those who worked for it (civil servants, welfare professionals). Such individuals were always keen to support new demands from new pressure groups if they seemed likely to generate yet more jobs and career opportunities within the welfare state itself.

The post-1979 Thatcher governments in Britain supported the New Right critique of the welfare state and this was reflected in many of their social and economic policies (Sullivan, 1994). Policies were being driven by an ideology with four main elements:

1. Market mechanisms should be used wherever possible, even if there cannot be a fully free market for the services.
2. Competition should be established between providers, and consumers should be allowed to opt out of state provision to sharpen competition, with the private and voluntary sectors where possible, but also between different public providers.
3. Individualism and individual choice should take precedence over collective choices and planned provision.
4. State provision should be kept to a minimum, to encourage those who can afford it to supplement state provision or opt out. (Based on Flynn, 1989)

However, the first eight years of Thatcherism saw more rhetoric than action in terms of major welfare change. All this changed dramatically with the election of the third Thatcher government:

> A major offensive against the bureaucratic structures of welfare provision was launched in 1988 and 1989: years that in retrospect will be seen as critical in the history of British social policy. For it was then that the Government began to apply a programme of introducing internal or 'quasi'-markets to the welfare state. (Le Grand and Bartlett, 1993, p. 21)

More specifically these years saw a series of major reforms and reviews: the Education Reform Act 1988; the White Paper *Working for Patients* (Department of Health, 1989b); both the Griffiths Report (1988) and the White Paper on community care (Department of Health, 1989a); and two major housing acts.

So what are quasi-markets? Le Grand and Bartlett argue that all these reforms remain based upon state finance but that they propose radical change in systems of service delivery. State (near) monopoly provision is being either replaced or complemented through the development of a variety of private, voluntary and public providers, all operating in competition with one another. It is through the mechanism of the contract that 'the state, locally and centrally' is transformed 'into an "enabling" organisation, responsible for ensuring *that* public services are delivered, rather than producing it directly itself' (Deakin and Walsh, 1996, p. 33).

This is seen as the development of quasi rather than pure markets for a number of reasons on both the supply and demand side. In terms of supply, the multiple independent providers are not all privately owned nor are they all out to achieve profit maximisation. On the demand side, quasi-markets differ from conventional markets in that purchase is normally achieved not through money but through a voucher or earmarked budget, which are confined to the purchase of a specific service. Not only this, but purchasing decisions are often delegated to a third party (a care manager, a GP, or a health authority) rather than directly to the service user (Le Grand and Bartlett, 1993).

Post-Fordism and the community care reforms

It could be argued that this major restructuring of welfare was driven by the energy and dynamism of a particular prime minister with a vision of an enterprise culture. However, Margaret Thatcher resigned in November 1990 and, without Thatcher, it may turn out that there is no Thatcherism. Many of the quasi-market reforms were soon to experience difficulties of varying degrees of severity (Bartlett et al., 1994). However, the premiership of John Major saw no gradual return to a belief in the provision of services on a near-monopoly basis by public bureaucracies such as local government. There seems little chance of a complete reversal of policy despite a Labour election victory in May 1997.

How can this be explained? The depth of the crisis of welfare states in a number of countries was underlined by the earlier comment from Mishra. The need to revolutionise welfare is recognised by commentators of the centre and left as well as New Right theorists (Thompson and Hoggett, 1996; Coote, 1992). In other words, dissatisfaction with the welfare state of the 1950s, 1960s and 1970s goes much deeper than the New Right. Hadley and Hatch (1981) produced *Social Welfare and the Failure of the State: Centralised Social Services and Participatory Alternatives* in the early 1980s. As suggested by the title, their central thesis was that the centralised social services of the 1940s onwards had been a failure, the reason given being that they had developed into ossified bureaucracies which alienate and despise consumers, the very people such services had been set up to serve in the first place. As a way forward, they proposed an alternative structure of social services based on four main elements:

1. Plural provision. A greater proportion of all forms of social service should be provided by voluntary organisations, the one major exception being social security.
2. Decentralisation and community orientation of statutory services. The predominant mode of statutory provision should be the community-oriented one, implying flatter structures, a different interpretation of professionalism and reinforcement as opposed to replacement of informal sources of care.
3. Contractual rather than hierarchical accountability. In return for funding and the contracting-out of more services to voluntary organisations, government, both local and central, should exercise a stronger monitoring and inspection rôle than at present.
4. Participation and representation. The counterpart of greater monitoring and inspection should be the participation of consumers and providers in statutory decision-making.

This type of approach came increasingly to be referred to as welfare pluralism (N. Johnson, 1987). It differed from the New Right policy agenda because of its emphasis on public subsidy rather than self-provisioning and its suspicion of the private sector as a possible service provider.

Similar themes emerged in the body of work associated with those calling for a radical decentralisation of local government services. After their 1979 election victory, an early focus of the new Conservative government was the deficiencies of local government in general and Labour-run authorities in particular. At the same time, many socialists saw local government as a possible base from which to undermine the recent ascendancy of the right. At the very least, there was a need to defend public services against cutbacks, but for some the task was also 'to explore the socialist potential of local government and local political space' (Boddy and Fudge, 1984, p. 2). Such islands of successful socialism could be used to wean the general population away from its apparent growing scepticism about large-scale state intervention. These more radical Labour authorities were developing a range of new initiatives, relating in particular to employment, women, race and the decentralisation of services. It is the emphasis on decentralisation which most concerns us here.

A feature of the early defence campaigns was that service users, especially council-house residents, seemed remarkably reluctant to identify with councillors and activists in this struggle. This became a pivotal factor in encouraging a reconsideration of the relationship of service consumers to service providers in Labour-run local authorities. The emerging critique was very similar to that of Hadley and Hatch (1981). The culprit was 'centralised, state-run, functionally managed, public service provision' (Hambleton and Hoggett, 1984) which was generating growing dissatisfaction:

> This dissatisfaction rolls together concern about the remoteness of centralised decision-making structures, irritation with the insensitivity and lack of accountability of officers employed by the state, and discontent with the sectional and blinkered approach to problem solving and service provision often associated with departmental (or functional) organisational structures. (p. 4)

One response to such dissatisfaction was to decentralise services into neighbourhood offices in which rigid departmental boundaries could be broken down. Such initiatives usually included at least the aspiration to involve local residents more fully in the running of services. Initiatives developed in authorities such as Walsall, Hackney, Islington and Birmingham (Hoggett and Hambleton, 1987).

This critique of central bureaucracies had much in common with aspects of the argument put forward by those calling for privatisation or welfare pluralism. However, the proposed solution differed in that the concern was not to turn away from state provision but rather to change the way in which public services were provided: 'it involves shifting attention from the quantity of service provision to questions of quality and seeks to change the relationship between public servants and the public they serve' (Hambleton and Hoggett, 1984, p. 5). The aim was not only to improve the distribution, accountability and quality of public services, but also to raise political awareness. This was to be achieved primarily via the empowerment of the consumers and local residents through giving them more direct control over local services.

But where have the fresh organisational ideas of the New Right, the centre and the left come from, and why do all of them seem to stress devolved management, devolved budgets, cost centres, control by contracts and the need for more individually tailored services? In observing this phenomenon, Hoggett (1991, 1996) argued that the public sector reflects the private sector in its dominant forms of organisation. In the 1950s and 1960s, industry was dominated by the large-scale production of standard necessities (sometimes called Fordism). It is interesting to note that the newly created social services departments were often disparagingly called 'Seebohm factories' in the early 1970s. The recommendations of the Seebohm Report (1968) on local authority and allied personal services had led to large numbers of smaller welfare departments being consolidated into a single larger authority. A common concern was that this would lead to more rigid managerial and bureaucratic control over the discretion of field-level staff to agitate on behalf of their low-income clients (Bailey and Brake, 1975). In other words, social services staff were becoming workers in large social work factories.

However, the technological base of bureaucracy in the private sector was undermined during the 1970s by the emergence of flexible automation and information technologies. The result was that the late 1970s and 1980s saw a shift towards a greater degree of market segmentation based upon highly differentiated products with a much shorter lifespan than that associated with Fordist systems of production (Burrows and Loader, 1994). In terms of private sector organisation, this saw the development of what Peters and Waterman (1982) called 'tight/loose' systems of organisation in which the centre loosens its grip over many aspects of production so that it can more effectively control the essentials of values, culture and strategy. Contracting out, decentralised production units and localised cost centres have been made possible by the emergence of computerised management and financial systems. Fierce arguments exist over the extent of these changes and whether the term 'post-Fordism' manages to capture their thrust and/or diversity. Hoggett (1991) expresses the view that 'perhaps one of the few advantages of the term . . . is its agnosticism about the future, i.e. it suggests that we're more clear about where we're coming from than where we're going to' (p. 243). The search is on for what Hoggett calls post-bureaucratic systems of organisational control.

It is these core–periphery models which came to the British public sector in the late 1980s although in a form which reflected the New Right ideology of the Conservatives. The decentralisation of largely operational services was combined with a broader centralisation of government power and influence, so that

> Whilst operations have been devolved to business units such as schools, trusts or agencies, control over policy and the allocation

of resources has been increasingly concentrated within Whitehall, centralised but arm's-length agencies such as the Funding Authority for Schools . . . or the new regional arms of central government. . . . Increasingly, the centre does not simply prescribe performance targets for operational managers but offers incentives and sanctions for meeting targets. (Hoggett, 1996, p. 19)

Hence, in the policy area of community care, social service authorities were not only being encouraged to develop independent sector services but access to their social security transfer money was dependent upon 85 per cent of that money being spent on that sector.

This decentralisation–centralisation with the heavy surveillance of many publicly funded workers through contracts, audits and job specification, leads Hoggett to refer to the British public sector in the mid-1990s as a 'flawed' post-bureaucratic regime (p. 12). However, in his earliest writing on this subject, Hoggett stressed that

whilst contemporary processes of modernisation be technologically driven, they are not technologically determined. A variety of social choices are possible within the frame provided by a given techno-managerial paradigm. (1990, p. 15)

The election of a Labour government in 1997 offers possibilities of new choices to be made. What some of these might be is a central concern of the final chapter. The choice which is not available is a drift back to the old-style social services department or 'Seebohm factory'.

Conclusion

This chapter began by describing the run-up to the White Paper on community care in terms of some very specific concerns about the mushrooming costs of institutional care and the failure to run down large mental handicap and mental health hospitals. However, it has been argued that the resultant reforms need to be understood in terms of the major restructuring of the British welfare state in the late 1980s. The springboard for this was not the radicalism of the then prime minister but rather the impact of much broader global trends. These included not only growing doubts across the political spectrum about the efficiency and effectiveness of large-scale public bureaucracies, but also the emergence of radical organisational alternatives, drawn from the private sector and made possible by technological advances in information and budgetary systems. However, the approach to community care reform chosen by the Conservative government did reflect their distrust of the public sector, their dislike of public expenditure and their belief in the efficiency of markets.

4 Towards User and Carer Empowerment?

The key theme of the last chapter was to place the community care reforms within the context of the broad criticism of welfare state institutions being run in the interests of staff rather than consumers. Increasingly, commentators talk in terms of the need to empower those who use community care services (Braye and Preston-Shoot, 1995; Jack, 1995; Servian, 1996). Chapter 1 observed that both the White Paper on community care (Department of Health, 1989a, p. 4) and the subsequent practitioner guidance stressed that 'the rationale for this reorganisation is the empowerment of users and carers' (Department of Health/Social Services Inspectorate, 1991, p. 7). Job advertisements (see Figure 4.1) can now be found in which empowerment is not only listed as a task to be achieved but also incorporated into the very job title itself. The focus of this chapter is on the likelihood of such empowerment occurring.

USER EMPOWERMENT – PROJECT CO-ORDINATOR

The Leonard Cheshire Foundation, a leading care provider for people with disabilities, offers a range of services through its Care at Home Services, respite care, day services and residential homes. The Foundation currently provides services for approximately 8,500 people.

A grant has been received from the National Lotteries Charity Board to run a UK-wide project to empower the Foundation's service users. The principal aim of the project is to assist disabled people in developing their self-confidence and acquiring skills in management.

The Project Co-ordinator must have personal experience of disability and, because of the nature of the job, preference will be given to a disabled person. The Co-ordinator must have management experience including training and budgetary control.

Source: Précis of job advertisement in *Guardian Society*.

FIGURE 4.1   Job advertisement

The starting point is to consider what is meant by the term 'empowerment' and the contribution made to the debate by advocates of normalisation and ordinary life approaches and by the disability movement. Key issues are identified, such as whether or not all service users have common interests and whether or not the interests of users and carers conflict. The second half of the chapter looks at four different strategies for achieving empowerment: namely exit, voice and rights strategies and how these relate to the concept of empowerment through struggle.

What is empowerment?

There is no simple answer as to what does and what does not represent user empowerment, since it is a contested concept. However, most would argue that it involves users taking or being given more power over decisions affecting their welfare and hence it probably involves taking at least some power away from service providers, although this chapter will show how some writers (Servian, 1996; Oliver, 1996) draw upon the work of Foucault to stress that power is a relational concept rather than a zero-sum game.

Any discussion of empowerment has to consider the concept of power. Lukes (1974), in his illuminating analysis of this concept, outlines three main perspectives. The one-dimensional concept of power focuses on observable conflict and seeks to study whose preferences prevail. The two-dimensional view is more subtle in that it takes into account the way in which the powerful mobilise bias so as to ensure that the rules of the game operate in their favour so that they can keep some sources of conflict or potential conflict off the political agenda. However, Lukes argues the need to develop this perspective one stage further into a three-dimensional view of power which

> allows for consideration of the many ways in which potential issues are kept out of politics. . . What one may have here is a latent conflict, which consists in a contradiction between the interests of those exercising power and the real interests of those they exclude. These latter may not express or even be conscious of their interests. (p. 25)

In other words, the victims of non-decision-making may not always be aware that they are victims because they do not always appreciate their real interests. This perspective, if accepted, has major implications for the empowerment debate in community care. It suggests that creating opportunities for greater participation, dialogue and control over services will not be enough, since many services users and potential service users will not be fully aware of their real interests. It suggests that empowerment requires a general raising of awareness about how society discriminates against and oppresses older people and disabled people. Professional evangelists in the ordinary life and/or normalisation movement have always been centrally interested in this more subtle form of power. They have been concerned to identify the real interests of people with learning difficulties and then to fight for services which have the capacity to foster those interests.

Normalisation and ordinary living

There are several useful outlines available showing how the concept of normalisation originated in Scandinavia, was further developed in North America and subsequently transported to Britain by professionals attempting to act in the interests of people with learning difficulties (Emerson, 1992; Race, 1987). Normalisation was initially a straightforward concept which emphasised that services should attempt to deliver a high quality of life for users and that this required them to reproduce the life-style experienced by non-disabled citizens through such characteristics as the rhythm of the day, progression through the life course, the development of sexual relationships, self-determination and economic standards. In other words, normalisation was 'a statement about how services can reflect the basic rights of people with learning difficulties in an egalitarian society' (Emerson, 1992, p. 3).

However, North American theorists, such as Wolfensberger, introduced a more sociological perspective to normalisation theory by arguing that it should be much more concerned both with the way people with learning difficulties are portrayed and perceived by the public and with the need to develop socially valued rôles for such people (Wolfensberger and Thomas, 1983). The emphasis switched to the way people with learning difficulties are labelled and have rôles forced on them. The way forward was to improve both the social image of service users and their personal competence. Proponents of normalisation see this approach as having the capacity to empower people with learning difficulties through offering them self-determination.

Others have been less sure. Even if normalisation theorists attempt to empower, the driving force for achieving this is the professional. As Chappell (1992) argues:

> Normalisation offers a theory of how to improve services. As services are controlled by professionals, normalisation has enabled professionals to retain a key rôle in the debate about quality. It does not challenge the legitimacy of the professional rôle in the lives of people with learning difficulties. It has enabled professionals to adapt to deinstitutionalisation by developing new models of practice. It therefore continues to legitimise their authority. (p. 40)

This is a rather harsh view, given the overall beneficial impact of ordinary life and normalisation theory upon the quality of services provided for people with learning difficulties. It should be recalled that normalisation theory was a major factor in persuading policy-makers and professionals to reject hospital-based services in the UK (King's Fund Centre, 1980). However, real empowerment would require tackling the material poverty of people with learning difficulties rather than just marginally improving the services which provide shelter at night and 'recreation' during the day (Fulcher, 1996).

The fourth dimension of power

It can be argued that such gains can only be achieved through a process of struggle in which service users take the lead rather than await the intervention of enlightened professionals. Such struggles are about changing the relations of power.

Drawing upon the work of Foucault (1979), Servian (1996) refers to this as a fourth dimension of power in which power is no longer a thing to be won or lost but rather a process by which the identities of individuals are socially constructed, often by welfare professionals and welfare institutions. Such 'disciplinary' power has often been forged through the use of institutions such as school, prison and hospital with discipline in these institutions being made possible by the application of surveillance techniques. A key feature of the 1980s onwards has been the movement of people out of closed institutions into broader society. This has required the development of micro-techniques of power and surveillance for those in the community, such as assessment, diagnosis, screening, codification and categorisation, all of which serve to help define the client, and the nature of his or her problems, in technical, legislative and bureaucratic terms. Cohen (1985) has shown how a juvenile delinquency industry developed in America to run community-based systems of social control and surveillance and how they have been able to penetrate deep into the heart of working-class communities and especially into the lives of working-class youth. Prisons fail and so young men are diverted into community-based alternatives. These fail and so young men are diverted into community activities before they offend. And so on. In such a way young offenders and young people deemed at risk are sifted and classified, and hence Cohen's 'vision of social control . . . is the eternal case conference' (p. 185). The relevance of such an analysis to the 'new' community care is obvious.

As indicated, such power and social control is nevertheless seen as relational rather than absolute, so that

> The greatest achievement of power is its reification. When power is regarded as thinglike, as something solid, real and material, as something an agent has, then this represents power in its most pervasive and concrete mode. . . However, reified power will rarely if ever occur entirely without resistance. (Clegg, 1989, p. 207)

This resistance can take two forms. First it can involve 'resistance to the exercise of power which leaves unquestioned the fixity of the terms in which that power is exercised' (p. 207). The normalisation movement could be argued to involve this form of resistance because it seeks to change what professionals do rather than power relations between the professional and the service user. The second form of resistance is less common but more fundamental and involves the fixing of new relations of power. The UK disability movement can be seen as attempting this latter form of resistance.

Empowerment and the disability movement

Many professionals have become concerned about issues of empowerment because they are under growing pressure from users and their organisations. Campbell and Oliver (1996) provide an excellent account of the development of the disability movement in Britain. They chart the growth of traditional voluntary organisations such as the Royal National Institute for the Blind and the formation of single-issue pressure groups such as the Disablement Income Group. Both tended to be ineffective in terms of improving the situation of disabled people, who began to appreciate the need to establish their own organisations. More specifically, 1981 was the International Year of Disabled People and saw the establishment in Britain of the British Council of Organisations of Disabled People, which by the early 1990s comprised over 80 independent organisations. Equally important was the subsequent formation of Disabled People International. This organisation of disabled people was formed after Rehabilitation International rejected a resolution at its 1980 conference that at least 50 per cent of the members of each national delegation should be disabled people. Morris (1991) sees this as a crucial moment of fighting back which required a struggle for power between organisations of disabled people and organisations for disabled people: 'disabled people had to assert their autonomy and attempt to take power away from the professionals who controlled not only the disability organisations but also the individual lives of disabled people' (p. 175).

The theoretical starting point of the UK disability movement is their commitment to a social model of disability. This model is highly critical of previous definitions of disability because of their tendency to individualise and medicalise so that disability is seen as ultimately reducible to the functional limitations of disabled individuals (Oliver, 1996). In contrast to this, the social model of disability is based on the following distinction:

- *Impairment:* Lacking part or all of a limb, or having a defective limb, organism or mechanism of the body.
- *Disability:* The disadvantage and restriction of activity caused by a contemporary social organisation which takes no or little account of people who have physical impairments and thus excludes them from the mainstream of social activities. (Quoted in Oliver, 1990, p. 11)

Such an approach recognises that people have impairments but argues that it is society which disables them. This is through its imposition of, for example, segregated special schools rather than mainstream education; income maintenance benefits rather than access to the labour market; care management rather than direct payment schemes; and inaccessible housing rather than lifetime homes. The way forward is for disabled people to take control of their lives by gaining sufficient resources to decide how best to meet their own personal assistance needs rather than, as at present, being expected to live on poverty benefits and to receive care services under the control of welfare professionals or family members. Disability thus becomes a political issue in which disabled people are invited to join a struggle or social movement with a manifesto to win their right to be full citizens of the society in which they live (Campbell and Oliver, 1996).

Common needs? Common interests?

The disability movement, therefore, argues that the way forward is for disabled people to organise together and hence to act as capable agents rather than passive victims. Above all the focus is upon their common experience of discrimination by society which means they have a common interest in fighting for their civil rights to meet their common needs.

A number of disabled authors who support such a perspective have nevertheless pointed to certain tensions within the movement. At the core of these concerns is how to balance the emphasis upon shared agendas with the heterogeneity of sources of discrimination. Perhaps some of the fiercest comments have come from black disabled people (Begum, Hill and Stevens, 1994):

> I got fed up to the back teeth of being told by white disabled people that as black disabled people we shouldn't be concerned with issues of race and disability; that we should be concerned only with issues of disability because that was the fight; that was the most important element in our character. I am of the belief that black disabled people share a lot in common with white disabled people. We have lots of issues in common, but we cannot ignore the fact that to a very large extent there still is that added element of racism that we have to encounter as black people. I didn't think that the white disability movement was taking that on board. (Hill, quoted in Campbell and Oliver, 1996, p. 132)

One implication of such an analysis is that community care services and relations between welfare professionals and black service users need to be understood in terms of racism as well as disablism. This requires 'white cultural assumptions underpinning current community care policies being recognised, their limitations understood and their relevance to services for people . . . from black and ethnic communities challenged' (Baxter et al., 1990). Studies are now beginning to emerge which illustrate how the colour-blind nature of provision means that many potential recipients of services fail to come forward to express their needs. This in turn helps to perpetuate complacency about previous services and to encourage sweeping assumptions about the capacity and desire of black families to care for all its members without support from publicly funded services (Askham *et al.*, 1995; Ahmad and Atkin, 1996).

In a similar way to Begum, Hill and Stevens (1994) with regard to race and the disability movement, Morris (1996) has complained that disabled women are too often marginalised not only by non-disabled feminists but also by males who tend to dominate the disabled people's movement. More generally in terms of gender and community care, a number of authors have reflected upon the fact that most elderly service users are female and hence open to being patronised and marginalised by health and welfare professionals, especially if these are male (Arber and Ginn, 1995).

A rather different issue is whether the disability movement speaks for some kinds of impairment and health problem with greater clarity than for others. Thus, many 'survivors' may feel that discussion in the disability movement continues to place too much emphasis upon physical access issues rather than upon the key concerns of people with mental health problems. Also, Campbell and Oliver (1996, chapter 8) have recently acknowledged that the disability movement in the UK is unable to claim to be a mass movement at the present because some groups, especially other disabled people, participate hardly at all. This, of course, begs the issue of whether older people whose experience of impairment may often not occur until later life are ever likely to identify in large numbers with the social model of disability and its political action implications. How easily can the disability movement and organisations of disabled people represent the interests of older people who use community care services?

One difficulty may be that older people are more likely to believe that their impairments and ill-health do make a difference to their lives, and hence might be inclined to agree that

> there is a tendency within the social model of disability to deny the experience of our own bodies, insisting that our physical differences and restrictions are entirely socially created. While environmental barriers and social attitudes are a crucial part of our experience of disability – and do indeed disable us – to suggest that this is all there is to it is to deny the personal experience of physical or intellectual restrictions, of illness, of the fear of dying. (Morris, 1991, p. 10)

In any case older people are the least likely to organise themselves into user or campaign groups although there is some evidence that this is beginning to change (Carter and Nash, 1995). Older people seem to find it hardest to express dissatisfaction. Consumer surveys often generate very positive responses about services being received by older people although a much less clear-cut picture emerges when the interviewer explores levels of service satisfaction through a more in-depth discussion with the older person (Harrison and Means, 1990). In addition, it needs to be remembered that many older service users will have dementia and that this is likely to place limits upon their ability to communicate and to participate fully in a service user movement.

In making these points, there is a danger of caricaturing the common interests perspective. A political position which emphasises the shared experience of oppression of disabled people does not preclude a consideration of how other forms of oppression related to age, gender, race and sexuality can intersect with the experience of being a disabled person. Indeed, one fault that the recent disability literature cannot be accused of is a refusal to explore the implications of this for their movement (Barton, 1996; Campbell and Oliver, 1996; Morris, 1996; Oliver, 1996). Equally, the political emphasis upon a shared agenda of change does not mean that the implementation of this agenda for individuals will inevitably ignore individual needs and requirements. Thus, for example, the specific housing and support needs of a frail 85-year-old person will be different from those of a young deaf person who has just left the parental home, even though both solutions need to be committed to the principle of maximising their independence (Means, 1996a).

Finally, it should be stressed that the making of this argument is not inconsistent with recognising that although

> not all of the six million disabled people in Britain see themselves as part of the disability community, let alone as supporters of the aims or the tactics of the movement . . . [the] issues that the movement has placed on the political agenda such as rights, access, choice and control are issues relevant to the wider community. (Oliver, 1996, p. 150)

Users versus carers?

The last section raised some important issues about whether or not the needs of all service users are the same. However, there are equally fundamental issues about the relationship of empowerment of users to the empowerment of carers. One extreme position would be to argue that this is one and the same thing, but another extreme view would be to claim that users and carers always have conflicting interests.

To grapple with this issue, it is important to start by returning to the critique which has emerged regarding the assumptions made by central government about the rôles and responsibilities of carers, and especially female relatives who provide caring functions. The White Paper stressed that

> The Government acknowledges that the great bulk of community care is provided by friends, family and neighbours. The decision to take on a caring rôle is never an easy one. However, many people make that choice and it is right that they should be able to play their part in looking after those close to them. But it must be recognised that carers need help and support if they are to continue to carry out their rôle: and many people will not have carers readily available who can meet all their needs. (Department of Health, 1989a, p. 4)

Chapter 2 illustrated how one explanation of the neglect of community care services in the years after the Second World War was that government believed that such provision undermined the willingness of families to maintain caring rôles and so vast numbers of disabled and frail elderly people would be abandoned to the state at enormous cost. Such views changed only when research indicated that either services went to those without informal carers or their effect was to persuade carers that it was feasible for them to continue their caring activities longer than would otherwise be the case.

Chapter 1 outlined the extent to which caring rôles are performed by women and how feminists have argued that community care policies represent an intensification of the exploitation of women, since they involve a shift of responsibility from paid staff in institutions to unpaid care by largely female relatives in the community. Such a perspective raises the immediate issue of how best to move forward. One option would be a major expansion of domiciliary services and a more equitable sharing of caring rôles between men and women. However, Finch (1984) in her very influential article on non-sexist alternatives to community care argued that 'on balance . . . the residential route is the only one which ultimately will offer us a way out of the impasse of caring' (p. 16). In other words, the exploitation of women carers could only be overcome by persuading frail elderly and disabled people to accept high-quality institutional alternatives to living in their previous homes. Dalley (1996) has taken this argument considerably further by arguing that group living can be a positive and empowering experience if underpinned by a belief in collectivist principles.

This type of argument has been criticised on a number of fronts. Many commentators believe that it is impossible to make residential care an acceptable alternative to independent living to any but a very small minority of people (Baldwin and Twigg, 1991). The feminist literature on caring tends to concentrate upon certain types of care situation to the exclusion of others and, in particular, too little attention has been given to the co-resident carer (usually a spouse or long-term partner) where the sense of exploitation and lost labour market opportunities may be far less pertinent (Arber and Ginn, 1991). More generally their critiques are seen as failing to recognise the satisfactions of caring as well as the costs (Nolan *et al.*, 1996). Connected to this is the evidence cited by Fisher (1994) that the extent of the female imbalance in the caring rôle has been exaggerated, since the 1992 General Household Survey suggested that 2.9 million of the 6.8 million carers were men. Morris (1993) points out that the strict dichotomy between carer and cared for is misleading in that many disabled people are involved in active caring rôles.

Morris (1991) is quite clear about what service users perceive as the best way forward, despite the feminist critique of caring:

> Disabled and older people experience daily the inadequacies of 'community care' and would agree with everything that feminists such as Finch and Dalley say about the isolation, poverty and sheer hard work which too often characterises both their lives and that of their carers. However, disabled and older people as individuals and through their organisations have almost without exception put their energies into achieving a better quality of life *within* the community (taking this to mean outside residential care) and have thus maintained a (critical) support of community care policies – whilst recognising that the Conservative government may have some questionable motivations for promoting such policies. (p. 153)

Morris goes on to argue that feminists should be fighting alongside disabled people and their organisations for the full spectrum of support services which would enable people to remain outside or leave residential care. Such services would enable partners who care about a disabled person to make a positive choice as to whether or not they also wish to assist that person physically. This does not have to result in the bolstering of the dependency of female carers in the nuclear family, if access to extensive support services is a right for the disabled person irrespective of their family circumstances. The interests of users and carers do not inevitably have to conflict, so long as both are offered real alternatives.

However, the stress of the present community care system upon rationing means it is very far indeed from this state of affairs. And Morris (1991) warns that it is 'where the choice is between unsupported (or minimally supported) "family care" and residential care' that 'the physical and emotional suffering incurred by both parties to a caring relationship is often enormous' (p. 164). This ensures real tensions between users and carers over whose voice is being listened to by the statutory agencies, both in terms of individual care packaging and more strategic decision-making about priorities for service developments.

Tensions between users and carers can flow from a number of other factors and not just from resource shortages. Values and aspirations may be in conflict, and even where a sense of reciprocity exists between carer and disabled person this may become undermined in due course by the impact of ageing on one or both. Another issue is the need to recognise that users and carers may require different approaches to participation, especially in the area of learning difficulties. There has been a tendency to bias consultation at both the individual and strategic level towards the carer rather than towards the service user, as occurred in the All-Wales strategy for people with learning difficulties (McGrath and Grant, 1992).

The heterogeneity of carers and caring situations also needs to be recognised. Carers differ by age, gender, ethnicity and in terms of their relationship with the disabled person, and this has implications for the support services that they need (Nolan *et al.*, 1996). It is essential to recognise that 'caring situations vary widely in the extent and types of responsibilities, in the stage of life at which such responsibilities were taken on and in the constant or periodic nature of the need for caring' (Taylor *et al.*, 1992, p. 21). Hence, personal care may be the main feature of caring for a person with a physical impairment, but this is less likely to be the case in situations of mental ill-health. The parents of children with a learning difficulty and the partner of someone with dementia are at very different stages in the life course. Yet both these rôles tend to involve constant responsibilities, in contrast with the periodic caring required to support someone with a recurrent physical impairment or some types of mental health problem.

Strategies of empowerment

It is important to consider the degrees of empowerment which might be achieved by service users and carers and the different strategies or broad approaches which might be adopted for ensuring that such empowerment occurs. Table 4.1 illustrates the enormous variation in the degree or extent of control and influence that can be conferred on users or taken by them. There are very different views about how best to achieve progress up this ladder and not all would agree about the importance of all the steps. For example, Ramon (1991) argues that the term 'empowerment' should be reserved for situations where real power and control are taken by users. She complains of 'the use of the concept of empowerment by politicians, who are constantly cutting back on services and benefits available to people with disabilities' since they confuse 'buying power with empowerment' (p. 17). This under-lines the need to look at the four main approaches to achieving empowerment and the different assumptions that they make. These are:

1. Empowerment through 'exit';
2. Empowerment through 'voice';
3. Empowerment through 'rights';
4. Empowerment through 'struggle'.

The assumptions behind each of these approaches are considered in turn and their implications for the community care reforms are drawn out.

TABLE 4.1   Degrees of empowerment

HIGH	Users have the authority to take decisions
↑	Users have authority to take some decisions
	Users have an opportunity to influence decisions
	User views are sought before making decisions
	Decisions are publicised and explained before implementation
LOW	Information is given about decisions made

Source: Taylor *et al.* (1992) p. 3.

Empowerment through 'exit'

Several authors have drawn upon the work of Hirschman (1970) to distinguish between 'voice' and 'exit' models of user empowerment and consumer control (Means *et al.*, 1994; Taylor *et al.*, 1992). The 'voice' approach is critical where consumers want to remain with an existing provider but wish to improve the quality of the service being received, while 'exit' emphasises the importance of being able to switch services and move to alternative providers if empowerment is to occur. 'Exit' is essentially a *market* approach which seeks to empower consumers by giving them choice between alternatives and the option of 'exit' from a service and/or provider, if dissatisfied. The consumer, in other words, will be able to change provider, and if a large number of them make the same decision about the same provider then that provider will be punished for their inefficiency by going out of 'business'.

It should be noted that this 'exit' model does not, in theory at least, require a (quasi) market of providers. It would be possible for service users to be given the choice between a range of local authority services and hence the option of 'exit'. However, the community care reforms are based on a belief that such empowerment can only occur where provider competition for customers is generated from the involvement of the private and 'not for profit' sectors.

In any case, quasi-markets are a compromise approach for many 'exit' proponents. For Conservative governments and the 'New Right', the preferred system of exit is through self- provisioning. Their vision of an enterprise culture is based on low taxation and minimal state intervention and provision of services. Those who gain most from the wealth generated from this enterprise culture have two obligations. As citizens, they should be willing to make charitable donations to help those struggling to take advantage of the new opportunities. As individuals, they should develop a strategy through private pensions and insurance, both to ensure they could maintain a reasonable income after retirement, and to help them meet their future health and social care needs. Publicly funded services would be a residualised service for the less well off. These views and values were quite explicit in the Griffiths Report (1988):

> In looking at future options for the funding of community care, planning needs to take account of the possibilities of individuals beginning to plan to meet their own care needs at an earlier stage in life. . . Encouraging those who can afford to plan ahead to do so

should help to ensure that public resources are concentrated on those in greatest need. I therefore recommend that central government should look in detail at a range of options for encouraging individuals to take responsibility for planning their future needs. (p. 22)

This position was further justified on the grounds that the incomes and savings of elderly people were rising in real terms, and that this trend would continue because of the growth of occupational pension schemes.

How feasible is this purist model of 'exit' in which, for example, the elderly person with health and social care needs would, in the future, be able to shop around for a high-quality provider, drawing upon their own resources? Considerable doubts exist about the viability of this on the grounds that only a small minority of elderly people will have anything like the resources needed to meet all their needs in this way (Vincent, 1995; Groves, 1995). The main source of wealth for elderly people is home ownership and the Griffiths Report suggested this could be unlocked to help develop a greater degree of self-provisioning. Bosanquet and Propper (1991, p. 277) draw on data which suggest that housing assets of older people by the year 2000 may be as high as £279 billion and that the amount of equity owned outright by this group is likely to reach £240 billion. It is certainly true that a growing percentage of that equity is being used to enable older people to pay for their own residential and nursing-home care (Hamnett, 1995). However, there is less evidence that older people are able to self-provision if they 'stay put'. Since many elderly owner-occupiers have low incomes, they find it difficult to maintain their properties, yet alone self-provide for their health and social care costs through finding ways of releasing the equity stored in their homes (Davey, 1996). The above trends suggest that there will be no dramatic explosion in the income and ...... of most elderly people in Britain during the 1990s. If this is true of older people, it is even truer of younger disabled people, since most live on incomes below those of the rest of the population.

What are the options available to a central government committed to 'exit' models of empowerment in community care in a situation where the resources of most people do not allow for self-provisioning? One possibility is to assess the level of need of disabled people, and then to offer a voucher or benefit related to that need (and their existing resources) with which they could buy the services they wanted. The Independent Living Fund (ILF) was based on these principles and it gave disabled people substantial sums of money to buy care services.

The ILF was established as an independent trust to provide a weekly payment to those severely disabled adults who lost out from the abolition of additional requirements payments as part of the 1988 social security changes. It was initially expected that the ILF would provide a service for about 350 people and require a budget of around £5 million, yet by March 1991 it was helping 7,724 people with a budget of £54 million.

Research carried out on the experiences of ILF clients found they were able to use their ILF money to pull together a care package which met their needs in a way which fostered their sense of independence:

> The findings from this research challenge the assumption that disabled people are incapable of exercising effective choice and control over their own care arrangements. They also show that independent living is a relevant and important concept not only for the *young* disabled, but also for older people with many different kinds of disability, including the most severe. The experience of ILF clients . . . shows how, with enough money to have care assistance under their own control, or that of a chosen advocate, many disabled people can greatly improve the quality of their lives as well as stay out of residential care. (Kestenbaum, 1992, p. 78)

As such, the ILF experience can be used by central government and the New Right to justify a commitment to 'exit' models of empowerment.

Nevertheless, the Conservative government moved to phase out this scheme on the grounds of mushrooming cost. In April 1993, a much more limited scheme was introduced, with the government arguing that the ILF was always seen as a temporary response to the 1988 social security changes rather than a national system of cash payments to buy care for disabled people. The real concern of the then government was that such schemes generate high levels of public expenditure since it is difficult to deny payment to those who meet eligibility criteria. However, the Community Care (Direct Payments) Act 1996 was supported by the same government presumably on the grounds that such schemes would be run by local authorities within their finite budgets.

As we saw in Chapter 3, the main exit option of central government in community care was to develop a quasi-market in community care. The emphasis of the community care changes embodied in the 1990 Act is that social services need to stimulate a market in social care in which the voluntary, private and local authority sectors will compete to provide services. Assessment of individuals and the brokering in of appropriate care packages will be the responsibility of the care manager who will act as an intermediary between the user and the service provider. Enthusiasts argue that this will offer choice for the user and care manager at the point of pulling a package together as well as the prospect of replacing those parts of the package with which the user is subsequently dissatisfied.

Drawing on the theory of markets, Le Grand and Bartlett (1993) identified five conditions for success:

1. *Market structure:* for a conventional market to be efficient and offer genuine choice, there must be competition or the potential for competition. That is, there needs to be many providers and many purchasers, or at least the opportunity for new providers to enter and existing providers to exit from the market relatively costlessly.

2. *Information:* both sides of a market must have access to cheap and accurate information about the costs and quality of the service provided. Monitoring of quality is an essential part of any quasi-market system.

3. *Transaction costs:* these are the costs involved in drafting, negotiating and safeguarding packages and contracts. These costs need to be less than the efficiency gains achieved through developing quasi-markets in social care.

4. *Motivation:* for markets to work appropriately, providers need to be motivated at least in part by profit-making, whilst purchasers must be motivated to maximise the welfare of users.

5. *Cream skimming:* in order to achieve equity, markets must restrict opportunities for discrimination by either purchasers or providers in favour of the cheaper or less troublesome users (the cream): the relatively healthy, the less needy, the more self-sufficient.

It soon became evident that the introduction of quasi-markets in community care posed a number of problems. Competition in the market may be reduced by the existence of monopoly or near-monopoly social services purchasers and cosy relationships with dominant community care providers. Do users have the sanctions to upset these cosy relationships and demand that the authority exit to another contractor? Quality in welfare is notoriously difficult to monitor. If it is defined by purchasers and providers, there is no guarantee it will fulfil user needs. Information flow is constrained by the fact that many welfare choices are made by service users under duress or in crisis.

Many welfare providers are not commercially motivated and may find it difficult to give sufficient priority to the financial state of their provider unit. Why should purchasers (indirect consumers) have the direct interests of consumers at heart? And how will they know what the consumers' interests are? Finally, welfare services are particularly vulnerable to cream skimming. Chapters 5 and 9 take this argument forward by reviewing the extent to which the implementation of the community care changes is witnessing the emergence of the conditions specified by Le Grand and Bartlett for the successful operation of quasi-markets.

Empowerment through 'voice'

The limitations of 'exit' or market approaches to empowerment in community care are increasingly recognised, even by those who feel they have much to offer service users. One weakness is that the 'exit' literature is most easily applicable to those people who have been assessed as having a need which requires a publicly funded service. It has little to tell us about the processes by which certain groups and not others are defined as a priority for services, and it tells us nothing about how some potential service users will fail to come forward for assessment because of perceptions that care managers and service providers are hostile and prejudiced against certain groups and not others. Such subtle, and not so subtle, mechanisms may disempower large numbers of potential service users in a context where the small number who are receiving a service appear to have great choice, and hence confirm the value of quasi-market approaches. As such, 'exit' approaches appear to reflect a comparatively unsophisticated view of power when compared to that offered by Lukes or Foucault, as outlined earlier in this chapter.

Second, a quasi-market of social care providers may be helpful to users and potential users at the time of assessment in terms of generating choice. However, once a user begins to receive a service, 'exit' may appear a poor option even where there is dissatisfaction with the quality of service received:

> Exit is a blunt instrument, when the overall service may be what the consumer wants, but there are aspects of it which he/she would like changed, e.g. the time at which a home help arrives or the range of tasks he or she is able to do. (Hoyes *et al.*, 1993, p. 13)

There are two options in this type of situation. The purchaser can put pressure upon the service provider through the contract if one exists (that is, they can threaten contract withdrawal at a later date unless the service improves). Or the service user can exert an influence upon the service they receive through a user committee or other voice mechanisms. This seems a particularly important issue for those service users for whom 'exit' is not really an option or when 'exit' would impose very high costs. For example, some people receiving a mental health service do not have the right of exit because they are being detained against their will, but it remains crucial that mechanisms are developed by which their voice will be heard. Equally, the majority of elderly people in residential care or nursing home care would not consider moving to a new home as a realistic option.

In fairness to the government, the community care reforms introduced by the 1990 Act included a mixture of 'exit' and 'voice' mechanisms. The whole emphasis of community care planning is that social services as the lead agency are required to seek the views of others before deciding on the overall strategic direction, and users and carers have been included by the government amongst the key constituencies for consultation. Second, care managers are intermediaries between service users (or applicants) and the developing mixed economy of social care. As such, the user has the potential to influence the professional through a 'voice' mechanism which leads to the putting together and subsequent delivery of an appropriate and flexible care package.

This issue can be further conceptualised by drawing on the work by Hoggett (1992) who has developed a two axis diagram (see Figure 4.2) based upon four quadrants. The diagram distinguishes both between the degree of control/participation on offer and whether the 'voice' mechanisms are operating at the individual or collective levels. The diagram can be illustrated best by considering what is on offer in terms of 'voice' mechanisms to particular individuals. For example, with regard to a woman with a severe learning difficulty, the following set of questions would need to be asked:

> to what extent does she have influence over the construction of her own care or service plan (Quadrant 1)? As a user to what extent does she have influence over the manner in which these services are then delivered (Quadrant 2)? She may also be part of a group which receives a particular service (for example, they all attend the same day centre). To what extent is this group able to influence the way in

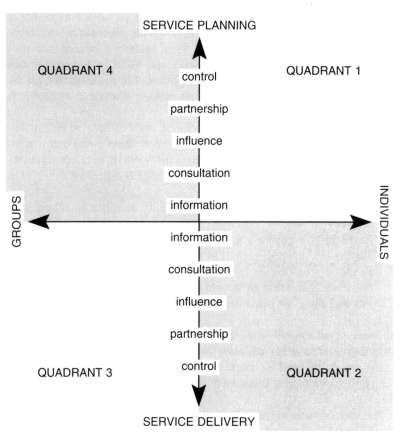

Source: Hoggett (1992) p. 19.

FIGURE 4.2   Dimensions of empowerment through voice

which this service is provided (Quadrant 3)? Finally, this woman will be one of many living in her area with similar needs and problems. To what extent is this group involved in the service planning process (Quadrant 4)? (p. 19)

The answers to these questions depend on the extent to which purchasers, providers and, crucially, care managers are willing to change the previous relations of power between themselves and service users.

At the individual level, there is no shortage of advice available to professionals about how to develop empowering practices in social care (Braye and Preston-Shoot, 1995). This literature covers not only communication skills, assessment skills and skills in the negotiation of care options but also the need to 'facilitate full participation [of the service user] in the process of decision making' (Smale *et al.*, 1993, p. 45).

It is interesting to note that the personal qualities deemed essential to empowering practice are often those long recognised in the mainstream social work literature. Thus Smale *et al.* (1993), in *Empowerment, Assessment, Care Management and the Skilled Worker*, list:

1. Authenticity – the care manager's ability to relate to others with integrity (p. 48);
2. Empathy – a person's ability to communicate understanding (p. 50);
3. Respect – the care manager's ability to communicate their acceptance and valuation of people irrespective of their personal qualities and social or professional position (p. 54).

If there are additional skills, these are often seen as either being about negotiating with other agencies in the mixed economy or more generally about the need to create a collaborative culture at the field level which includes service users as full partners (Beresford and Trevillion, 1995).

In terms of voice at the collective level, the new system of community care planning was a significant development in that it created opportunities for local authorities to consult users and carers in a way that had not previously occurred. All social services authorities had to publish their first community care plans by 1 April 1992. The White Paper stated that 'local authorities will be expected to produce and publish clear plans for the development of community care services, consistent with the plans of health authorities and other interested agencies' (Department of Health, 1989a, p. 6). The subsequent policy guidance pointed out that Section 46 of the National Health Service and Community Care Act 1990 required local authorities to consult health agencies, housing agencies, voluntary organisations, private agencies, user groups and carer groups, but that no attempt would be made to specify the most appropriate machinery for achieving this (Department of Health, 1990, p. 14).

How have local authorities responded? Glendinning and Bewley

(1992) studied 99 of the first plans produced. They found that the vast majority of local authorities made use of the joint planning machinery with health authorities, and extensive consultation took place with voluntary organisations, but only 16 per cent of plans stated clearly that user groups had been involved in the planning structures and this was usually at working group level only. They concluded that extensive and creative attempts had been made to publicise the plans, particularly in their draft and final stages. However, less attention had been directed to ensuring that disabled people, whether as service users or local residents, were actively involved in the actual planning process itself.

Subsequent case study research showed local authorities making some progress in terms of a more substantial involvement of service users and carers in the community care planning process. Thus, one review of 40 user and carer groups' involvement in community care planning in four different local authorities generated a mixture of positive as well as negative comments as a result of changes made for consultation about the 1993–4 plan (see Figure 4.3). Bewley and Glendinning (1994), in their own follow-up research, found conflict over the issue of the representativeness of service users nominated for committees, professional control of agendas, too little time for service user representatives to consult other members of their organisations, and the organisation of meetings tending to reflect professional norms and needs. One result of this was that people with learning difficulties, older disabled people, people with sensory impairments and disabled people from minority ethnic communities were all likely to be excluded from consultation mechanisms.

One required response is for much greater creativity and thought to be given as to how such 'groups' might be drawn more centrally into the community care planning process. For example, Martin and Gaster (1993) described how one local authority set about winning the 'trust' of black and minority ethnic organisations in terms of becoming involved in the community care planning process. Thornton and Tozer (1994) profiled a range of initiatives (such as forums, networks, teleconferencing) for involving older people in planning and evaluating community care, although they still felt it necessary to conclude:

> We have identified few initiatives designed specifically to include physically frail or disabled older people, and only one for mentally frail or confused older people. On the whole, older people are assumed to be a homogeneous group. (p. 71)

Negative comments	Positive comments
'They were less successful at putting the plan together, however, and in our view the process was inefficient, and late, and the end product was inadequately reviewed – I still haven't seen the final version.'	'To start with, involvement of disabled people was tokenism, but now the social services department does work with users.'
'I assume we've been overlooked.'	'There is now a mutual confidence which has not always been there.'
'It's all cosmetic stuff.'	'The format which social services decided to use is rather clumsy in our opinion, but within this constraint the drafts show a reasonable reflection of our input.'
'The plan is wordy, too long, and written in local government speak. It should have been written in a way that involves service users rather than simply producing a report with nice photographs.'	'Some of our criticisms of the 1992/93 plan were incorporated into the 1993/94 report. We believe the publicity for the consultation meetings was better and that more opportunity was given . . . to comment.'

Source: Means and Lart (1994, p.320).

FIGURE 4.3   Views of user and carer groups on their involvement in community care planning in four local authorities

There is still a long way to go before the full range of service users have anything like an adequate input into the production of community care plans.

In some ways a more fundamental issue is not the quality and depth of consultation but whether the community care plan itself is a significant document in terms of shaping and influencing the local strategic development of community care services. One possibility is that the plan is only being produced because of the statutory requirement to do so. Hoyes and Means (1994) warned of the danger that the really important purchasing and commissioning decisions might continue to be made by small numbers of managers from social services and health, uninfluenced by the community care plan to which service users may have given so much time. This suggests the focus of collective voice debates should be on mechanisms of consultation with service users and carers over the strategic commissioning of services of which the community care plan is only one component.

Overall, the prerequisites to enable user and carer groups to have a strong collective voice over the local development of community care services are not yet fully in place. Drawing upon the work by Taylor *et al.* (1992), it is possible to identify what some of these need to be:

1. *Access* means considering whether users and carers have the facilities to get to key planning meetings, whether the venues are physically accessible and what the cost implications (including child care and sitting expenses) are of attendance.

2. *Information* is part of access. People cannot make choices if they are not informed about key meetings and they cannot give an informed view without information. Such information must be presented clearly, attractively and in good time – translated into minority ethnic languages where necessary, and into Braille, large print or on to tape. At meetings, British sign language translation, loop systems or lip-reading should be available as appropriate. Interpreters may need to be trained if they are not to reflect existing power structures. Information needs to capture people's attention if it is to be used. Local authorities should use a variety of channels for disseminating information, and publicising its meetings and policies, including broadcasting. The essential foundation for this is a comprehensive map of user and carer groups, backed up by a good, up-to-date mailing list.

3. *Clarity* about the degree of influence on offer is essential since people need to know the scope and limits of the contribution they can make. If people are to contribute effectively, they need to know what it is they are expected to contribute and what the outcome will be.

4. *Support and advocacy* are necessary because many people are not used to being asked for their views. To contribute effectively they may need advocacy, especially if they do not have verbal communication skills or have learning difficulties. This advocacy needs to be independent. Development resources and training are needed if people are to have the confidence and skills they need to speak up, especially in consultation structures.

5. *Timing* must be considered since it is essential to allow sufficient time for people to form views and to feed them back and for material to be translated as appropriate. With consultation structures this is especially important as representatives will need to

sound out their constituencies. It is also essential to consult early in the decision-making process, before too many vested interests have been created. Otherwise, the process of consultation is in reality one of ratification.

6. *Results:* Social services authorities should commit officers and members at a high level to ensure that consultation can influence decisions. Users should be given an input into the agendas of meetings they attend. Users should be told at the earliest opportunity what has happened as a result of any meeting or consultation exercise.

7. *Commitment and structures:* If users are to have an input to decision-making, institutions concerned with planning, purchasing, assessment and delivery will need to transform their decision-making processes accordingly and provide the mechanisms for users to be involved. These should allow for a variety of inputs to reflect the different interests and capacities of users. Experience suggests that unstructured open groups are best for exploring needs and generating ideas; a small structured group is better at translating ideas into well-argued implementation strategies.

Rights and empowerment

In his discussion of a 'voice' approach to empowering a woman with a severe learning difficulty, Hoggett (1992) argued the need not only for options/alternatives and advocacy/representation as preconditions but he also claimed that she needed 'a right/entitlement to a service in the first place' (p. 19). This brings us to the issue of rights and empowerment.

For the New Right, 'rights' are essentially the right of individuals to pursue their own goals and objectives, and to meet their own needs, free from intrusive intervention from the state. This view is taken by de Jasay (1991) who goes on to argue that the alternative approach of the collectivity giving rights to individuals suffers from the fact that a right for one person is an obligation for another, and the temptation is to campaign for rights which one will be the beneficiary of or for which one will not have to pay directly. De Jasay does not believe government has the capacity 'to strike the balance between the advantage of those who get the rights and the burden of those who must assume the obligation' (p. 43).

The opposite perspective is taken by many in the disability move-ment. They believe an 'exit' approach to empowerment through self-provisioning is meaningless for those on low incomes, while many 'voice' approaches fail to work because they do not address the imbalance of power between the service user and the professional. Hence, service users are treated in patronising and stigmatising ways as they attempt to prove their eligibility for a service which is then delivered in a standardised and uncaring way. For example, Kesten-baum (1992) in her study of ILF clients found that

> the choice and control they valued so highly could not in their experience be provided by statutory authorities. It is not simply a matter of resource levels, though these are very significant. As important are the qualities that any large-scale service-providing organisation would find hard to deliver: choice of care assistant, flexibility, consistency, control of times and tasks, etc. (p. 77)

Many in the disability movement believe that the way forward from this situation is to argue for a rights-based approach to cash and/or care for disabled people. Hence the concern is to argue for much more than a right to fair treatment and consideration (often called procedur-al rights) and rather to push the case for legally based rights. They see this as needing to cover not only the right to appropriate services or the cash to buy those services, but also a right to an income which ensures material comfort and an environment which does not disable those with impairments.

As already outlined, a key justification for this view voiced by the disability movement is that, as disabled people, they have a right to participate fully in society and to be full citizens of that society (Campbell and Oliver, 1996). Such a perspective has also been sup-ported by the left-wing think-tank, the Institute of Public Policy Research. Coote (1992) has summarised the social rights perspective in the following way:

People do not start out on the proverbial 'level playing field': many have disadvantages, of which some are constructed and avoidable, while others are inherent or insuperable. Welfare policies should therefore aim to minimise the avoidable disadvantages and compensate for the others, in order to equalise the 'life chances' of all. The idea of 'life chances' is closely linked to the idea of individual empowerment as a requirement of citizenship. Citizenship entails being able to partici-pate in society, to enjoy its fruits and fulfil one's own potential, and it

follows that each individual citizen must be equally able (or 'empow-
ered') to do so. (p. 4)

The difficulty of this perspective lies in moving away from general-
ities about social rights to the specification of what these might be.
Authors such as Cranston (1976) have long argued that social rights
could never be enforceable in the same way as civil rights because they
are not universal. For example, the meaning of any right to medical
care would vary enormously in content according to which society one
was in or what time period one was talking about. Equally, no society
could possibly meet every medical need of every single citizen at all
times. Social rights are expensive and have to be rationed, even if you
believe in high public expenditure, unlike the New Right theorists.

However, it is easy to exaggerate such difficulties, since many of the
same issues exist with regard to the enforcement of civil and political
rights. Plant (1992) has pointed out that 'there must be a right to the
protection of civil and political rights, but there cannot be a right to the
services of a policeman, as these are subject to the same problems of
scarcity as doctors and teachers' (p. 21). He goes on to argue:

> The idea of rights in the public sector provides a new way forward
> between the market and democracy as two models of empowerment.
> This is not to decry either markets or democracy, only to say that
> there is a case for looking at a new way and seeing how far we can
> get with it. If these rights can work and be made clear and enforce-
> able, whether they are rights to have certain procedures followed, or
> actual rights to resources, then this would clearly be a more direct
> way of empowering the citizen than either the market, or bureau-
> cratic regulation, or greater democratic accountability. (p. 28)

However, service users have only limited rights under existing community care legislation. Some carers have a right to an assessment under
the Carers (Recognition of Services) Act 1995 although not to a
subsequent service response. Another important exception is the
Disabled Persons (Services, Consultation and Representation) Act
1986 which addresses 'rights' in a wide range of different ways:

> the right of a disabled person to be represented in dealings with a
> local authority by a person authorised to speak on his or her behalf;
> the right of a disabled person to demand full assessment of his or her
> need for services provided by a local authority; the right to receive a
> written statement, following an assessment of what services the local

authority intends to provide or why it proposes not to provide services; the right of disabled persons' carers to have their needs taken into account; and the right of disabled people's organisations to be consulted before any person is co-opted to a formal committee to represent disabled people's interests. (Barnes *et al.*, 1990, p. 114)

In addition, we have seen how the National Health Service and Community Care Act 1990 established a mandatory complaints procedure whereby users and carers can challenge the fairness with which they have been treated by their social services authority. But these examples seem only to offer the hope of procedural justice rather than any prospect of substantive rights.

However, a number of lawyers have begun to specialise in community care law with a view to testing out through the courts exactly what substantive rights are enshrined in the existing 'hotch potch' of legislation. The view of Roberts (1992) has been that it is rights to assessment rather than to services which have been strengthened under the 1990 Act, since section 47(1) states that

where it appears to a local authority that any person for whom they may provide or arrange for the provision of community care services may be in need of any such services, the authority (a) shall carry out an assessment of his needs for those services; and (b) having regard to the results of that assessment, shall then decide whether his needs call for the provision by them of any such services,

while Section 47(2) goes on to state:

If at any time during the assessment of the needs of any person under sub-section (1) (a) above it appears to a local authority that he is a disabled person, the authority (a) shall proceed to make such a decision as to the services he requires [under section 2(1) of the Chronically Sick and Disabled Persons Act 1970] without his requesting them to do so, and (b) shall inform him they will be doing so and of his rights under the Disabled Persons (Services, Consultation and Representation) Act 1986.

Roberts interprets this to mean that 'the duty of a local authority in relation to assessment will be strengthened, but the nature and content of the services which can, or must, be provided remain unchanged' (p. 16).

Not all community care lawyers shared this gloomy assessment of the 1990 Act. Some believed the wording of Section 47 means that it may be able to establish that a disabled person has a right to a service once assessed by a local authority as having a need. However, recent judicial judgments suggest that Roberts is probably correct. The decision of Gloucestershire County Council to withdraw services from some clients on the grounds of budgetary constraints has been declared legal by the House of Lords although judicial reviews of other cases have seemed to stress the rights of the client over the local authority (Thompson, 1997).

This type of welfare rights approach in a hostile political climate does generate tactical dilemmas. Conservative governments were not going to concede to many, if any, of the demands of the disability movement. Even under the new Labour government, local authorities will continue to face an enormous gap between the limited resources made available for community care and the expansive objectives of the legislation (see next chapter), and we suspect that some gap between need/demand and resources will always exist, irrespective of the attitude of central government to public expenditure. Therefore, in the short term, and possibly in the longer term, community care will be about the language of priorities rather than (or as well as) the language of rights. Local authorities have no alternative but to establish priority groups for a service and to deny services to others. However, we feel local authorities should be honest and clear to users, and their organisations, about these priority processes and show their commitment to user empowerment by funding networks of user advocacy and representation groups. Priority systems need to avoid discrimination based on prejudice towards certain groups and individuals, and decisions need to be open to challenge.

Empowerment through struggle

The existing community care legislation, therefore, gives few if any substantive rights to service users, and the last section has suggested that clear substantive rights are unlikely to be conceded by future governments because of the party political consensus about the need to control public expenditure. However, the fourth dimension of power discussed earlier in the chapter stressed its relational nature and the scope this creates for struggle and resistance. It is only through struggle and resistance that the old relations of power can be challenged and ultimately shifted so that perhaps the affordability of rights will become more widely recognised.

The UK disability movement believes that by working with other movements of oppressed groups it may be possible to achieve a new vision of a genuinely democratic society (Campbell and Oliver, 1996). Indeed, it is through the process of struggle and involvement in the movement that a process of politicisation and education occurs for individual disabled people, and hence their appreciation of the need for fundamental change within society based on an acceptance of their right to be fully participating members of that society. In terms of community care, the individual needs of disabled people can only be met once they have won the right to have access to the resources to put together their own personal assistance arrangements.

We are fully supportive of the need for empowerment through struggle. However, it might seem to imply that any disabled person who rejects this agenda is seen as falsely conscious of their real interests (Lukes' third dimension). But this does risk defining many service users as passive victims or dupes. In the context of race and disability, Stuart (1996) has complained that

> Unfortunately, the literature on disabled people from black and minority ethnic communities continues to characterise them as passive victims of racism and disablism. To ensure that the community care legislation works best for these disabled people it is important to remember that they are actors too. As actors their views and opinions may or may not coincide with the 'problems' characterised in the literature. Disabled people, whether black or white, are the product of neither racism nor disablism alone. They have wider concerns and interests, which cannot always be accounted for within these twin prisms of oppression. (p. 103)

This may lead some to wish to challenge what in our section on the fourth dimension of power we called the relations of power through involvement in social movements. But others will decide not to do this. They may limit their resistance to challenging the exercise of power by professionals within the existing community care system by manoeuvring and negotiating an appropriate care package for themselves. This may not be revolutionary but it is a form of struggle which still deserves respect and support. This may be the only realistic option available to the frailest and most isolated, many of whom will be elderly. Indeed, their 'empowerment' may well remain dependent on the skills of care managers and other professionals in the community care system despite the justified criticism so often made about their attitudes and behaviour towards service users (Barnes and Walker, 1996, p. 385).

Conclusion

The first half of this chapter looked at the contribution of the disability movement, and to a lesser extent normalisation theorists, in raising the issue of empowerment for service users to the top of the community care agenda in the UK. The second half assessed four markedly different strategies for achieving empowerment, namely through exit, voice, rights and struggle. Despite the obstacles to achieving a rights-based approach, we have no doubt that such a perspective is essential for the empowerment of service users and of carers. This is for two main reasons. First, unless disabled people and full-time carers have a right to an adequate income, they will experience poverty and not empowerment. Second, procedural rights may be less preferable than substantive rights, but strong procedural rights can protect users and carers against the arbitrary power of professionals. We also recognise that what little progress has so far been made has been largely through the willingness of the disability movement to engage in political struggle.

However, the community care reforms are more concerned with issues of 'exit' (for example, developing a mixed economy) and 'voice' (such as community care planning) than 'rights'. Hoyes *et al.* (1993) argue that if this system is to operate to the best advantage of the user, this requires that authorities should

1. stimulate a market of diverse providers which offers choice to users and carers;
2. ensure the provision of advice, information and advocacy to help service users and carers through this range of services and to help them assert their claims to a quality service;
3. develop service standards and definitions of quality in conjunction with users and carers;
4. promote and encourage mechanisms which supply service users with the opportunity both to develop their own services and to have a say in existing services (user committees and so on);
5. provide accessible channels for user and carer groups to engage with the community care planning process.

Figure 4.4 illustrates how such requirements might be further fleshed out with a checklist for assessing the responsiveness, flexibility and accessibility of services. The rest of the book underlines how far most local authorities have still to go in terms of stimulating an adequate range of services and introducing user-centred care management systems.

Are service users and/or disabled people's organisations being regularly consulted on their views about the service?

Is information about the service available in Braille, large print, on audio and video tape?

Is information about the service available in minority community languages, including accessible formats?

Does the service have minicom/textphone facilities? Have receptionists and other key staff been trained in its use?

Are BSL interpreters and lip speakers available, and those skilled in Makaton and other speech and non-speech methods of communication?

Are minority community language interpreters available?

Are premises wheelchair accessible (i.e. designated parking, level access, wide enough doorways, wheelchair accessible toilets)?

Are premises within easy reach of bus stops? Is there free parking close by for users?

Does the service offer access to independent advocacy support?

Have workers at all levels received disability equality training?

Does the service vary according to the needs of the individual?

Can the service change according to the changing needs of an individual user?

Can the service user choose the timing of appointments/service delivery?

Is the service provided age-appropriate?

Does the service take account of preferences re gender of staff who have personal contact with users?

Does the service take account of cultural/religious requirements of users? Is appropriate training provided for staff?

Does the service's workforce reflect the community that it serves? If not, what steps are being taken to ensure that it does?

Are measurements of quality developed in consultation with service users?

Does monitoring/evaluation/auditing involve service users?

Is information about complaints procedures available to all service users? Are complaints procedures easy to use?

Source: Morris (1995b), pp. 39–40.

FIGURE 4.4 Checklist for responsive, flexible, accessible services

5 Leaders at Last: The Changing Rôle of Social Services

Chapter 3 looked at Sir Roy Griffiths' recommendation that social services authorities should be given the lead agency rôle for community care and how this proposal was eventually accepted with reluctance by central government. Chapter 4 outlined the limited progress that has so far been made in achieving the empowerment of service users and carers. This chapter considers the story of reform implementation by social services and tackles a number of central questions. Have social services been willing and able to stimulate a mixed economy of social care provision? Are social services developing internal purchaser–provider splits? Are systems of care management evolving which are driven by needs rather than the availability of a limited number of traditional services?

The above questions are addressed by drawing upon the emerging literature on the implementation of the community care reforms. Much of this material illustrates the limited progress that has so far been made in terms of developing needs-led assessment, involving users in community care planning, stimulating a mixed economy of social care, and so on. However, any judgement about the performance of social services departments as the lead agents in community care needs to be set against an awareness of the difficult climate which has faced social services authorities in their attempts to implement the reforms.

Managing change in a climate of uncertainty

We have already described the history of neglect associated with social care services in England and Wales. As a result, social services authorities were not only being asked to implement a complex reform package, but they were doing this in a context where existing service provision in the early 1990s was often woefully inadequate. They were soon warned by the Audit Commission (1992) that they faced 'a cascade of change' with the clear implication that they risked being swept away if the pace and timing of changes were not thought through by individual departments. It is to the credit of all those who work in the personal social services that, on the whole, such disasters have been avoided. This is especially true when one considers the different aspects of uncertainty and pressure faced by social services since the passing of the 1990 Act.

Political uncertainty seemed initially to have been overcome with the return of a Conservative government after the 1992 general election. If a Labour government had come to power, they would have wanted to reverse the NHS reforms and they might have wanted to challenge the emphasis within the community care reforms on developing markets through internal purchaser–provider splits and the contracting-out of former local authority services. Such a possibility encouraged some Labour-controlled local authorities to delay their thinking on future structures until the outcome of the 1992 general election was known.

However, the 1992 election result did little to resolve or reduce overall tensions between central government and local government. In many Labour and Liberal Democrat authorities, in particular, these tensions created an immensely stressful climate for senior managers as they attempted to respond to the often conflicting advice, suggestions and instructions from central government and from local politicians. This continued right through to the 1997 election with the Conservative government publishing proposals for a further major reduction in the provider rôle of social services (Department of Health, 1997a) together with a report questioning the lead agency rôle of social services in mental health provision (Department of Health, 1997b) only weeks before the calling of the election. The early and extensive lead for the Labour Party in national opinion polls combined with their ambiguity about which elements of the reforms they would change also served to generate uncertainty.

Closely linked to political uncertainty has been the issue of *financial stringency*, both in terms of local government finance overall and community care funds in particular. The funding system for community care is highly complex (Lunt *et al.*, 1996) and in terms of money available to social services draws upon such diverse elements as the revenue support grant, the council tax, the special transitional grant (see previous chapter) and income generated through charges. All of these components have to be mediated through the budgetary process of individual authorities in order to produce an agreed budget for each new financial year. The squeeze from central government on all forms of public expenditure has meant that local authorities have often had to cut services, withdraw grants, impose service charges or freeze posts in order to stay within agreed budgets. As Becker (1996) succinctly puts it, 'the social care business, particularly within local authorities, is in crisis, partly because of the increasing real costs of meeting ever-growing statutory responsibilities and demands for care, and because the resources for the job are inadequate'.

Thus, the revenue support settlement for 1996–7 led to 68 of the then 119 English local authorities having to make service cuts of £166 million from the previous year with the hardest hit area being services for elderly people where cuts of £39 million were made (*Community Care*, 25 April–1 May 1996, p. 3). In addition, these authorities were making efficiency savings of £69 million through job cuts, cheaper contracts and tightening administration costs while £27 million was being raised through increased service charges.

The knock-on consequence of this financial stringency has often been bad publicity over both charging for care services and over grant levels to the voluntary sector. Thus, the mid-1990s saw the emergence of a debate about the rationale for and fairness of charging for such services as home care and day care. This research has shown service users to be confused by charging policies, hostile to the principle of charges, yet often afraid to speak up:

> Seema worries about being able to pay for her care but she does not feel strong enough to do anything about it. She has spoken to people who are refusing to pay for their carers, and who said that they would fight to keep their care. Seema would not be prepared to do that. I don't think I can take on all this, there's too much pressure on me. Because I used to, you know, I used to be [a] fighter and wanting to do, but nowadays, you know, I haven't got like a – if I start to think too much my ulcer comes up and I feel all uptight in my joint and my neck. (Quoted in Chetwynd *et al.*, 1996, p. 80)

Equally problematic for social services authorities has been the impact of financial stringency on relations with the voluntary sector. Although the community care reforms opened up enormous possibilities for the voluntary sector (see later discussion) they have also made voluntary organisations (and indeed private sector ones) very vulnerable to the 'ups and downs' of social services as they become the prime purchaser of their services (Russell *et al.*, 1996; Taylor *et al.*, 1995). Thus, the 1996–7 budget of Liverpool social services involved a reduction of

£950,000 in funding for the voluntary sector leading to the closure, for example, of a 'good neighbours' scheme for 4,000 elderly and disabled people run by Age Concern Liverpool (Cervi, 1996).

The third area of pressure concerns *dependence upon others* in that social services can only be successful in implementing the community care reforms with the co-operation of a wide range of other organisations with local purchasing and providing responsibilities. This includes both health agencies (health authorities, NHS Trusts, GP fundholders) and housing agencies (housing associations, housing authorities). The implications of this for social services as the lead agency in community care are explored in some detail in the next two chapters. It also includes a dependence on the rules and regulations of the social security and housing benefit systems in terms of the financial viability of various housing and support arrangements (hostels, sheltered housing, group homes) for service users (Griffiths, 1997). A change in benefit regulations can soon undermine the viability of existing provision:

> Imminent rent reviews for vulnerable people in supported housing mean thousands could lose their tenancies. . . Benefits are set to be slashed next month, threatening many schemes providing homes for some of the 500,000 people in supported housing across Britain. (*Inside Housing*, 21 March 1997, p. 3)

In the end, the return of a Labour government resulted in a reversal of this decision. Social services authorities need to develop facilities and enabling skills if the community care reforms are to be successful, yet they do this in a context where these efforts can so easily be undermined by policy changes (sometimes but not always imposed by central government) relating to the other key community care players.

This links into the final area of pressure, namely *organisational uncertainty*. A review of local government boundaries was initiated in the early 1990s with an initial emphasis from central government on the desirability of abolishing those authorities which were seen as somehow artificial entities (for example 'newer' counties such as Avon, Cleveland and Humberside), together with the need to extend the number of single-tier arrangements whereby all local authority services are provided by a single unit of administration (unitary authorities). In Wales twenty-two unitary authorities were established in April 1996 out of the previous eight county councils and thirty-seven districts. Local government reorganisation (LGR) in England will not be completed until

1998 and has involved a much wider mix of new arrangements to replace the old two-tier authorities:

- the retention of some two-tier arrangements of counties and districts (of which a few will retain pre-1996 boundaries such as Lincolnshire);
- the creation of unitary authorities (some being split off from a pre-existing county which then becomes a smaller 'hybrid' two-tier county alongside unitary urban areas, such as a 'new' Hampshire alongside unitary Southampton and Portsmouth councils);
- the abolition of some counties and their replacement by entirely new unitary authorities, for example the replacement of Cleveland by Middlesbrough, Stockton, Hartlepool and Redcar and Cleveland;
- the creation of some largely rural unitaries such as Rutland, Herefordshire, the Isle of Wight and East Yorkshire. (Based on Craig and Manthorpe, 1996, pp. 2–3)

The resultant disruption to social services has been enormous. For example, April 1997 saw the establishment of social services departments in the new unitary authorities of Thamesdown, Stoke on Trent, Darlington, Derby, Leicester, Rutland, Milton Keynes, Luton, Brighton and Hove, Poole, Bournemouth, Southampton and Portsmouth. Each of these will have had to appoint a new Director of Social Services (or equivalent) and management team who in turn will have needed to review with councillors the most appropriate approach of the new authority to the implementation of the community care reforms. Craig and Manthorpe's research on the impact of LGR on community care suggests that 'the process of transition' has generated 'uncertainty, political tension, service planning blight and disruption to working arrangements' (p. 32). This is not only amongst social services staff but also within those voluntary agencies whose very survival depends upon grants and contracts from social services.

Establishing the new funding regime

In the first edition of the present volume, we outlined in some detail the arrangements for transferring money from the social security budget to individual local authorities and expressed some doubt as to whether the new system would work.

By and large, it has to be said that local authorities have been successful in taking over financial responsibility from the social security system for those people about to enter residential or nursing-home care who are entitled to a public subsidy to help meet the costs of that care. The resources of such people are being assessed, the local authority contribution is being decided and appropriate payments are being made. The new funding regime is now fully operational in all local authorities.

However, to make this point is not to claim that the new funding regime is without its problems. The most obvious of these was touched upon in the last section, namely that it is an underfunded regime which means that local authorities will refuse to fund or part-fund a place in residential or nursing-home care to some dependent people seeking such support. This is especially likely to happen towards the end of the financial year as individual social services authorities struggle to stay within agreed budgets. There is also growing resistance from the public to the idea of means-testing for residential and nursing-home care especially when it involves a calculation about the value of the owner-occupied family home.

Another important point relates to the complexity of some of the new assessment and fee payment systems and their dependence upon the willingness of social workers and other field-level staff to take an increased rôle in the means-testing of clients. This can be illustrated by explaining the system in operation in a London borough during early 1996 (Means and Langan, 1996). The majority of social services assessments in this borough were organised through six area offices which have a high degree of delegated budgetary control. Assessment and care management tasks were the responsibility of care plan co-ordinators (CPCs) who included social workers, home care managers and occupational therapists.

Where clients were deemed to be in need of residential or nursing-home care, a financial assessment was made to ascertain how much, if any, public subsidy the person was entitled to from social services. The client was normally expected to fill out the financial assessment form themselves, although help was often provided by relatives and/or the care plan co-ordinator. The form was then sent to the incomes section of the finance department of the borough.

The incomes section was required to assess the charge within ten days. The CPC would be notified of the assessed charge on a form which had to be signed by the CPC and the client and returned to the incomes section. After taking up their residential or nursing-home place, the client would then be billed by the incomes section so as to collect her or his contribution to the overall fee. However, the incomes section had no involvement in paying fee income to independent sector homes. Instead, it was the responsibility of each home to claim fees from the appropriate social services area office, which in turn arranged payment via the exchequer division of the finance department.

Such complex systems generate difficulties. They require good collaboration between field-level staff and finance/revenue staff to work properly, and yet research suggests these relationships are often problematic. Langan and Means (1995) found many social workers resenting 'the money rôle being passed on to us' and were often failing to fill in all the required information on financial assessment forms for 'the bureaucrats at head office'. They also found that

> revenue and finance staff were often equally scathing about a social services culture and a social work profession which denied the importance of collecting the client contribution in terms of the overall financial health of the local authority. Such views were sometimes tinged with anger because of feelings that the impact of the community care changes had involved as great an increase in workloads for their sections as it had for field-level social services staff. (p. 40)

The consequences of such tensions for service users and carers must be worrying, given the complexity of many people's personal and house-hold circumstances. This is especially true where there is a need to allocate joint income, joint savings and especially joint assets between the person being considered for residential or nursing-home care and the person or people who used to live with them. The outcome of assessment might vary according to whether it relates to a married couple living together, a couple living together but not married, a couple separated but not yet divorced, or a carer who lived in. Equity and fairness is hard to maintain in such circumstances and perhaps almost impossible in situations where there are negative stereotypes held about each other by field-level social services staff and finance/ revenue staff.

The particular concern of Langan and Means (1995) was the implications of these new charging systems for elderly people with dementia. They found that local authorities were only just beginning to grapple with this issue, with staff showing little awareness of the range of legal safeguards available such as enduring power of attorney, receivership and appointeeship. Most worryingly, people operating systems of payment to independent sector and local authority homes often gave little thought to the vulnerability of residents with dementia. For example, where elderly people with dementia are in receipt of social security benefits, the correct procedure is for the person most able to handle their money to request to become an appointee through filling out the appropriate Benefits Agency form (Lavery and Lundy, 1994). Both local authorities and independent home proprietors can apply to do this where relatives are not available. However, local authorities vary considerably in their own willingness to take on this rôle and in their level of concern about whether it is an appropriate rôle for independent sector homes. Overall, local authorities

> seemed to be primarily concerned with the need to establish effective revenue collection strategies when taking on appointeeship or receivership responsibilities rather than from a desire to protect vulnerable elderly people and to act as advocates on their behalf. This was perhaps most obvious in the metropolitan authority which held the pension book for all but six of its LA residents on the grounds that payment was 13 weeks in arrears and residents and carers would be unable to cope with this new payment system. At the same time, it had a policy of not becoming an appointee of any residents within independent homes. (Means and Langan, 1996, p. 251)

This was despite the fact that both specialist guides (Jenkins, 1996) and central government advice recommended that independent homes should not take on appointeeship rôles because of their need 'to be protected from accusations of misuse and mismanagement' (Department of Health/Social Services Inspectorate, 1993, p. 12).

This section has looked at some of the issues raised by the implementation by local authorities of the new funding regime for residential and nursing-home care. However, it must be remembered that an important aspect to the community care reforms was the need to not only target such care at those most in need, but also to ensure that stay-at-home options were explored and developed even for very dependent people. This was to be achieved through the introduction of user-driven care management systems, the development of an internal purchaser–provider split and the encouragement of a mixed economy of social care. The rest of the chapter addresses what progress local authorities are making with each of these.

Establishing care management

The White Paper stressed that a primary objective of the community care reforms was 'to make proper assessment of need and good case management the cornerstone of high-quality care' (Department of Health, 1989a) while the subsequent policy guidance devoted a whole chapter to this issue (Department of Health, 1990).

The policy guidance outlined the three stages of a proper care management system, namely:

1. assessment of the circumstances of the user, including any support required by carers;
2. negotiation of a care package in agreement with users, carers and relevant agencies, designed to meet identified need within available resources;
3. implementation and monitoring of the agreed package, together with a review of outcomes and any necessary revision of services provided.

As explained in earlier chapters, the implied critique of past approaches was that they involved slotting people into a limited number of inflexible and traditional services which often did not meet their needs or which were organised to meet the requirements of service providers rather than service users and carers. The policy guidance argued that the new system of needs-driven assessment and care management could overcome these major weaknesses in existing practice and achieve no less than six major objectives:

1. ensuring that the resources available (including resources transferred from social security) are used in the most effective way to meet individual care needs;
2. restoring and maintaining independence by enabling people to live in the community wherever possible;
3. working to prevent or to minimise the effects of disability and illness in people of all ages;
4. treating those who need services with respect and providing equal opportunities for all;
5. promoting individual choice and self-determination, and building on existing strengths and care resources; and
6. promoting partnership between users, carers and service providers in all sectors, together with organisations of and for each group. (Department of Health, 1990, p. 23)

The policy guidance was soon followed by further government reports offering advice on the details of establishing care management systems (for example, Department of Health/Social Services Inspectorate, 1991).

So far, it might appear that care management is like 'mum's apple pie', an uncontroversial positive development for users, carers and professionals alike. Later in this section we will outline the hesitant progress made by authorities towards implementing care management strategies, but, to appreciate some of the reasons for this, we need to understand the background and some of the disputes which exist about the way care management should be organised, whom it should be aimed at and what it might be able to achieve.

The approach of the Department of Health to care management was heavily influenced by the positive research findings of the Personal Social Services Research Unit (PSSRU) at the University of Kent in their evaluation of care management pilot projects in Thanet (Kent) and Gateshead (Davies and Challis, 1986; Challis *et al.*, 1988). Both were aimed at frail elderly people at risk of entering residential or nursing-home care. Hudson (1993) provides a clear description of the basis of the Thanet scheme:

Social workers with considerable experience of work with elderly people and with smaller caseloads than usual were given access to a decentralised budget. The money could be spent on a variety of services not normally available through the social services system but the social workers (in effect acting as care managers) were required to cost the packages of care which they organised. Although there was freedom to construct the packages of care considered to be most appropriate to the needs of clients and carers, this had to be within the overall constraint of two-thirds of the cost of a place in a residential home. A particular feature of the care packages was the interweaving of informal care (such as relatives who were willing to handle finances) with semi-formal care (such as a helper to visit daily) and the formal statutory services. (p. 4)

Just under 100 frail elderly people were supported through this care management service in Thanet and their experiences were compared to a matched group receiving services in the conventional way from a neighbouring area in Kent. The results were overwhelmingly positive (as they were in the subsequent Gateshead experiments). The probability of death within one year and of admission to long-term care within one year was halved and the probability of continuing to live at home was doubled. Informal carers felt less exploited and more supported, while perceptions of wellbeing on the part of service users were improved. All of this was achieved at lower cost than if residential care had been supplied as the main option.

However, at least three complications have arisen in interpreting these results in terms of their general implications for the reform of community care in England and Wales. First, queries have been raised about the robustness of the methodology in terms of whether or not too many problematic clients were filtered out from the experimental group. Second, a conclusion that care management has much to offer frail elderly people does not indicate whether or not the same positive effects will occur for all other groups. Third, there has been a great deal of care management experimentation and so there are now several different models on offer rather than just the Kent/Gateshead approach. Each of these issues is considered in turn.

Fisher (1990–1) has pointed out how the research team excluded 110 of the originally identified cases by using criteria such as clients keen to enter care, carers being unwilling to share care and so on, leading him to suggest that some key practice dilemmas were not addressed. A second linked point is whether or not 'success' with frail elderly people wishing to avoid residential care can be translated into 'success' for a much wider range of elderly people and also to the other main user groups. Indeed, the PSSRU research team have warned repeatedly that this is an approach which can benefit certain types of users in certain types of situations, rather than an approach which should be applied to all users, or even to all users with the most complex needs. Hence, their justification for screening large numbers of elderly people from their original case samples is almost certainly that they have known all along that care management cannot keep everyone in the community and out of residential care at low cost and within tolerable levels of burden for carers. Therefore, Davies (1992, p. 20) is unapologetic about the fact that the Thanet experiment was based on the principle of offering 'case-managed care for selected users', who were essentially people who were 'at high risk of *inappropriate* and *avoidable* admissions to institutions for long-term care' (author's emphasis). Davies complains that Kent Social Services Department abandoned this clear focus after 1987 and tried to develop a much more general approach to care management which was doomed to fail. It can be argued that the community care reforms were based upon the same generalist assumptions.

The third complication facing local authorities as they considered their care management implementation strategy was that available care management models were much wider than just the Thanet/Gateshead approach. One reason for this was that the DHSS established in 1983 twenty-eight pilot 'care in the community' projects designed to help long-stay hospital residents move to community settings (see Chapter 6). These pilot projects covered people with learning difficulties, mental health problems and physical impairments as well as people with age-related problems. Cambridge (1992) stressed the enormous variety of service delivery arrangements which emerged from this initiative with a key dimension of variation being whether the care management pilots were based in social services, in a health setting or within multi-disciplinary teams. Also, several of the models chosen stressed the need for care managers to act as advocates or brokers on behalf of clients. They should not be constrained by the resource dilemmas of the statutory agencies, but rather should be based in independent or semi-independent organisations (see Chapter 6 for further discussion of this issue).

Thus, local authorities found themselves facing considerable uncertainty and disagreement about what care management was and how it might be able to help within the new community care arrangements. Was care management something to be applied to all clients, all clients with complex needs or clients in very specific situations? Should care managers be located inside or outside social services? Are they advocates on behalf of clients, rationers on behalf of social services, or both? Should assessment only be carried out by social workers, or also by other professional groups such as home care organisers, community nurses and occupational therapists?

In fairness to central government, there was recognition of the complexity of what was being asked for and social services were reassured that change needed to be spread over several years. The full extent of the implementation challenge was perhaps best summarised by the Audit Commission's (1992) report on *Community Care: Managing the Cascade of Change*. This report opened by outlining how, under previous systems, the user was expected to fit in with existing service requirements, and the service received was often more dependent on which professional received the initial request for help rather than on actual needs, even for people in very similar situations. Hence, an occupational therapist referral would be assessed as requiring an occupational therapy service, while the same person, if referred to home care, might be defined as requiring a home help. However, the simple decision to place user and carer needs first had sparked off a cascade of change, as illustrated by Figure 5.1. The central point about this figure was not only the scale of change required, but also the order in which the changes might have to be tackled. Key strategic decisions had to be made about how to stimulate a mixed economy of care, and whether or not to develop an internal split within social services between purchasers and providers. These decisions then had to be underpinned by new and appropriate financial, structural and procedural arrangements. Social services authorities also needed to develop new assessment systems and forms which were needs-driven and which were acceptable to a wide range of agencies. Decisions had to be made about who would be a priority for services in the light of likely resource levels. And thought would have to be given as to how wide a range of staff within and outside social services might perform the rôle of care manager. All this had to be tackled before a needs-led assessment and care management system could be put into operation. As the Audit Commission (1992) explains, 'a process of change has been set in motion which will turn organisations upside down' (p. 19).

Under these circumstances, it is perhaps not surprising that most authorities have taken considerable time to establish care management and that the resultant systems show enormous variation, which is often closely linked to different approaches to developing (quasi) markets in social care. Thus Hoyes *et al.* (1994) looked at the initial approach of four authorities and found the following:

1. Devon

Devon made an early decision to separate the purchasing and provision of all its functions, including childcare, at the level of its then 32 district offices. Three pilots were established in 1990–1 with a view to these informing a phased county-wide reorganisation over a three-year period. Care management teams for adults were composed of a wide range of staff, including social workers, occupational therapists and home care organisers. Community mental health and learning disability teams included community nurses, whose care management work was managed by social services although they were employed by the health trust. Care management teams were perceived as purchasers, with responsibility for a locality or client group. Care management was a service all users received with different degrees of professional involvement according to the complexity of their needs and care packages.

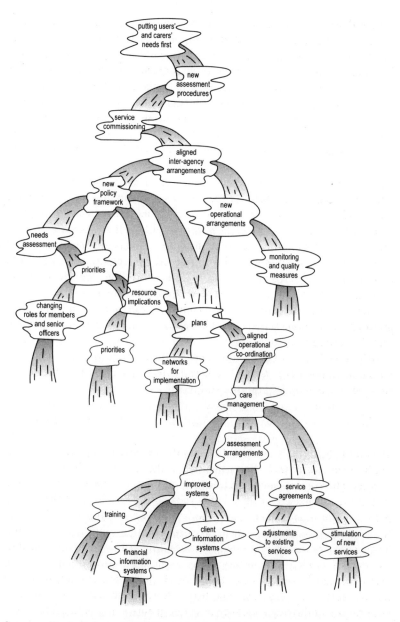

Source: Derived from Audit Commission (1992) p. 38.

FIGURE 5.1   The cascade of change

By the end of the research period, care management teams and a purchaser–provider split had been established throughout the county, although there had been delays in the delegation of budgetary control to some teams. Also, the county was planning further structural changes to consolidate and strengthen the purchasing function, and to develop and support the management structure of the in-house providers. The main effect of this restructuring would be a reduction in the number of districts from 32 to 19, and the establishment of a managerially separate provider division, known as 'Community Services – Devon'.

2. Hammersmith and Fulham

During 1991 this inner London authority began the process of separating out its purchasing from its providing functions. These changes have been consolidated with the setting-up of a Commissioning Unit within the Quality Assurance and Planning Division and the appointment in mid-1992 of a new assistant director to oversee its development. The borough and the health authority were reviewing the joint planning structure, with the possibility of moving more formally towards joint commissioning.

All grants and service agreements were to be administered by the Commissioning Unit. A Quality Standards Unit had been in existence since January 1993 and quality standards were being developed for in-house residential care; domiciliary care standards would follow.

Care management was initially introduced fairly cautiously through a small number of pilot schemes covering most of the main client groups. These were superseded by a comprehensive new system introduced on 1 April 1993. The principle had been to keep commissioning functions separate from the assessment and purchasing rôle of frontline staff.

Following assessment, care managers put together a proposed package of care. This was then submitted to a budgetholders' meeting which included colleagues from the health authority. This decided whether departmental criteria were met and then agreed in-house provision and/or released money for external providers. Budgetholders were middle managers in the field-work division. However, the aim was to delegate budget responsibility to frontline managers, starting with care in the community packages from April 1994.

If residential care was required, the care manager had access to a list of approved residential care provision developed by the Commissioning Unit (although they could select others subject to financial constraints). The care manager notified the Commissioning Unit of the selected choice and, subject to vacancies, a contract was placed and admission arranged. The Commissioning Unit also monitored the contract. A similar list was likely to be developed for domiciliary care.

3. Oxfordshire

A major restructuring of the social services authority took place in autumn 1992, when its five geographical divisions were reduced to three and a clear central commissioning arm was established, headed by an Assistant Director (Commissioning and Planning). Within each of the three divisions, new care manager teams for adults were formed, composed of social workers, occupational therapists and home care organisers. Community mental health and learning disability teams included community nurses and social workers. However, unlike Devon and St Helens, most team members retained a mixture of purchaser and provider functions and so the split occurred *within* teams. Former home care organisers had become full-time care managers with no management rôle for home care staff. Home care services were managed as provider units and were a separate cost centre within the department.

Senior managers felt it would risk the stability of high-quality in-house provision if individual care managers were budgetholders and provider units operated as separate trading accounts. However, it was expected that budgets would be released on an evolutionary basis over a period of years. In the immediate future, however, most services would be drawn off centrally negotiated contracts. The department has been very cautious over releasing any transitional grant money for non-residential use because of uncertainties over demand for residential and nursing-home provision. Senior management devised a mechanism for setting prices for 1993–4 within bands of service specification. There was a list of all homes with the price for each specification band, and the care managers could spot-purchase to the agreed price on this list, with the user topping up if the actual price was higher.

Even before the community care reforms had started, all social services funding of voluntary organisations was subject to three-year service agreements, negotiated with individual providers. These included agreements for day care services for people with mental health problems and for elderly people. Contracts existed with Crossroads care attendant schemes and there was a small number of private domiciliary care agencies, used on a very local basis to supplement the department's home care service.

4. St Helens

This authority had a traditional service delivery structure with social work teams, home care teams and occupational therapists involved in both assessment and care delivery. However, in April 1993 a radical purchaser–provider split was introduced into the community care work of the department, with care management teams becoming the 'purchasing arm' of the authority. These new teams were composed of a mixture of social workers, home care organisers and occupational therapists. Team leaders allocated referrals to one of five priority bands which defined the speed of response from the care manager. Subsequent packages had to be costed by the care manager (all services were given shadow unit costs) and agreed by the team leader, who had to refer upwards if the proposed package was above agreed ceilings. Places in independent residential and nursing homes were bought on a spot-purchase basis by care managers, using Department of Social Security price guidelines.

St Helens had a tradition of local authority provision of services. However, development plans for all services were generated in 1988 and these identified the need for new services and a more diverse range of providers. By the time the fieldwork commenced, the local authority had developed a number of service agreements with the voluntary sector and this included a Crossroads care attendant scheme and day care provided by Age Concern.

Movement in this direction had continued, but only modestly, and no major change in this situation was expected in the near future for two main reasons. First, the local authority remained very proud of its own services (especially home care provision) and most members were not willing to consider contracting out such services. Second, St Helens received a low sum from the social security transfer formula in 1993–4 and had also faced major expenditure cutbacks as a local authority. This had limited the scope for developing new services outside existing local authority and voluntary sector provision.

A similar spread of approaches to the development of care management was identified by Lewis and Glennerster (1996) in their study of five local authorities. In general they also found progress to be slow, with the feasibility of applying care management to all client groups being one major problem, and how to mesh care management into the broader purchasing and enabling strategy of each authority being another.

Care management systems have continued to evolve as enthusiasm waxes and wanes for different approaches to assessment and the extent to which the care manager should literally act as the purchaser of

1. empower both the user and carer – inform fully, clarify their understanding of the situation and of the role of the assessor before going ahead;
2. involve, rather than just inform, the user and carer, make them feel that they are full partners in the assessment;
3. shed their 'professional' perspective – have an open mind and be prepared to learn;
4. start from where the user and carer are, establish their existing level of knowledge and what hopes and expectations they have;
5. be interested in the user and carer as people;
6. establish a suitable environment for the assessment, which ensures there is privacy, quiet and sufficient time;
7. take time – build trust and rapport, and overcome the brief visitor syndrome. This will usually take more than one visit;
8. be sensitive, imaginative and creative in responding – users and carers may not know what is possible, or available. For carers in particular, guilt and reticence may have to be overcome;
9. avoid value judgements whenever possible – if such judgements are needed, make them explicit;
10. consider social, emotional, relationship needs as well as just practical needs and difficulties; pay particular attention to the quality of the relationship between user and carer;
11. listen to and value the user's and carer's expertise or opinions, even if these run counter to the assessor's own values;
12. present honest, realistic service options, identifying advantages and disadvantages and providing an indication of any delay or limitations in service delivery;
13. not make assessment a 'battle' in which users and carers feel they have to fight for services;
14. balance all perspectives; and
15. clarify understanding at the end of the assessment, agree objectives and the nature of the review process.

Source: Nolan and Caldock (1996) pp. 83–4.

FIGURE 5.2   Benchmarks for assessment practice

individual care packages. It is certainly possible to point to individual examples of creative and flexible responses to the needs of service users:

> A young [disabled] woman . . . had been enabled to take part in swimming, relaxation and Tai Chi groups, using local facilities and volunteers where necessary. This reflected the authority's aim to move from a model of day provision dominated by more traditional, statutory day centres. These activities had become such a part of this woman's life that she no longer regarded them as part of her package. (Hoyes *et al.*, 1994, p. 19)

The development of assessment skills in care managers is crucial to this kind of creative and imaginative care package and there is growing consensus on what the benchmarks of good assessment practice are (see Figure 5.2). However, it is one thing to agree these benchmarks but it is another to create an environment in which they can flourish.

A number of factors continue to make the establishment of such an environment problematic to achieve. Many care managers and other field-level staff 'are experiencing the pain of major organisational change but few of the benefits' (Hoyes *et al.*, 1994, p. 14), resulting in alienation and cynicism towards the community care reforms. What seems to be happening is that the knock-on consequences of financial stringency are undermining the delivery of a care management system based on the principles laid out in the policy guidance (Department of Health, 1990) and the assessment benchmarks as proposed by Figure 5.2.

Above all, care management systems have become dominated by debates about which types of client should be a priority for a care package. Hence, there is much talk of eligibility criteria and the priority matrix, as social services authorities continue to define ever more narrowly the number of people they claim they are able to provide a service for (see Figure 5.3). Some authorities use the twin concepts of risk and dependency to create priority bands with the 'acceptable' cost of a care package being reduced according to which band one is allocated to:

> Buckinghamshire Social Services Department is adopting a risk/ dependency approach, as part of a 'banding' system, around high, medium and low levels, attaching cost ceilings for care within each band. The authority has carried out an option appraisal of banding methods. A dependency/risk model has been tested by staff. Feedback has been very positive and encouraging, with staff finding the

method straightforward to use. It provides an effective way of placing people into high, medium and low categories. Each band is assigned a maximum spend per case, as follows:

- High priority – the average net cost of residential care plus 20 per cent premium if spent on community services, enabling people to stay in their own homes;
- Medium priority – 60 per cent of the average net cost of residential care; and
- Low priority – 30 per cent of the average net cost of residential care.

(Quoted in Audit Commission, 1996a, p. 12)

Older people

Priority 1   To provide appropriate community-based services in order to reduce the requirement for some older people (including those with carers) with complex needs to enter residential or nursing home care on a long-term basis.

Priority 2   To support carers who themselves may need support to enable them to continue caring.

Priority 3   To enhance the quality of life of carers and users.

People with learning difficulties, HIV/Aids, mental health problems and alcohol/drugs problems, physically and sensory impaired people and homeless people

Priority 1   To meet the needs of people with complex social care needs who are presently unable to stay in their own homes.

Priority 2(a)   To enhance the ability of people to live independently of their families where this is their choice.

Priority 2(b)   To rehabilitate people from small-scale hostel-type accommodation into the community where this is their choice and their needs can be met in this way.

Priority 2(c)   To support carers who themselves may need support to enable them to continue caring.

Priority 3   To enhance the quality of life of carers and users.

Within existing budgets, it is not expected that it will be possible to purchase services to help people who fall in the Priority 3 categories.

FIGURE 5.3   **Order of priority for people living in the community: example of a priority matrix**

The end product of this has been numerous highly complex assessment forms in which 'criteria that define those needing care with sufficient precision to limit expenditure in a predictable way may well be too complicated for people to understand or operate on a day-to-day basis' (Audit Commission, 1996a, p. 11).

Such forms have been a generator of much ill-will amongst those expected to use them, especially when linked to the collection of information about the personal resources of clients in order to estimate service charges (see previous section). Field-level staff feel care management has meant more paperwork and more bureaucracy or, as one third-tier manager told Lewis and Glennerster (1996):

> I think people have felt weighed down by paperwork . . . and they feel the department wants to turn them into administrators and financial processors. All the emphasis is on filling out forms, and a lot of staff are saying That isn't what I was trained to do. (p. 140)

We have already seen how such resentment can be especially acute where social work trained staff are being asked to fill out financial information as part of an assessment for service charges. This can be further illustrated by the following quotation from a care manager talking about the problems of financial assessment where the client has dementia:

> I've got one now. She knows she's got a bank book and she knows it's in [this city]. She doesn't know what's in it. And I've just sent a letter to revenue – I know it's a bank, I know it's [this city]. That's her name. Your problem! (Quoted in Means and Langan, 1996, p. 253)

Such anger can be partly explained by the feeling that the counselling aspects of social work are being squeezed out of care management by the emphasis upon targeting, financial assessment and the co-ordination of care (Phillips, 1996). This concern was raised by field-level staff in the research of both Lewis and Glennerster (1996) and Hoyes *et al.* (1994) with the latter remarking that feelings of loss and bereavement in clients 'are not easily alleviated just by the provision of practical help, and may benefit from counselling and social work support' (p. 29). Yet it is this very traditional counselling rôle that many field-level staff feel has become undervalued within the care management system.

Another factor frustrating the development of a creative user-centred care management system has been the lack of computer-based information systems to underpin the purchasing of complex care packages and their subsequent monitoring. There is much talk of the contract economy and spot purchasing while Chapter 3 looked at debates about post-Fordist organisational forms, but the harsh reality is that numerous social services authorities have developed care management systems based upon the devolved purchase of services with completely inadequate IT and information system back-up (Bovell *et al.*, 1997). The end result has often been further frustration for care managers.

Information is, of course, a crucial issue for the whole of the community care system and not just for care management. This is bringing us towards the need to consider the extent to which social services authorities are establishing a clear purchaser–provider split, and the extent to which a mixed economy is emerging. There is little point in having user-centred care managers if all they have to purchase is a limited set of services from a 'set list' (Hoyes *et al.*, 1994, p. 36). Therefore, the next section considers the extent to which social services authorities have been implementing purchaser–provider splits as a starting point for generating markets in social care.

Establishing purchaser–provider splits

It should be remembered that the importance of developing purchaser–provider splits within social services departments was emphasised in the White Paper on community care (Department of Health, 1989a) and in the subsequent policy guidance (Department of Health, 1990), with the latter stressing that

> In practical terms in developing the enabling rôle authorities will need to distinguish between aspects of work in SSDs concerned with
>
> • the assessment of individuals' needs, the arrangement and purchase of services to meet them
> and
> • direct service provision. It will be important that this distinction is reflected within the SSD's management structure at both the 'macro' level (involving plans to meet strategic priorities as a whole) and at the 'micro' level (where services are being arranged for individuals).

> (Department of Health, 1990, pp. 37–8)

It can be argued that the purpose of this proposed split was twofold. First, it would ensure equality of treatment for alternative suppliers and the authorities' own services in terms of the identification of service costs. Second, it would increase the fairness of consumer choice, since the care manager would feel distanced from in-house provision and hence under no pressure to recommend its take-up in preference to those services available from alternative suppliers.

The Department of Health subsequently commissioned the consultants, Price Waterhouse, to produce a report which offered advice on options and implementation strategies. This report identified three different approaches to developing a purchaser–provider split (Price Waterhouse/Department of Health, 1991). These were:

1. Separation of purchaser/commissioner and provider functions at strategic level only. Here the split is very much at the macro level with headquarters staff contracting with area offices to provide assessment, care management and direct services, within a block contract. The contract would be at a high level of generality even though targets might be set for unit prices and activity levels. The report felt that this was only a transitional option since it did not fully meet the policy objectives.

2. Separation of purchaser/commissioner and provider functions at senior management team level. In this approach, the Director of Social Services would be the only post combining both purchaser/ commissioner and provider functions, Assistant Directors would head separate hierarchies including fieldwork teams (on the purchaser side) and establishments (on the provider side). Purchasers would agree which services were to be supplied by providers to individual clients so that service agreements or contracts would be at the micro level.

3. Separation of purchaser/commissioner and provider functions at the local level. This model involves a series of separate purchaser/ commissioner and provider teams operating under a combined management structure at the area level, an approach likely to appeal to those authorities which have already undergone considerable decentralisation of budgets and decision-making. Care management teams would take new referrals, assess need and put together packages of care, taking account of resource limitations. They would purchase appropriate care packages from in-house providers or independent suppliers.

The report recognised that all three models posed major implementation challenges and that all three models had major strengths and weaknesses. For example, the first model minimises disruption but fails to separate assessment from provision. The second model achieves a much clearer separation but the purchasers are very centralised and there is a danger of managerial duplication. Model three is potentially the most responsive to local needs, yet is highly complex, placing high demands on middle managers and on information systems.

How have local authorities responded to this challenge? The twenty-five authorities studied by Wistow *et al.* (1992) from April 1990 to May 1992 had made little progress on clarifying their position in relation to the purchaser–provider split:

> Only two had already achieved some degree of split, and another had conducted a small pilot project. Of the others, one had no intention of such a reorganization, and seven were not intending to introduce such a split unless forced. (Two were hoping for a Labour government before April 1993, when full implementation of the 1990 Act is required, but councils run by each of the main political parties were represented among the reluctant. Most saw the split as an inevitable fact of life, but, faced with so many other pressures, welcomed the delay.) The other sample authorities expressed intentions which ranged from a cautious 'possibly, but slowly' approach, to a definite commitment to a split whose details had yet to be agreed . . . Directors of social services were almost universally more enthusiastic than their political masters about splitting the purchasing and providing functions. (p. 31)

In their follow-up study of the same authorities, based on 1993 data, Wistow *et al.* (1996) found that there was still a reluctance to go for the most radical purchaser–provider split options because, as one Assistant Director put it, 'the last thing we wanted to do was to chuck the organisation up into the air . . . and go through a massive organisational change' (p. 76). However, what had been happening was a devolving of purchasing power down social services departments so that team managers and/or care managers were now the most likely staff to make purchasing decisions both from internal/in-house providers and from external independent sector providers of social care services. However, just one of the case studies ran the in-house provision through a full trading account while only four had shadow trading accounts.

This suggests social services authorities have been selective in their embracing of the philosophy of the White Paper with regard to purchaser–provider splits. They are keen for their own services such as home care and residential care to become more responsive to the needs of clients through placing purchasing power in the hands of team managers and care managers. At the same time, they seem reluctant to fully expose their own in-house services to unprotected competition from the private and voluntary sectors in the belief that this could undermine existing high-quality provision. To understand this issue fully, it is necessary to take a detailed look at the extent to which local authorities have been attempting to stimulate alternative suppliers.

Establishing a mixed economy of social care

The main focus of the White Paper on community care (Department of Health, 1989a) was on the need for local authorities to develop their lead agency rôle through the skills of enabling rather than through service delivery. The responsibility of the local authority was to create a market in social care through maximising the service delivery rôle of the voluntary and private sectors. This market would initially be strongest in residential care, but would subsequently be expected to expand to the provision of domiciliary services. Any study of advertisements in the personal social services is likely to lead one to conclude that considerable progress has been made (see Figure 5.4). This section looks at emerging research evidence on whether this is really the case.

From the outset, it is important to remember that, in many ways, a mixed economy of social care has always existed. The National Assistance Act 1948 established a new system of local authority residential homes, but left powers with local authorities to fund places in residential homes run by the independent sector, while it allocated the primary rôle in the development of domiciliary services to voluntary organisations (see Chapter 2). Although the reasons for this are complex, one key factor was a desire to develop a post-war rôle for organisations like the Women's (Royal) Voluntary Service, the British Red Cross Society and National Old People's Welfare Committees (now Age Concern) which had all developed extensive welfare services during the Second World War (Means and Smith, 1985). However, local authorities became frustrated at the failure of voluntary organisations to develop coherent authority-wide provision for services such as meals-on-wheels, day care and visiting/counselling schemes. This cre-

SOCIAL SERVICES DEPARTMENT

TENDERS FOR THE PROVISION OF
(i) OCCUPATIONAL THERAPY ASSESSMENT
and
(ii) DOMICILIARY CARE SERVICES

As part of their Service Development Strategy, Surrey Social Services Department are intending to subject elements of their care services to competitive tendering. Interested parties are invited to submit their expressions of interest in tendering for contracts for one or both of the above services.

Expressions of interest should be made in writing no later than 29th September 1995 to:

Mr. R. Thorpe, Project and Contracts Manager, Social Services Department, Surrey County Council, A.C. Court, High Street, Thames Ditton, Surrey KT7 OQA

**Expressions of Interest for Tenders in
Respect of a Housing with Care Service for
Adults with Learning Disabilities**

The Director of Social Services is seeking expressions of interest from experienced companies/organisations with a proven track record in the provision of residential and day care for adults with learning disabilities.

The Service will provide a range of high quality and innovative residential and day care support to Service Users living in small community units in the north of the City of Westminster. It is proposed to package the contract in two parts and shortlisted companies/organisations will be invited to tender for one or both parts of the contract. The two parts are as follows:

Part one   Residential care of fourteen frail, elderly people with severe learning disabilities and high care needs, living in three units.

Part two   Residential care of eight mobile adults with moderate learning disabilities and high care needs living in three houses.

The contract will commence in August 1997 for a period of five years.

Those companies/organisations wishing to express an interest in being considered for the short list of prospective tenderers should write to Contracts Manager, Social Services Department, 7th Floor, Westminster City Hall, 64 Victoria Street, London, SW1E 6QP requesting an information pack and questionnaire (Expressions of Interest). The deadline for receipt of requests for the information pack and questionnaire is Friday 11th October 1996 and the deadline for receipt of the completed questionnaire (Expressions of Interest) is noon on Friday 1st November 1996.

Interested companies/organisations are invited to an informal meeting on Thursday October 17th 1996 at 2 pm at Westminster City Hall where there will be opportunities to receive information and to seek clarifications about the Service.

Source: *Guardian Society*, 6 September 1995, p. 59, and 2 October 1996, p. 47.

FIGURE 5.4   Tendering and the mixed economy of care

ated what one commentator called 'a wind of discontent in the town halls' (Slack, 1960). Chapter 2 described how this was a factor in the gradual extension of local authority powers to provide such services. However, the rôle of the independent sector was never completely squeezed in terms of these traditional services for elderly and physically disabled people, while large voluntary organisations such as MENCAP and MIND began to emerge as service providers for other groups, usually with the aid of grants from the local authority or through joint finance monies. Finally, Chapter 3 illustrated how the social security system funded a major growth of private sector residential and nursing-home care in the 1980s.

Table 5.1 illustrates not only the extent of social services funding of non-statutory organisations in the late 1980s, but also the great variation in the extent of that funding between different local authorities. Thus, social services departments faced very different starting points with regard to the further developments of a mixed economy of social care within their areas. However, it is this development which was at the heart of their enabling responsibilities, as stressed by the White Paper on community care, and which involved a major cultural shift for both local authorities and voluntary organisations in terms of the emphasis upon making markets and control through contracts (Forder *et al.*, 1996; Wistow *et al.*, 1996).

As already indicated, the inherited market structure varied enormously between areas. The uneven distribution of private and voluntary residential homes, with a concentration in seaside resorts, was graphically demonstrated in *Making a Reality of Community Care* (Audit Commission, 1986). The independent market in domiciliary services was far less developed in nearly all authorities, with few large suppliers and many small ones. Local authorities had had little experience of contracting-out in this field, although if future services were to be based on individual packages of care for people in their own homes these were bound to assume greater importance. The White Paper recognised these potential supply problems, stating that one of its key objectives was 'to promote the development of a flourishing independent sector alongside good-quality public services'. Moreover, social services departments were expected to make clear

where such providers are not currently available, how they propose to stimulate such activity. In particular, they should consider how they will encourage diversification into the non-residential sector. (Department of Health, 1989a, p. 23)

TABLE 5.1 Local authority social services department funding of non-statutory organisations as percentage of total expenditure, 1988–9[1]

Authority type and statistics[5]	General contributions to voluntary organisations			Contracts with private and voluntary organisations		
	ELD[2] %[5]	MH/LD[1] %[5]	ALL[4] %[5]	ELD[2] %[5]	MH/LD[3] %[5]	ALL[4] %[5]
Inner London mean	2.6	1.1	3.2	7.1	27.2	8.0
Outer London mean	0.6	1.0	1.1	5.0	16.9	7.1
Metropolitan district mean	0.3	0.7	1.1	1.4	4.1	3.0
Shire County mean	0.8	1.5	1.4	2.8	10.0	3.8
All authorities mean	0.8	1.1	1.4	3.2	11.2	4.6

Notes
1. Allocations expressed as percentages of relevant total client group expenditure.
2. Services for elderly people.
3. Services for people with mental health problems or learning disabilities.
4. All personal social services.
5. The percentage given is the mean for the local authorities in the category.

Source: From Knapp *et al.* (1993) p.8.

However, stimulating new and diversified markets is not easy. The voluntary sector expressed fears about losing autonomy and flexibility and about compromising its advocacy and campaigning rôles; smaller groups in particular did not always feel up to the demands of bidding for and fulfilling contracts (Deakin, 1995; Taylor *et al.*, 1995). The government recognised the need for authorities to continue to provide core grant funding to voluntary organisations to underpin administrative infrastructure and development work, but it was questionable whether social services authorities would choose to spend their limited resources on this rather than the purchase of particular services. Diversification from residential provision appeared to be a logical step for many suppliers, especially if demand was shrinking. However, it would not necessarily be a straightforward move for small, or even larger, organisations whose experience was limited to providing care in an institutional setting (Wistow *et al.*, 1996).

If a local authority was to stimulate a market, it would need to do more than contract-out its own residential care. Interventions required on the supply side included help with business development grants;

subsidies and credit for start-up and working capital; training; and licensing and regulation. Local authorities could attempt to influence the market by the way in which they related to service providers. For example, to what extent were local authorities willing to draw upon the rhetoric of user-centred services and the mixed economy to support the growth of voluntary organisations 'where services are provided for minorities by minorities' (Atkin, 1996, p. 150)? For conventional markets to operate efficiently, perfect competition required that there should be neither a monopoly (one or few providers) nor a monopsony (one or few purchasers). It was likely that in some areas, for some services, the social services department would be the only purchaser. Whilst this might make it easier for the authority to dictate terms, it might also deter potential providers from entering a market where they would be dependent on a single buyer. On the other hand, if an authority, for the sake of administrative convenience or economy, chose to enter into block contracts with one or two providers, they risked squeezing out other smaller providers and could find themselves faced with a monopoly and in a very weak position. Authorities needed to consider to what extent they were able and would wish to guard against these situations by, for example, operating care management systems which devolved responsibility and resources to many purchasers, and by encouraging many suppliers by undertaking the interventionist strategies such as those described above.

Several studies have examined the attitudes of senior managers and members towards the move to a system of service delivery which relies more and more upon the contracting-out of social care services to independent providers. One of the earliest studies was by Hoyes and Means (1993b) who carried out a small number of interviews in two shire counties in the period June to November 1990, to ascertain attitudes to the community care reforms. In both case studies, respondents saw the need for a further contracting-out of services and they expected this process to gather pace over the next five years. But others emphasised their belief in the quality of existing local authority services.

The first detailed study of these issues was the investigation referred to earlier into the implementation of the community care reforms in twenty-five local authorities which was funded by the Department of Health (Wistow *et al.*, 1994). This research highlighted not only the wide range of mixed economy options available to social services authorities (see Table 5.2) but also the wide diversity of attitudes to the ten options identified in the research:

While it would be wrong to generalize too freely, there were some clear and largely predictable rankings in attitudes towards these options. Thus most Labour authorities preferred d to e, and strongly preferred e to f. Indeed, option f was a non-starter in some authorities. If the possibility was mentioned, they also ruled out j and were often unhappy about h. To take another example, most Conservative authorities supported option g, expressed some practical but not ideological reservations about h, and usually liked the idea of e and f in principle even though elected members had some difficulty supporting the sale of facilities in their own wards. Option c hardly ever received support from either officers or members, and it was too early for local authorities to make any judgements about the viability of option j. These are gross generalizations, and only rarely were two authorities alike. Indeed, one of the strong conclusions to emerge from our study was that generalizations along party political lines are often hard to sustain. (Wistow *et al.*, 1992, p. 30)

TABLE 5.2   Potential alternative modes of provision of community care

a.	Continuing local authority provision as it is currently organised, with no planned changes to the management, funding or regulation of activities.
b.	Continuing local authority provision with reorganisation of the SSD along the lines of a purchaser-provider split of some kind and to some degree.
c.	Management or staff buyouts of some local authority services.
d.	Floating off some services to a not-for-profit trust which allows the local authority to retain some degree of control, though with eligibility for Department of Social Security payments.
e.	Selling off services, perhaps at a nominal price, to voluntary organisations (new or already working in the authority) which act independently of the authority, except for any service agreements or contracts.
f.	Selling off services to private (for-profit) agencies (new or already with a presence in the authority) which act independently of the authority, except for any service agreements or contracts.
g.	Encouraging (or perhaps simply not stopping) voluntary or not-for-profit organisations setting up new services.
h.	Encouraging (or perhaps simply not stopping) private (for-profit) agencies setting up new services.
i.	Considering health authorities as potential providers for some social care services, such as residential care for elderly people or people with mental health problems.
j.	Bringing NHS trusts into the supply picture.

Source: Wistow *et al.* (1992) p. 30.

Not only did attitudes to the options in Table 5.2 vary widely, but implementation strategies were being pursued with some caution in terms of developing internal purchaser–provider splits, tendering out services and stimulating markets in social care. The end result was caution in the vast majority of the twenty-five case studies in which a selective approach to the diversification of supply was being adopted involving a preference in most authorities for working with voluntary and not-for-profit agencies. However, at the time of the fieldwork in 1991, four authorities had still not clarified their view about contracting out, two were 'conscientious objectors', and three were 'proven enthusiasts', determined to implement their policies rapidly.

Wistow *et al.* (1996) have continued to monitor these twenty-five authorities well into the main implementation phase of the community care reforms. By late 1993 considerable change could be identified, so that whereas 'in our 1991 interviews we identified only three authorities as market enthusiasts, the fieldwork in 1993 identified only three authorities in which the disadvantages of a social care market were thought to outweigh the potential advantages' (p. 34). However, this enthusiasm for moving away from near-monopoly local authority provision still fell a considerable way short in nearly all authorities from a desire to achieve a point of non-provision, so that most wished to remain one provider among many within a much expanded local mixed economy of social care. Even the majority of Labour-run local authorities in this study were becoming market pragmatists who saw the many opportunities opened up by a cautious move towards a more mixed economy system.

Finally, the second phase of the research pointed to local authorities beginning to increase their knowledge and information about both need and supply while also increasing in confidence in terms of their individual purchasing strategies (Wistow *et al.*, chapters 4 and 5). However, their ability to map the market might have improved but the research conclusion was still that 'areas of ignorance still exceeded the areas of knowledge' (p. 69), perhaps not surprising given what was said in the previous section about the inadequate IT systems available in most social services departments. On the need side, key gaps tended to include the lack of work on projected future need across client groups and the paucity of information on client groups other than elderly people. On the supply side, much more was known about residential and nursing home care provision compared to the providers of other services.

Despite these continuing weaknesses it is quite clear that a mixed economy of social care has continued to develop further and that this has included domiciliary services as well as residential and nursing-home care. The Local Government Management Board (LGMB) are tracking community care expenditure and their 1997 report found that the independent sector accounted for 52 per cent of the community care budget in 1996–7 compared with 40 per cent in 1993–4. It also found that independent sector provision for day and domiciliary services continued to expand, being responsible for 10 per cent of the overall social services budget for older people in 1996–7 and 16 per cent of the budget for younger adults (Edwards and Kenny, 1997).

Such findings are supported by the 1996 survey of independent sector providers of home care services who are affiliated to the United Kingdom Home Care Association (UKHCA). This generated replies from 266 organisations or 26 per cent of the membership, the vast majority of whom were small recently established for-profit organisations:

> Sixty per cent of organisations are providing services to less than 100 clients and just five per cent had more than 500 clients on their books. Only 4 per cent of respondents were providing more than 25,000 hours of service per month and 74 per cent fewer than 5,000 hours. Around 6 per cent of providers had been in business for less than one year, 23 per cent for between one and two years and just 10 per cent for more than ten years. (Young and Wistow, 1996, p. 18)

This mushrooming of small agencies had been stimulated by the desire of local authorities to contract-out some of its home care work to the independent sector. However, most of these small providers found such business to be sporadic with no clear flow of cases and that small profit margins were being offered for working with often complex cases. The resultant high turnover of staff risked undermining the quality of provision and caused many of these providers to be pessimistic about the future of their organisations.

This illustrates one of the key tensions faced by social services authorities as they have attempted to develop a mixed economy of social care. The emphasis of many authorities on placing purchasing decisions at the level of the care manager, and their team leaders, encourages a system of spot contracts or purchase which may be very user-centred but which can have the effect of undermining the financial viability of small independent sector providers. Against this, agree-ments from social services to block purchase services from established providers can have the effect of limiting the services available for the care manager to draw upon. Senior managers with overall strategic responsibilities for purchasing have been learning how to develop and work with local (quasi) markets, not only in terms of the block versus spot-contract debate but also in terms of how detailed to make contract conditions so as to ensure they develop in a way which generates high-quality appropriate responses to the needs of local service users (Forder *et al*, 1996).

A linked topic addresses the question of which stakeholders should be involved in these and related purchasing issues. In the early stages of the reforms there was a view from many social services authorities that they should not discuss their purchasing intentions with independent sector providers. There is now a growing recognition of the importance of factors such as trust between purchasers and providers and the fact that the providers have an enormous amount of information about service users because it is staff from their organisations who are most likely to be in direct day-to-day contact with them (Lewis *et al.*, 1996; Means, 1996b).

However, there are dangers in such developments unless this is balanced by a strong input from service users and carers. It needs to be remembered that the overall aim of locally based mixed economies of social care should be the development of user-centred provision which seeks to empower service users and carers. The previous chapter suggested that it was through the community care planning process that service users and carers were expected to have an influence on shaping purchasing strategies along with other key stakeholders such as health agencies, housing agencies and independent sector organisa-tions.

A number of early studies looked at community care planning from the perspective of the extent to which service users and carers were being drawn genuinely into the planning process (see previous chapter). The general message seemed to be that real progress was being made but there was still a long way to go before genuine influence could be achieved.

However, cynicism about community care plans is not uncommon, with some of this relating to ambiguity about their objectives (Hudson, 1996). Are they a glossy user-friendly document for the general public? Or the plan which steers and justifies the whole community care purchasing strategy of the local authority? Hoyes and Means (1994) have pointed out the growing interest in joint commissioning and purchasing strategies with health and have argued that this raises real dilemmas about how the input of users and carers will be structured into these new arrangements. They suggest that different authorities will opt for combinations of the following:

- User and carer groups and perhaps only the more professionalised, will remain part of the revised joint planning/commissioning/purchasing systems but voluntary sector organisations will tend to be excluded from these mechanisms, as a provider interest.
- The planning input of user and carer groups will occur mainly at locality level within a macro framework created by key purchasers from social services and health (whether this framework will be empowering or a straitjacket is open to question).
- Social services will plan overall strategic direction with health but claim to balance this with stimulating a variety of *ad hoc* initiatives by which user and carer groups can have limited influence on services on the ground, such as involvement in training schemes, advocacy initiatives, design of forms.

And they conclude:

> The worst scenario would be a community care planning system which falls into growing disrepute with user and carer groups because it is seen as irrelevant to where the real decisions are made.
>   The best outlook would be for health and social services to ensure that community care plans are a genuine expression of purchasing intentions . . . and that this includes a strong and continual dialogue with local user and carer groups. (p. 23)

This brings us to the issue of social services' relationship to health, the subject of the next chapter. A judgement about the extent to which social services are 'the leaders at last' in community care requires a detailed consideration of their continuing problematic relationship with health care agencies.

Conclusion

This chapter has looked at the progress so far made by social services as the lead agency in community care in terms of establishing a new funding regime for residential and nursing-home care, developing care management systems, promoting a mixed economy of social care and introducing purchaser–provider splits. The overall message is that social services authorities have approached these tasks with some caution, so that full implementation still has a long way to go, even in the late 1990s. This can be partly explained by the size of the task required of them, partly by ambivalence about how far to go down the (quasi) market route and partly by the immensely difficult climate in which they have been working. The final chapter considers to what extent the election of a Labour government in May 1997 will radically change the implementation agenda.

6 The Health Dimension of Community Care: Towards Collaborative Working?

Chapters 3 and 5 focused primarily on the implications for social services authorities of the community care changes outlined in the 1989 White Paper (Department of Health, 1989a). This chapter takes a different perspective by considering its implications for the health dimension of community care. Has the clear identification of social services as the lead agency for all the main service user groups reduced tensions with health care agencies? What are the key issues, such as hospital discharge arrangements, which could continue to cause trouble? What are the main obstacles to effective working together between health and social care agencies in the late 1990s?

The health care and community care reforms

The central thrust of *Working for Patients*, the White Paper on the future of the National Health Service (Department of Health, 1989b), was the creation of internal or quasi-markets which, it was claimed, would generate efficiency and be responsive to the consumer. The creation of such a market required the separating-out of health purchasing from health providing activities. The NHS changes brought in by the National Health Service and Community Care Act 1990 were highly complex and have been discussed in detail elsewhere (Ham, 1994). Essentially, health authorities no longer provide or manage health care services; they now operate strategically and purchase services through contracts:

> The delivery of services and their management is the responsibility of NHS Trusts which are legally separate and independent bodies. Health authorities agree contracts with the Trusts for service provi-

137

sion, set broad quality standards and monitor performance. Among them may be found acute and specialist hospital trusts, community health service trusts, mental health services trusts, learning disability trusts or any combination of these in one trust. (Harrison in Means *et al.*, 1997, p. 14)

A further complication relates to GP fundholders, who have the power to make contracts with NHS trusts for specified services on behalf of their practice populations so that a significant part of the health care budget lies outside the direct control of the health authority. At the time of writing, further uncertainty has been created by the confirmation in the Queen's May 1997 speech to Parliament that the Labour government intends to abolish internal markets in the NHS although it was not clear what that would mean in practice. The creation of any further GP fundholders was also put on hold. However, the Audit Commission (1996b) study of GP fundholding showed that one in three practices was involved in the scheme in 1995–6 which formed a total of 2,200 funds in England and Wales. The study estimated that half the population would be covered by some form of GP fundholding arrangement by 1996–7.

The early 1990s was thus a period of considerable upheaval as new health care structures were created and health care staff were redesignated. This created major difficulties for social services authorities as the lead agents in community care, since such disruption made it very hard to establish a coherent dialogue with health care managers about the proposed community care changes. This is important since the community care changes emphasised the continuing central importance of health care and health care professionals in terms of assessment, service delivery and strategic planning.

Caring for People (Department of Health, 1989a) allocated a whole chapter to outlining the rôles and responsibilities of the health service within the proposed new system of community care provision. This was justified on the following grounds:

Community care is about the health as well as the social needs of the population. Health care, in its broadest sense, is an essential component of the range of services which may be needed to help people to continue to live in their own homes for as long as possible. (p. 33)

More specifically, it was explained that health care professionals would continue to have a major rôle to play in assessment even though the

co-ordination of multidisciplinary assessment was to be the responsibility of social services.

The health care professionals involved in such assessments would
sometimes be hospital-based, such as psychogeriatricians when an
elderly person with dementia was the focus. However, they were more
likely to be primary health care staff. For example, the White Paper
recognised that the general practitioner (GP) was in regular contact
with most people with community care needs so that close liaison
between GPs and social services staff would be essential for referral
and assessment purposes. Community nursing staff such as health
visitors, district nurses and community psychiatric nurses were seen by
the White Paper as equally crucial in assessment procedures, the
development of care arrangements and the provision of care once a
package of services had been designed. However, this encouragement
was counterbalanced by a warning that expensive nursing skills should
not be wasted on non-specialist tasks which could easily be done by
others.

The White Paper recognised that not everyone with health and social
care needs could remain in their own homes even with high levels of
support. Some would require continuous health care and it was claimed
that this would remain the responsibility of health authorities. However, this statement ignored the increasing reliance of the NHS upon
private nursing homes as a means of releasing acute hospital beds and
closing long-stay beds. The funding of these places for those on low
incomes was primarily a social security rather than a NHS responsibility and, of course, the White Paper proposed a shift of responsibility
from social security to social services in the future. This was an
inevitable source of future tension between health and social services
which is considered in detail later in this chapter.

As emphasised in the previous chapter, the White Paper placed a
high emphasis upon community care planning as the mechanism for
setting out the strategic direction of individual social service authorities, and again the rôle of health authorities and other health agencies
was underscored. It was stressed that social services authorities would
be expected to liaise with and consult health authorities and family
health services authorities, among others, in the production of plans,
while health authorities were told that they

> will be expected to prepare plans setting out their community care
> policies and the arrangements they propose for securing community
> services and community care. It will be for health authorities to

decide whether these plans would best form part of their overall plans or should be produced separately as a joint exercise with the relevant local authorities. But their key contents and resource assumptions will need to be shared and agreed with the social services authority. (p. 43)

It was left to individual social services authorities and health authorities to decide if the old systems of joint planning provided a helpful or unhelpful structure for tackling these new planning tasks.

Finally, the White Paper on community care had a considerable amount to say about the future funding and provision of services for people with mental health problems. It pointed out that the policy of successive governments since the publication of the White Paper on *Better Services for the Mentally Ill* (Department of Health and Social Security, 1975) had been the development of locally based rather than hospital-based provision. However, it was recognised that 'there are legitimate concerns that in some places hospital beds have been closed before better, alternative facilities are fully in place' and it was admitted 'some reports also suggest that, at times, patients have been discharged without adequate planning to meet their needs in the community' (Department of Health, 1989a, pp. 55–6).

Three main proposals were made for addressing these problems. First, health authorities were told that continuous health care must be available to all discharged patients, which would require individual care programmes to be agreed by both health and social services. Second, health authorities were reminded that money from the sale of mental illness and mental handicap hospitals could be used to provide capital to develop new facilities in the community, although the dilemma that these facilities were needed before the hospital could be closed, and hence sold, was recognised. Third, a new system of funding limited additional local authority social care services for people with mental health problems was announced through an earmarked grant.

This section has illustrated the extent to which the White Paper on community care proposed a system of provision dependent on collaborative working between social care and health care staff at both the strategic and operational levels. The importance of collaboration was recognised by the White Paper, which devoted a short chapter to this issue (pp. 49–52). It was argued that the proposed changes would help to clarify the respective rôles of health and social care agencies so that tension and conflict could be greatly reduced. In some areas the distinction between health and social care remained blurred, but health and local authorities would 'need to decide locally about how they share objectives, responsibilities and the funding of different services' (p. 50). Is collaboration as simple as this to achieve?

Collaborative working: the theory

Any review of the extensive literature on joint working would lead the reader to conclude that the White Paper on community care was very optimistic about the prospects for positive collaboration between social services authorities and health care agencies. As Webb (1991) brutally explains, 'exhortations to organisations, professionals and other producer interests to work together more closely and effectively litter the policy landscape' yet the reality is 'all too often a jumble of services fractionalised by professional, cultural and organisational boundaries and by tiers of governance' (p. 229).

One key difficulty is that governments have often been happy to extol the virtues of collaborative working without ever bothering to address the very real obstacles which exist from the point of view of the proposed collaborating partners. As Hudson (1987) explains:

> From an agency's viewpoint, collaborative activity raises two main difficulties. First, it loses some of its freedom to act independently when it would prefer to maintain control over its domain and affairs. Second, it must invest scarce resources and energy in developing and maintaining relationships with other organisations when the potential returns on this investment are often unclear and intangible. (p. 175)

Thus in order to commit themselves to joint working, agencies need to be persuaded that it is only by this route that organisational objectives can be achieved. They have to be convinced of the possibility of what Huxham (1996) calls 'collaborative advantage'.

Hudson (1987) suggests there are three main strategies available to foster collaborative working despite these problems. These are co-operative strategies (based on mutual agreements), incentive strategies (based on 'bribes' to encourage joint working) and authoritative strategies (agencies or individuals are instructed to work together). In the past, the tendency of government has been to request organisations such as social services authorities and district health authorities to collaborate on various initiatives. The alternative authoritative approach usually suffers from the fact that sanctions are weak and that there are numerous devices available to agencies and individuals by which reluctant partners can subvert or undermine policy initiatives.

Incentive strategies, however, have considerable potential. The authors of this book were involved with colleagues in the evaluation of a Health Education Authority (HEA) funded regional alcohol education programme which was met initially by a mixture of indifference and hostility from most of the seven councils on alcohol and the twelve health promotion units covered by the initiative. Nevertheless, these negative beginnings were overcome when the HEA agreed to fund 50 per cent of the salary costs of a network of district co-ordinators to develop local alcohol education strategies (Means *et al.*, 1990). However, these incentives needed to be substantial to overcome a previous history of distrust and hostility.

In general, Conservative governments have proved astute at learning how to manipulate the behaviour of local authorities through a mixture of incentive and authoritative strategies. With regard to collaborative working between health and social services over the resettlement of hospital patients, joint finance initiatives can be seen as an incentive strategy where the incentives were continuously increased yet still failed to overcome the main obstacles to joint working. The new funding regime for residential care and the mental health specific grant suggested that the government had moved to a more authoritative approach where key monies are withheld if certain collaborative tasks are not completed successfully. The danger of this approach for the government is that it generates resentment rather than goodwill, especially if social services perceive health authorities as exploiting unreasonably the pivotal rôle allocated to them by central government.

Hudson's work is focused in the main on co-ordination and collaboration between agencies, and yet there is equal concern about how to promote better co-operation on a day-to-day basis between health and welfare professionals involved in providing services for community care clients (Owens *et al.*, 1995). These relationships can be equally problematic and some of the reasons for this have been pulled together by Means *et al.* (1997):

- **Stereotypes** – different professional groups often hold negative stereotypes about each other. The more entrenched the stereotypes, the harder it will be to develop joint working.
- **Cultural differences** – in addition to stereotypes, there are real and very important cultural differences between professional groups in

terms of how they understand and respond to need. These cultural differences include the use of jargon particular to each profession. In terms of joint working between health and social care professionals, there are clear tensions between the medical model and the social care model over how best to respond to the needs of service users.

- **Disagreement about rôles and responsibilities** – if professionals disagree over their respective rôles, responsibilities and competences, then this is likely to be an obstacle to effective joint working at the local level. This is sometimes referred to as a lack of domain consensus (Hudson, 1987).
- **Misunderstandings** – professionals often have only limited knowledge about other professional groups or other organisations with which they wish to liaise and work. They simply misunderstand the priorities, organisational structures, cultures and working practices of fellow professionals. There is a lack of network awareness.

A further complicating factor is that individuals have the capacity not only to undermine joint working through what is sometimes called 'street level bureaucrat' behaviour (Lipsky, 1980) but also to foster such activity. The policy studies literature indicates that some professionals are adept at encouraging joint working. Such individuals are sometimes referred to as 'reticulists' (Friend *et al.*, 1974) while the Audit Commission (1986) called them 'champions of change'. They are skilled at mapping policy networks and identifying the key resource holders and fellow enthusiasts, both from their own and from other agencies (Means *et al.*, 1990). They tend to feel comfortable working above their hierarchical position, and they are willing to operate in a way not bounded by narrow organisational self-interest.

It might be expected that members and senior managers in social services authorities would feel increasingly able to support such individuals as they move from being the monopoly providers of services to a more enabling rôle in which a broad range of organisations can be expected to take on service delivery functions. It is widely recognised that the traditional systems of bureaucratic and hierarchical management are no longer appropriate, and that the centre needs to allocate more power and discretion to its periphery and to other locally based organisations (see Chapter 3). As a result, Smith *et al.* (1993) argue that a developmental philosophy of management is required which would offer field-level staff support on a number of grounds (training, time allocation) to establish collaborative field-level initiatives. Although not writing specifically about joint working, Smale

(1996) supports such a view and argues that good managers can develop their ability to get innovative practice accepted and implemented through using what he calls the innovative trinity:

• mapping the people to identify all the key players
• analysing the innovation to plan action
• understanding the context to use it to your advantage.

However, we have already stressed that it is much easier for such innovators to move forward where the collaborating agencies and professionals have similar values and culture and where there is domain consensus such as agreement on rôles and responsibilities. In addition, Webb (1991) suggests that the existence of trust built up through previous successful joint activity can be a crucial factor in helping any new collaborative initiative towards a successful outcome.

What are the prospects for effective collaborative working between health and social services when judged against these criteria? To make a judgement about this, it is first necessary to explore the long history of distrust between health and social care agencies and how this relates to tension and conflict over their respective domains.

Who should lead? Historical perspectives

Within the confines of this chapter, it is possible to give only a glimpse of the ongoing debate about who should take the lead co-ordinating rôle in community care. Prior to the late 1970s, the central rôle of health care professionals with regard to people with learning disabilities and mental health problems was rarely questioned. However, the debate over lead agency rôles for elderly and physically disabled people goes back much further. Certainly, by the mid-1960s, Titmuss was able to say:

> In all this discussion at the present time of who is responsible for what, the family doctor is being cast for the rôle of co-ordinator, mobiliser, director, stage manager and leader of community care . . . Others, however, are seeing the medical officer of health performing this rôle partly on the grounds that the family doctor is too busy and is trained as a clinician and medical diagnostician. Still others propose that the chief welfare officer should assume some or most of these responsibilities. (1968, p. 100)

In other words, should such services be led by health care professionals or social care professionals? Medical officers of health were responsible for local authority health departments, and hence were left with the residue of local authority health functions after the removal of hospitals from local government responsibility under the National Health Service Act 1946. Consequently, they had the prestige of being medically qualified but the problem of overseeing a declining empire (Means and Smith, 1985). Several medical officers of health attempted to counterbalance this by arguing that residential care and domiciliary services under the National Assistance Act 1948 should be under their control rather than that of a chief welfare officer who was not medically qualified. For example, Irvine (1950), Medical Officer of Health for Dewsbury, argued for combined health and welfare departments on the grounds that 'the transference of old people from a home to a hostel, from a hostel to hospital, and vice versa can be most readily effected when the decisions lie with medical men [*sic*] who understand the medical basis of the case' (p. 74).

Although the Guillebaud Report (1956) on the costs of the National Health Service supported the idea of combined health and welfare departments, the authority and prestige of medical officers of health continued to decline. Attention began to switch to the general practitioners as the potential leaders of community health and welfare services. This debate was sparked off by concern about the administrative separation of the GP from community-based health provision such as district nursing, midwifery and health visiting, all of which remained the responsibility of medical officers of health and local authorities until the 1974 health care reforms. The Gillie Report (1963) on the rôle of the family doctor argued that the family doctor was

the one member of the profession who can best mobilise and co-ordinate the health and welfare services in the interests of the individual in the community and of the community in relation to the individual. (p. 9)

The achievement of this was seen as requiring teamwork between the GP and the preventive health and welfare services of the local authority. The GP needed to be trained into how best to use such staff 'as his [*sic*] ancillary staff in the home' (p. 38).

Many disagreed. Titmuss (1968, p. 100) pointed out 'there is as yet little evidence that in his [*sic*] day-to-day medical work the family doctor is moving, or wishes to move, in this direction' since consultation rates with elderly people had fallen since 1948. The Royal

Commission on Local Government in Greater London (Herbert Report, 1960) agreed that the GP should be the clinical head of the domiciliary team but that it was 'the day-to-day work of the district nurse, health visitor and home help, the ancillary services such as laundry and chiropody, and the voluntary services such as meals-on-wheels that makes it possible for so many old people to remain in their own homes' (p. 158). The Royal Commission felt the GP could neither provide these services nor co-ordinate their delivery. Such services required an administrative head within the local authority to ensure the availability of these services and their overall co-ordination. In other words, they needed co-ordination by a welfare rather than a medical professional. Against this, others felt the only sensible arrangement was to combine general practitioner and local authority health services. Such a 'community health authority' could become 'the friendly rival of the hospital' (Brockington, 1963, p. 1145).

These arguments were about who should be the clinical and administrative leaders of what in those days was referred to as the domiciliary care team. The eventual restructuring of these services in the early 1970s was based on assumptions about the distinction between health care services (GP, health visitor, district nurse, etc.) and social care services (social worker, home help, etc.). The National Health Service Act 1973 was an attempt to tackle some of the perceived ineffectiveness associated with the NHS structure created by the 1946 Act. Brown (1979, p. 6) claimed the local authority health services were seen as 'a rag-bag of functions' that needed to be integrated into the hospital and general practitioner services. The 1973 Act was a mechanism by which 'the local authority services were nationalised and brought under the same management as hospital services' (p. 22). District nurses and health visitors were no longer to work in a local authority department but were rather to be responsible to a district nursing officer who would be a member of the district management team of the newly formed district health authority. It was the district nursing officer who would have primary responsibility for the allocation of district nursing and health visitor staff. This might or might not involve their location in GP practices. The post of medical officer of health was abolished. Each district management team instead included a community physician whose task was to assess needs and evaluate service provision within the community.

With regard to local authority services, the leadership rôle fell to the Director of Social Services and social services departments from 1 April 1971. As seen in Chapter 2, the early 1970s saw a major extension of the powers of local authorities to provide services and support for elderly people and disabled people. Local authority welfare departments had become increasingly interested in employing those with social work skills to help in deciding how to prioritise elderly people wishing to enter residential care, and they had begun to argue that such skills could help in preventing elderly people even entering such care, especially if backed up by appropriate domiciliary support such as home care and day care. As early as the late 1960s, Brown (1972) felt 'many welfare departments were finding a growing affinity with children's departments, for example, rather than with health' (p. 51). Their subsequent coming together into social services departments should therefore not surprise us.

The logic of the eventual split between health and social care services through the two Acts was clearly explained by Lord Balniel, in a debate on the Local Authority Social Services Bill:

> It is a demarcation based on primary skill. It is a demarcation so that on one side there should be services which are primarily medical in content and, on the other side, the services which are primarily social in content. I do not think one can try to separate services along the lines of . . . some being for children and some being for the elderly. It is the primary skill which is the only conceivable logical line of demarcation in this field. (Quoted in Means and Smith, 1985, p. 338)

Yet this view and the actual reforms had at least two major weaknesses. First, they increased rather than decreased the complexity of service delivery. District nursing was no longer a local authority responsibility yet it remained separate from the administration of GP services despite the creation of family practitioner committees under the 1973 Act. How was all this to be co-ordinated effectively from the point of view of service users? This remained unresolved in 1973 and it remains unresolved twenty-five years later. Second, the demarcation line between health care and social care has always been disputed territory, in terms of both institutional provision and of domiciliary services. The reforms of the early 1970s did not end the debate and it remains a contested area in the late 1990s.

What is health care? What is social care?

With regard to institutional care, a key debate has always been over the meaning of the term 'in need of care and attention' within the National

Assistance Act 1948. Godlove and Mann (1980) argued that the authors of the 1948 Act did not envisage residential homes 'as being adequate for people suffering from incontinence, serious loss of mobility, or abnormal senile dementia'. These were health problems requiring placement in a hospital or nursing home. Yet an important aspect of the history of welfare services since 1948 has been the shift of definition of 'care and attention' to include those suffering from these illnesses and medical conditions (Means, 1986).

The early debate on this issue was sparked off by two factors. First, the 1950s saw shortages of residential accommodation, caused by capital restrictions on the building of new homes. Second, the same period saw concerns about the high cost of hospital provision within the newly created National Health Service. A number of questions began to be asked. Were expensive hospital beds being blocked by the lack of residential accommodation, or were local authorities being swamped by residents in need of constant nursing care? Was there a group not catered for in the existing legislation so that they were 'stranded in the no man's land between the Regional Hospital Board and the local welfare department – not ill enough for one, not well enough for the other?' (Huws Jones, 1952, p. 22). Was there a need for a national system of rest homes or halfway homes that catered for this special group?

As early as 1953, the Minister of Health (Iain Macleod) described this whole area 'as perhaps the most baffling problem in the whole of the National Health Service' (quoted in Means, 1986, p. 94). This problem was considered in depth by both the Guillebaud Report (1956) into the costs of the National Health Service and the Boucher Report (1957) on services available to chronically sick and elderly people. Both dismissed the idea of halfway houses since it was an approach which would generate yet more confusion about the respective rôles of health care and social care institutions. The better plan was to expand local authority residential care in a form which would enable such homes to cope with the needs of those labelled as 'infirm' rather than 'sick'. This approach was supported by the government, which attempted to specify the responsibilities of local authorities and hospital boards with regard to frail and sick elderly people. Ministry of Health Circular 14/57 stated that local welfare authorities were responsible not only for 'active elderly people' in need of residential care but also for:

1. care of the otherwise active resident in a welfare home during minor illness which may well involve a short period in bed;

2. care of the infirm (including the senile) who may need help in dressing, toilet and so on, and may need to live on the ground floor because they cannot manage stairs, and may spend part of the day in bed (or longer periods in bad weather);
3. care of those elderly persons in a welfare home who have to take to bed and are not expected to live more than a few weeks (or, exceptionally, months).

Hospital authorities were given their own list of responsibilities by this circular. These included the chronic bedfast, the convalescent sick and the senile confused. At first glance, 'the partly sick and partly well' were no longer in no-man's-land. They would increasingly be directed to local authority residential accommodation even though this was meant to be a form of social rather than health care provision.

However, Circular 14/57 was only a working guide and was riddled with problems of interpretation. As one of us has asked previously:

> Could one always decide if a bedfast resident would die in three months or three years? How clear cut was the distinction between the senile and the senile confused? At what point did spending part of the day in bed justify a resident being labelled as bedfast and thus requiring admittance to a hospital? How could one know if removal to a hospital was inhumane? (Means, 1986, p. 96)

It seems likely that the reality of the situation was that both hospitals and local authorities remained keen each to persuade the other to accept responsibility for as many cases as possible.

In other words, the circular could be used as a bargaining tool by the professionals involved in specific cases, but it did not by itself point to whether a person should end up in a hospital bed or a residential home. Elderly people had few rights in this situation and many were placed in specific types of institutional care, according to the balance of power of the various health and social care professionals involved in their care. Later circulars made further attempts to clarify responsibilities, but by the early 1980s the actual placement of elderly people in different types of institutional care still bore little relationship to any 'objective' assessment of their material and social needs (Wade, Sawyer and Bell, 1983).

Debates about the health and social care divide with regard to community health and welfare services have perhaps been less fierce but they have been no less important. The health and social care reforms of the early 1970s suggested means by which a service could be defined either as a community health service, and therefore part of the NHS, or as a community welfare or domiciliary service which was the responsibility of the social services authority. Hence district nursing became split from home care in terms of the responsible authority. This left unresolved who should have the power to co-ordinate a coherent package of services from both sides of this divide on behalf of the client. Several studies have underlined the resultant lack of co-ordination from the perspective of the service user (Allen *et al.*, 1992). Others have argued that there are major overlaps in the work carried out by many of these community health and welfare professionals (Clarke, 1984). Such overlaps are particularly evident between district nurses and home care staff, especially as the home care service has changed from being a cleaning/domestic service to a personal care service. This generates ludicrous attempts at the local level to distinguish between whether a user needs a bath for medical or for social reasons, since the former is the responsibility of a district nurse or aide while the latter is the responsibility of a home help or assistant. Clarke's solution was to call for combined health and welfare departments as in Ireland.

The last two sections have underlined the long-term lack of domain consensus about the respective rôles of health care and social care agencies, as well as the history of rivalry over resources. The impact of *Working for Patients* (Department of Health, 1989b) and *Caring for People* (Department of Health, 1989a) was to make joint working even more important than previously, yet to do this while at the same time encouraging a further shift in health and welfare boundaries. For example, it has already been seen how social services authorities have taken over the funding of people in nursing-home care. The rest of this chapter looks at specific areas where tensions have emerged between health and social services as a result of these changes, and the extent to which resultant difficulties have been overcome.

Hospital discharge and the changing rôle of the NHS

Hospital discharge arrangements for those entering care and for those returning home were seen from the outset as a major issue in the implementation of the community care reforms. The Deputy Chief Executive of the National Health Service Management Executive and the Chief Inspector of the Social Services Inspectorate set local authority and health care agencies eight key tasks for 1992–3 in terms of the initial implementation of the community care changes. These included ensuring the robustness and mutual acceptability of discharge arrangements. Subsequently, the handover of social security transfer monies to individual social services authorities became dependent on signing hospital discharge agreements with their health authorities. At one level, this emphasis on improving hospital discharge arrangements deserves to be welcomed since research was pointing to major inadequacies in discharge arrangements for people with support needs returning to their own homes:

> One in three of the people in the sample said they had not been asked how they would manage at home after their discharge. Two-fifths were told about the discharge either the day before or on the day it was due to happen. (Neill and Williams, 1992, p. 74)

However, it is likely that the priority given to hospital discharge issues has been driven by the necessity to avoid bed blockages in the acute hospital sector, rather than from a concern to ensure the capacity of the care manager to offer appropriate care options after hospital treatment.

In fairness, considerable efforts have been made to improve the way health and social care professionals work together over hospital discharge issues. This has included the production of a hospital discharge workbook (Henwood, 1994) which stresses that good practice is resource efficient (for example it reduces readmission rates to hospital) as well as essential if the following requirements of the Patient's Charter are to be met:

> before you are discharged from hospital a decision should be made about any continuing health or social care needs you may have. Your hospital will agree arrangements for meeting these needs with agencies such as community nursing services and local authority social services departments before you are discharged. You and, with your agreement, your carers will be consulted and informed at all stages. (Quoted in Henwood, 1994, p. 4)

Undoubtedly, the workbook has helped to increase the number of situations in which this satisfactory outcome is achieved. However, research continues to identify the overwhelming pressure to achieve a speedy discharge from hospital, so that, for example, occupational therapists find themselves under pressure to cover issues of safety but to neglect the wider needs of the person returning home (Clark *et al.*, 1996).

A key reason for this relates to the changing rôle of the NHS. It has moved away from the direct provision of long-stay beds and there is a growing emphasis upon day surgery. Those entering hospitals for acute care will be discharged after major surgery far more speedily than was until recently deemed feasible or desirable. This, combined with the emphasis in NHS performance indicators on 'throughput' and reduced waiting lists, creates an inevitable tension with a care management system where the emphasis is upon a considered holistic assessment of the needs of the client (Wistow, 1995).

However, the tension goes much deeper than just assessment. The discharge of patients back to their homes very soon after major illness and/or surgery places enormous additional demands upon carers, primary health care services and upon the community care budgets of social services departments. The Griffiths Report (1988) stressed community care objectives needed to be realistic and reflect available resources. Instead, major new responsibilities have fallen to social services as a result of the knock-on consequences of changes in the NHS, and these have not been supported by adequate additional resources. These resource tensions create a difficult environment for joint working between health and social services at both the strategic and operational levels. Indeed, it has placed tensions not just on the hospital/social services interface but also on the interface of social services with the general practitioner and the rest of the primary health care team. They are increasingly required to work together to support very ill or very frail people to live in the community despite their past poor history of joint working. One of the key sources of friction remains the dispute about where health care ends and social care begins. More specifically, there is often disagreement about the respective rôles of staff such as district nurses and home care workers, with a clear desire on the part of both parties to reduce or control the costs which fall on their budgets as well as considerable confusion for clients about who is helping them and why (Baldock and Ungerson, 1994). This requires us to look more specifically at shifting health and social care boundaries, initially in terms of continuing care.

Continuing care and the changing health and social care divide

Between 1982 and 1993–4, the number of NHS beds fell by almost a quarter (Wistow, 1995, p. 233) and by far the vast majority of these were long-stay beds. The NHS began to place more and more reliance upon independent sector nursing and residential homes, initially under-pinned through the social security budget, and since 1 April 1993 through the budgets of social services departments.

However, this brings us starkly to the issue of why local authorities rather than the NHS are being asked to fund a nursing service. As Henwood (1992) points out:

> Despite the claim that the responsibilities of the NHS are unchanged, nursing home care is apparently now viewed as social care, not health. Is this contradictory, or are we to accept that there is a real distinction between those needing nursing home care for reasons of ill health and those needing it for other reasons? Surely this is playing *Alice in Wonderland* games with words and semantics. (p. 28)

Such a situation was bound to encourage health authorities to run down their remaining nursing-home and continuing-care bed provision. Another certainty was that some local authorities would deny they had a responsibility for some people referred to them from acute hospitals, on the grounds that their needs were essentially those of health care and not social care.

The boundaries between health and social care had shifted once more, with people previously perceived as ill now being increasingly defined as having social care needs which are the responsibility of the local authority and not the NHS. Henwood (1992) had a very unflattering, yet almost certainly correct, explanation for this further shift in boundaries. Health care under the NHS has to be free. Social care can be charged for, and increasingly local authorities have to charge the full economic price of care to the better off. The responsibility for funding long-term health and social care was thus being shifted covertly on to users and their families. Social services authorities and health authorities were being left to struggle with the consequences of this shift. This has emerged as one of the most significant features of the health and social care reforms of the 1990s.

Henwood points out that the ageing of the elderly population combined with policies designed to delay entry into residential care had created a new client group which is not clearly the responsibility of either health or social care services. Using words very similar to those of Huws Jones (1952) some forty years previously (see earlier discussion), she refers to them as 'the borderline people, the partly sick and partly well, who are perceived as too sick for residential support and not ill enough for hospital care' (p. 24). Who should pay for their continued maintenance in the community or make the decision about the most appropriate type of institutional provision?

The Conservative government responded to this situation by setting out *NHS Responsibilities for Meeting Continuing Health Care Needs* (Department of Health, 1995a) through circular HSG(95)8 in a similar way to which circular 14/57 (Ministry of Health, 1957) had attempted almost forty years previously. The circulars outline key services which health authorities and GP fundholders must continue to arrange and fund (see Figure 6.1). In terms of which patients should receive such services, the circulars stressed that after a multidisciplinary assessment and consideration of local eligibility criteria, the consultant (or GP in some community hospitals) in consultation with the multidisciplinary team would decide whether:

(a) the patient needs continuing in-patient care arranged and funded by the NHS because:
   – either he or she needs ongoing and regular specialist clinical supervision (in the majority of cases this might be weekly or more frequent) on account of:
   – the complexity, nature and intensity of his or her medical, nursing or other clinical needs;
   – the need for frequent not easily predictable interventions;
   – or because after acute treatment or in-patient palliative care in hospital or hospice his or her prognosis is such that he or she is likely to die in the very near future and discharge from NHS care would be inappropriate;

(b) the patient needs a period of rehabilitation or recovery arranged and funded by the NHS to prepare for discharge arrangements breaking down;

(c) the patient can be appropriately discharged from NHS in-patient care with:
   – either a place in a nursing home or residential home or residential care home arranged and funded by social services or by the patient and his or her family;
   – or a package of social and health care support to allow the patient to return to his or her own home or to alternatively arranged accommodation. (p. 9)

Individual health authorities and NHS trusts were given a timetable for translating the above into local policies, with health authorities needing to have arrangements to review decisions on eligibility for

- specialist medical and nursing assessment;
- rehabilitation and recovery;
- palliative health care;
- continuing in-patient care under specialist supervision in hospital or nursing home;
- respite health care;
- specialist health care support to people in nursing homes or residential care homes or in the community;
- community health services to people at home or in residential care homes;
- primary health care; and
- specialist transport services.

FIGURE 6.1 Services to be arranged and funded by health authorities and GP fundholders

NHS continuing care available from 1 April 1996. Conservative governments had encouraged a massively reduced rôle for the NHS but had become concerned that this trend had gone too far. The circulars were designed to ensure agreed local policies would establish 'a line in the sand' beyond which this withdrawal would not go.

This greater clarity and the establishment of a review procedure was welcomed by such organisations as the Association of Directors of Social Services, Age Concern (England) and the Carers National Association (*The Independent*, 24 February 1995, p. 4). However, some commentators remained sceptical about whether this national framework could be turned into agreed local policies which had the subtlety to resolve who should fund what aspects of the health and care packages of the most complex cases (Wistow, 1996).

The lead rôle in the provision of mental health services

From the outset, there was no shortage of people sceptical of the competence of social services authorities to play the lead rôle for people with mental health problems as proposed by the White Paper on community care. Thus, the British Medical Association (1992) indicated that 'there is concern . . . that most local authorities lack the skills and expertise to take on the responsibility for supporting mentally ill people in the community' (p. 30). Glennerster, Falkingham and Evandrou (1990) went further by arguing that it made much more sense for health authorities to take the lead rôle through their purchasing functions since they 'could buy in facilities and workers from whatever source it wished' (p. 101) including organisations like MIND or the local authority.

In any case the likelihood of social services being able to take on this lead rôle has also always seemed problematic because of the development of the care programme approach (CPA) as a parallel system to care management for developing user-centred care plans. CPA was introduced in order to provide a clear framework for the care of people with mental health problems outside hospital. Health authorities in collaboration with social services authorities are expected to agree their local CPA approach, which must have four main elements:

- systematic arrangements for assessing the health and social needs of people accepted by the specialist psychiatric services;
- the formulation of a care plan which addresses the identified health and social care needs;
- the appointment of a key worker to keep in close touch with the patient and monitor care;
- regular reviews and, if need be, agreed changes to the care plan. (Department of Health, 1995b)

However, since the vast bulk of care programme staff were employees of health care agencies, the relation of CPA to the new system of care management was always likely to be a further source of domain confusion and tension between health and social services.

Increasingly, reports and research on mental health services began to identify this as a major obstacle. Thus, the Mental Health Foundation (1994) report, *Creating Community Care,* referred to

> confusion about the responsibilities of health and local authorities, and there are deficiencies in health and social care. Services are delivered through three parallel systems (care management, the Care Programme Approach and section 117 of the Mental Health Act). Systems must be simplified and clear lines of accountability established. (p. 7)

In addition, the Audit Commission (1994) pointed out that too many resources remained locked into hospital provision, the development of community services was patchy and service management and co-ordination had to be improved.

Such concerns achieved a very high profile in the mid-1990s for two linked reasons. First, the number of single homeless people was growing and it was clear that a high percentage of these had mental health problems (Bines, 1994). This was bound to lead to concern that people were leaving psychiatric hospitals (or failing to get into them) and drifting into homelessness because of a failure to offer appropriate community services and support. Other research showed that mentally disordered offenders were another group at risk of homelessness because of the poor co-ordination of services on discharge (Lart, 1997).

Second, these concerns were dramatically heightened by a number of mass-media portrayals of people with severe mental problems who had killed either care workers or members of the public. For example, on 9 October 1993 John Rous, diagnosed as suffering severe schizophrenia, killed Jonathan Newby, a twenty-two-year-old graduate, working as a volunteer for the Oxford Cyrenians. Ten months previously, Jonathan Zito had been stabbed on the London Underground by Christopher Clunis, also diagnosed as schizophrenic. Reports into both these incidents pointed to a lack of specialist expertise, poor co-ordination of services, a failure to respond to warning signs and a lack of long-term accommodation specifically targeted at those with the most severe mental health problems (Davies Report, 1995; Ritchie *et al.*, 1994).

The initial response of government was to provide good practice guidance on joint working in this area (Department of Health, 1995b) and further changes to the law. In terms of the latter, the Mental Health (Patients in the Community) Act 1995 established a new system of supervised discharge for many of those leaving hospital with the most severe mental health problems. In February 1996 this was followed up with the announcement of a 'new "asylum" plan for severely mentally ill' which would provide 24-hour nursing care for at least 5,000 of the most disturbed mentally ill patients in some 400 new residential homes' (*The Independent*, 21 February 1996, p. 1).

In terms of good practice, the Department of Health (1995b) issued *Building Bridges: A Guide to Arrangements for Inter-Agency Working for the Care and Protection of Severely Mentally Ill People,* whose starting point was:

There has been continuing anxiety, particularly over the last two or three years, concerning the care and treatment of severely mentally ill people in the community. A number of suicides, homicides and other serious incidents have understandably led to great public and professional concern. (pp. 8–9)

The guide outlines the legislative framework, specifies the rôles of key agencies (health service purchasers, local authorities, health service providers and other agencies) and discusses how these need to be related to the working of the care programme approach on an inter-agency basis (see Figure 6.2). It is stressed that the care programme approach and care management are based on the same principles and so 'the two systems should be capable of being fully integrated' (p. 56)

PROCEDURE/ PROVISION	Applies to:
Care Programme Approach (CPA)	All people accepted by the specialist psychiatric services.
Care Management	All people subject to the CPA who have associated social care needs.
Supervision Registers	People subject to the CPA who are severely mentally ill and who may be a significant risk to themselves or others.
Section 117 After-care	Patients discharged following detention under sections 3, 37 (whether or not with restriction under section 41), 47 or 48 of the Mental Health Act 1983. All will be subject to the CPA and some may also be on a supervision register.
Guardianship	Patients subject to guardianship under sections 7 or 37 of the Mental Health Act 1983. All will be subject to the CPA, some may be on supervision registers and some may be subject to section 117 after-care.
Supervised Discharge	Certain patients who have been detained under the Mental Health Act 1983. All will be subject to the CPA and section 117 after-care and most will also be on a supervision register.

Source: Department of Health (1995b) p. 91.

FIGURE 6.2   Relationships between the care programme approach and other key processes and provisions

as long as each client has an agreed single care plan and single key worker in a system where there is:

- an initial screening process which is applied consistently, irrespective of the route by which the individual enters the system;
- a jointly agreed set of criteria for allocating CPA key workers/care managers to ensure the most effective deployment of professional skills on a cross-agency basis;
- a clear definition of the responsibilities of the key worker/care manager's co-ordinating rôle.

The 'culprit' was being defined as a failure in joint working caused by lack of agreement on rôles and responsibilities and poor awareness of each other's networks. Until these deficiencies were resolved, the message of *Building Bridges* is that some people with severe mental health problems would continue to slip through the 'net' of available support into homelessness and possibly worse. However, the guide assumes existing arrangements could be made to work.

However, the agenda of the Conservative government towards the end of its period of office had turned back yet again to the issue of lead agency and whether or not this pivotal rôle should continue to be entrusted to social services. *Developing Partnerships in Mental Health* (Department of Health, 1997b) outlined four options for change, namely:

1. *The Mental Health and Social Care Authority* – a new kind of authority would be established, responsible for planning, commissioning and purchasing health and social care which would neither be a health nor a local authority.
2. *Single Authority Responsibility* – either health authorities (most likely) or local authorities would be designated as the single agency responsible for planning, commissioning and purchasing mental health and social care.
3. *A Joint Health and Social Care Body* – health and local authorities would establish a joint body to plan, commission and organise the contractual framework for delivering mental health and social care services.
4. *Agreed Delegation* – health and local authorities would be able to delegate particular functions or responsibilities to each other.

The report concluded by seeking 'views . . . on which, if any, of these options would be supported' (p. 27).

There have been a number of criticisms about how Conservative governments fostered this debate about the future of mental health services. Some of these related to the continued reluctance of government to allocate sufficient resources to develop the full range of required services (Mental Health Foundation, 1994). Others have been highly critical of how policy has become driven by a small number of high-profile cases of people with severe mental health problems who have killed others. This has the effect of obscuring the pain and suffering experienced by those with mental health problems as a result of the prejudices and hostility of the general public (Rose, 1996). Such commentators are increasingly able to draw on research which shows that well-thought-out care programme and management systems have much to offer people with severe mental health problems (Newton *et al.*, 1996) if the prejudices of the general public could be overcome. There is also concern that the media and government emphasis upon those with the most severe problems leads to a neglect of the needs of the vast majority of people who need support because of mental health problems, and who are extremely unlikely to ever be a major perpetrator of violence on others. As Manthorpe and Stanley (1997) put it, 'a blinkered focus on psychiatry' has been allowed to undermine the necessity 'to acknowledge the ubiquity of mental health problems and the need for flexible services' (p. 7). It could also be argued that such an approach has reinforced stereotypes about 'the mad and the bad'.

Community care planning and joint commissioning

One of the themes running through the mental health debate is the lack of community services to support the objective of providing care in the community rather than in long-stay hospitals. This has led to a high emphasis upon the need for health and social services to work together on joint purchasing strategies. What progress has been made on this across the main client groups? Not all the evidence is bleak in this respect since research evidence suggests that, in many areas, an excellent dialogue between health and social services has emerged as a result of the community care planning process (Hoyes *et al.*, 1993; Wistow *et al.*, 1996), especially where health and social services boundaries are coterminous or nearly so (Hudson, 1992). If nothing else, social services managers and health service managers have developed a greater network awareness, and a greater appreciation of each other's priorities and preoccupations than existed before.

Many community care plans are jointly published by the social services authority and the health authority. Many have tried to achieve domain consensus over rôles and responsibilities. For example, the community care plan for St Helens not only outlined the broad definitions of social care and health care which were agreed by a working group of health and social services managers, but then went on to apply these to nearly 150 specific tasks. Social care was defined as interventions designed to meet one of the following needs:

1. Practical assistance in daily living, including provision of food, warmth, clothing, environmental support and assistance with personal care such as washing, dressing, bathing and going to the lavatory.
2. Practical advice and help in coping with day-to-day problems and counselling when needed.
3. Specific teaching and guidance in order to acquire new abilities and skills or to reinforce existing ones; these are often included as part of programmes of rehabilitation for people with severe physical or learning disabilities, for people with mental health problems and for young people as part of their preparation for leaving care.
4. Specialised programmes of care assessment, treatment and rehabilitation which aim to produce substantial changes in the individual's functioning so that they can live more freely, independently and with integrity.
5. Protecting children from risk and using legislative powers only where individuals are at risk of endangering themselves or others.

However, the St Helens plan accepted that social care would often be provided by health care professionals and that activities definable as health care would often be delivered by social care professionals:

> Care in the community is a composite of elements of health and social care delivered to the individual and his/her family and/or carers. Elements of this care will be delivered within a health care model and others within a social care model, neither framework being exclusive in its function by either health and social services personnel. (St Helens Metropolitan Borough Council Personal Services Department, 1992, p. 43)

Some have felt that such local guidelines are only the start. Collaboration needed to penetrate much deeper than this, and the appropriate strategy was for the development of joint commissioning strategies between health and social care agencies. Thus Knapp *et al.* (1992) argued that

> From a procedural standpoint, joint commissioning improves the prospects of moving to clearer and more consistent eligibility criteria. It should raise mutual awareness, foster co-operation rather than competition, and weaken previous tendencies to pass the buck – to shunt people and costs on to other agencies. For example, joint commissioning of residential and nursing home care would provide the opportunity to achieve a much more appropriate balance between congregate and community care across the health and social care system as a whole. (p. 29)

For both those in residential or nursing home care and those still in the community, joint commissioning was felt to be a positive-sum game since it involved 'the pooling of sovereignty to achieve ends which individual agencies are less likely to secure alone' (p. 30).

This appears to be a classic definition of when collaboration is likely to work (see previous discussion) yet at the same time the high opportunity costs of what needs to be resolved for this strategy to work must be recognised. Complex procedures of assessment and financial accountability need to be established largely because the legislative framework does not allow for the genuine pooling of budgets. Local authority members may be resistant and this may frustrate health service managers. Structures in the health service along the lines of purchaser–provider splits have been largely defined by central government and have been fairly consistently applied throughout the country. However, Chapters 3 and 5 illustrated the lack of central government guidance for local authorities over such issues in community care, and hence very different organisational responses have developed. It may be difficult to obtain agreement on the best balance between macro or block purchasing and micro commissioning by field-level care managers. Joint commissioning is much easier to develop where boundaries are coterminous than where they are not. And it is most feasible where health and social care agencies are building upon existing goodwill and trust, rather than in the context of past distrust.

However, by the mid-1990s the Conservative government had become convinced of the great value of joint commissioning and was keen to offer advice on how obstacles could be overcome. Both *An Intro-*

duction to Joint Commissioning (Department of Health, 1995c) and *Practical Guidance on Joint Commissioning* (Department of Health, 1995d) distinguished between joint commissioning (two or more commissioning agencies act together to co-ordinate commissioning), joint purchasing (two or more agencies co-ordinate the actual buying of services) and joint provision (agencies jointly provide a service) with a clear view that effective joint commissioning was likely to lead on to the second two activities. These documents set out the main topics which had to be addressed for joint commissioning to work in practice (see Figure 6.3). The overall message was that the Department of Health (1995c) remained committed 'to helping authorities achieve the potential benefits for service users and their carers that effective joint commissioning can bring' (p. 9).

Some commentators remained sceptical. Hudson (1995), for example, recognised the detailed work that had gone into the practical guidance (Department of Health, 1995d) but stressed the wide range of stakeholders requiring co-ordination as well as the size of the obstacles to be overcome, especially where there was a past history of distrust between agencies. He concludes that 'joint commissioning may be a case of misplaced enthusiasm' because 'collaboration has been oversold as a potential solution to problems of policy, management and practice' (p. 247). He feels the aim of joint commissioning is often to achieve consensus between agencies when what is really needed is an acceptance of the inevitability of strong elements of conflict, an acceptance that might allow joint commissioning 'to progress beyond the level of incantation of simple precepts' (p. 247).

As recognised by the Practical Guidance, one area where conflict is common relates to how best social services can draw GP fundholders into the joint commissioning discussions:

> It has often been difficult enough to liaise with one, or maybe two, health authorities, but a large county can find itself with more than 200 individual GP practices to consider. Making sure that social services' voice is heard when decisions are made about buying care for elderly people and people with learning difficulties or mental health problems becomes a nightmare. (Eaton, 1997, p. 18)

The favoured solution of the Practical Guidance was to stress the advantages of giving joint commissioning more of a focus upon smaller localities which relate well to the catchment areas of GPs, although Hudson (1995) warns that health authorities and social services

- **Getting started.** Agencies should start with initiatives that will deliver early benefits for the key stakeholders, without taking on all the most intractable problems at the outset. Some early wins build confidence.
- **Developing a shared vision and strategy.** Although authorities may be opportunistic in their development of joint commissioning, it is best set in the context of a shared overall vision and strategy. This is vital if they are to move beyond initiatives focused on special funding, such as joint finance, to commitment of mainstream funding.
- **Different forms of joint commissioning.** Joint commissioning initiatives can be grouped in terms of the focus for the commissioning activity, and often the categories overlap. Some joint initiatives focus on commissioning for selected user groups, while others focus on particular services, localities or individual service users. Each form of joint commissioning has particular benefits and limitations.
- **Establishing joint working mechanisms.** The first step is to secure effective joint working at individual officer level between agencies, through rôle clarity, targeted joint teamwork on key issues, and improved understanding and communications. There are arguments for giving the Joint Consultative Committee (JCC) a central rôle, revitalised if necessary to integrate it into the mainstream. If this is not possible, any new mechanism must relate to the JCC statutory functions, minimising any duplication.
- **Involving members and non-executive directors.** These key stakeholders must be fully engaged if joint commissioning is to deliver its full potential by moving into mainstream agendas. They should be involved from an early stage, so that they are able to influence developments. However, there are wider agendas which can lead to tensions, as well as differences in decision-making processes. These must be recognised and managed.
- **Involving independent sector providers.** These have a key rôle to play in developing more effective service responses, and in identifying emerging issues and problems that commissioners need to be aware of in planning future services.
- **Project managing implementation.** Joint commissioning is a tool for securing change, and changes in the process and content of commissioning services across several agencies requires careful management. Applying project management principles will help in turning shared strategy into action.

Source: Department of Health (1995c), p.6.

FIGURE 6.3 Making joint commissioning happen in practice

departments may have a different view of locality, locality purchasing may result in a loss of economies of scale, and inequalities in service availability between localities within the same social services authority may become exaggerated. A recent review of links between primary health care and social services confirmed how slow progress continued to be and called for a strong national lead (Thistlethwaite, 1997). How to mesh GPs and primary health care teams into community care remains as problematic as ever.

Collaboration: an assessment of progress

What are the future prospects for effective collaborative working between health and social services? What does the situation look like when judged against such factors as cultural differences, domain consensus, network awareness, absence of alternative resources and the existence of trust? Some positive points can be made. Considerable amounts of community care money have been linked to proof of collaboration over issues such as hospital discharge by central government. However, this authoritative strategy by central government of enforced collaboration will backfire if it generates distrust and resentment from social services towards health authorities and health trusts. It is often difficult for health care managers to respond flexibly to the concerns of social services when they have been monitored so rigidly by central government against specified targets in areas such as hospital discharge.

Where good working relationships have developed between key managers in social services and the purchasing side of the health authority, this tells us nothing about working relationships elsewhere, in areas such as joint working on assessment and care package delivery for individual service users. Here progress may depend more on whether both sides feel they are gaining from taking a collaborative rather than a competitive or defensive stance. In this respect, it was seen that the provision of mental health services remains an area fraught with difficulty for those who aspire to a collaborative approach. With regard to network awareness, the NHS reforms did disrupt existing networks, and hence network awareness. However, the process of community care planning has proved to be an excellent opportunity to repair this situation in many areas.

The situation with regard to trust is likely to vary enormously. Some social service authorities and health authorities have managed to build up trust and mutual respect over a long period of time. In other areas, the opposite is true. Where trust is at a low ebb between agencies, Webb (1991) advises that any new attempt to work together should be modest, low-risk and easy to achieve. This will maximise the chances of success and hence help to build improved relationships, leading to a capacity to tackle larger-scale projects in the future. Yet the requirements of central government with regard to joint working over community care between health care and social care agencies are far from modest from the point of view of those agencies trying to bury a history of conflict and distrust.

It is unclear whether health care and social care agencies are reducing their cultural differences and overcoming past stereotypes. However, what may be happening overall is that health service managers and social service managers are finding that they have more and more in common with each other, and the same may be true of a range of professionals working at field level. Perhaps one of the great implementation challenges of the future will be the need to tackle the growing gap and disenchantment of field-level staff with their managers, and vice versa. It is also clear that GPs fit into this picture very uneasily. They consider themselves to be clinicians, but ones who are in essence running small businesses. Most have neither the time nor the inclination to feed into more strategic debates. This is an area where domain consensus and network awareness remain almost entirely absent.

Indeed, domain consensus remains as elusive as ever over the boundaries between health and social care. In the 1990s, these boundaries shifted once again, and this is creating an enormous potential for conflict between health and social care professionals at both the strategic and operational levels. The consequences of this have been especially problematic for social care professionals. The shifting boundary has placed increased financial pressures upon them at a time when the community care reforms raised expectations from service users and carers. Whether the temptation to settle for conflict will be avoided will depend upon the qualities of managers and operational staff. 'Champions of change' who have not lost sight of the needs of the service user will want to tackle these dilemmas in a collaborative way. Street-level, and office-level, bureaucrats will not.

In general it seems certain that the coming years will see further extensive debate about the respective rôles of health and social services in community care. Enormous interest has been shown in 'the revolution' in Dumfries and Galloway in which social services and health board staff will share offices from September 1997 with a longer-term aim to achieve common budgets and a jointly trained pool of staff (*Community Care*, 29 May–4 June 1997, pp. 8–9). The Labour government which came to power in May 1997 is committed to review a range of health and social services interface issues (see final chapter).

7 Housing and Community Care

The Griffiths Report (1988) paid little attention to housing issues and merely stated that the responsibilities of housing agencies should be limited to arranging and sometimes managing the 'bricks and mortar' of housing need for community care purposes (p. 15). However, the White Paper on community care (Department of Health, 1989a) differed considerably from the Griffiths Report in this respect. 'Suitable good quality housing' was seen as essential to social care packages (p. 9) and it was argued that 'social services authorities will need to work closely with housing authorities, housing associations and other providers of housing of all types in developing plans for a full and flexible range of housing' (p. 25).

This chapter focuses on housing issues from the perspective that housing is an essential element of community care. However, the emphasis of the chapter is not solely on the politics of what is usually called 'special needs' or supported housing, but will also include a consideration of much broader issues such as the meaning of home and the impact of general housing policies upon frail elderly and disabled people.

The meaning of home

Community care policy in the United Kingdom is based on the belief that nearly everyone prefers to live in ordinary housing rather than in institutions because institutions lack the capacity to be a home. Higgins (1989) went so far as to argue that the very concept of community care should be abandoned because 'the real distinction is actually between the institution and home which differ markedly in terms of their core characteristics' (see Table 7.1). Ordinary houses (homes) are preferable to institutions because they offer more privacy, informality, freedom and familiarity. The rest of this section explores theoretical thinking about the home and goes on to consider the implications of this for the users of community care services.

TABLE 7.1   The key characteristics of institutions and home

Institutions	Home
1. Public space, limitations on privacy	1. Private space, but may be some limitations on privacy
2. Living with strangers, rarely alone	2. May live alone or with relatives or friends, rarely with strangers
3. Staffed by professionals or volunteers	3. Normally no staff living there but they may visit to provide services
4. Formal and lacking in intimacy	4. Informal and intimate
5. Sexual relationships discouraged	5. Sexual relationships (between certain family members) accepted
6. Owned/rented by other agencies	6. Owned/rented by inhabitants
7. Variations in size but may be large (in terms of physical space and numbers living there)	7. Variations in size but usually small
8. Limitations on choice and on personal freedom	8. Ability to exercise choice and considerable degree of freedom
9. Strangeness (of people, place, etc.)	9. Familiarity (of people, place, etc.)
10. 'Batch' or communal living	10. Individual arrangements for eating, sleeping, leisure activities which can vary according to time and place

Source: Higgins (1989) p. 15.

In doing this, one is immediately struck by the complexity of the term 'home' and how it relates to living in specific buildings. Thus Rapoport (1995), drawing on the work of Hayward (1976), shows how the simple question 'what does home mean to you?' can generate the following wide set of responses:

1. as a set of relationships with others;
2. as a relationship with the wider social group and community;
3. as a statement about self-image and identity;
4. as a place of privacy and refuge;
5. as a continuous and stable relationship with other sources of meaning about the home;
6. as a personalised place;

7. as a base of activity;
8. as a relationship with one's parents and place of upbringing;
9. as a relationship with a physical structure, setting or shelter.

The extensive literature on the home emphasises how responses will vary according to gender, class, ethnicity, country and age of the respondent, and that ideas about 'home' are constantly changing and evolving within any given society (Means, 1997a).

Gurney and Means (1993) point out that the late 1980s and early 1990s saw a fierce debate within urban sociology about the meaning of home, although it paid little attention to elderly and disabled people. The background to the debate was a belief in the emergence of a new 'middle mass' in British society (Pahl, 1984) with shared goals and aspirations, one of which was the desire to be owner-occupiers. Britain had become, as Saunders (1990) put it, *A Nation of Home Owners*. In terms of concepts of home in the UK, Saunders argued that owner-occupiers identified their house as a home and 'a place where they feel relaxed and where they can surround themselves with familiar and personal possessions' (p. 272). Council tenants, on the other hand, associated 'home' much more with their relationships with family and neighbours. He concluded from this that the great strength of owner-occupation was its capacity to enable people to express themselves and their identity in a private realm which was free from surveillance.

The strength of Saunders's work is that it brought to the fore debates about the meaning of home. However, his work is highly contentious and generated several critiques even prior to the collapse of the housing market in Britain which underlined that owner-occupation could be the cause of misery through negative equity and mortgage foreclosure (Forrest *et al.*, 1994) rather than always a wonderful source of security. Gurney and Means (1993) criticise Saunders by drawing on the work of Hayward (1976) and others to show how the complexities of the meaning of home cannot be reduced to the kind of generalisations about tenure used by Saunders. They argue for a greater emphasis upon what Gurney (1990) has called the emotions of home. For some, this has negative connotations since home is where elder abuse and the abuse of other vulnerable adults can take place free from surveillance (Biggs *et al.*, 1995). However, for the majority, home is where suppor-tive and loving relationships between kin and non-kin relations most often take place.

The importance of such positive emotions of home for older people is well demonstrated by the research by Langan, Means and Rolfe

(1996) on 31 elderly households from a range of tenures. Several of the respondents stressed home as a place of privacy and refuge:

> Mr: It's a place of retreat really.
> Mrs: . . . and home's always been a place where you want to go back to, however humble it is. Even when we go to town, we're still glad, well I am, to get back . . . It's a place of our own. (p. 6)

Another respondent saw home as a place where you had 'freedom to do what you want, when you want' (p. 6).

It has often been shown that many older people see home in terms of a strong emotional attachment to a specific house lived in for much of the life course:

> Home was the old armchair by the hearth, the creaky bedstead, the polished lino with its faded pattern, the sideboard with its picture gallery, and the lavatory with its broken latch reached through the rain. It embodied a thousand memories and held promise of a thousand contentments. It was an extension of personality. (Townsend, 1963, p. 38)

Such views may at first appear dated and hence irrelevant to present-day debates. However, thirty years later, Australian researchers were uncovering similar sentiments among some older Australians when invited to talk about their homes:

> The home is often a collection of memories. One woman comments, 'I'm very fond of it; it's got lots of memories.' Another man, on the thought of moving, remarks, 'all the memories are here; well, I can keep going and I'd just as soon stay here'. (Davison *et al.*, 1993, p. 51)

The Langan, Means and Rolfe study (1996) found similar views from many of those who had lived a long time in one house. One such woman reflected that 'I only get out of it for two or three hours and I can't wait to get back' (p. 6). In this study, such emotions and feelings were not restricted just to owner-occupiers. An 89-year-old had lived in the same three-bedroomed flat for 43 years. She felt she had 'all my home comforts' being in a quiet town block 'with no noisy teenagers running all over the place' (p. 6). She had no intention of moving into sheltered accommodation.

However, in placing this emphasis upon the link between 'feeling at home' and attachment to specific houses, great care must be taken not to overgeneralise. There is strong evidence that the majority of older people do manage to re-establish a sense of home when they move into good-quality sheltered housing (Riseborough and Niner, 1994). Two of the ten households who moved into sheltered housing in the Langan *et al.* (1996) study, stressed that they felt at home because they felt secure from burglaries and theft while another stressed it 'started to feel like home when my old friends visited me here' (p. 7).

There is also extensive evidence that owner-occupiers who move to a different part of the country on retirement establish a sense of home in their new accommodation and environment. Again drawing on the Langan *et al.* study, two households had moved from the Midlands to Lake District villages. One stressed that 'I love my little cottage, you know' while the other stressed the friendliness of her village which also had excellent facilities including a shop and easy access to a GP practice. It seems likely that many middle-class older people are used to moving house periodically for career and other reasons, and perhaps have always seen their house as an asset through which wealth can be released as a result of trading down in later life (Means, 1997b). Such individuals are likely to have learnt the skill of how to transport one's sense of emotional security from one building (home) to another.

Very little research has been carried out on the meaning of home to older people in rented accommodation. Are attachments to particular homes less strong? Certainly, elderly council tenants are often under pressure to move from their house where they brought up their children in order to release family housing to those on the waiting list. Many such tenants have been willing to consider a move to modern prestigious sheltered housing schemes (Means, 1997b), yet seem increasingly willing to reject offers from older schemes, many of which are becoming hard to let (Tinker *et al.*, 1995). However, very little is known about the emotional feelings experienced by older people on leaving rented accommodation. One key factor is almost certainly the quality of rented accommodation lived in in the past, and the extent to which there has been a single 'family' home rather than a whole series of moves into different rented accommodation during the life course. For many elderly people, their present rented accommodation may hold little emotional attachment and for some the memories may be largely negative. A move in later life may represent an opportunity to actually establish a sense of home for such people.

Another key issue for elderly people irrespective of whether they rent or own is likely to be whether the proposed move is to a home or to an institution. Willcocks, Peace and Kelleher (1987) suggest that strong emotions and attachments to their houses are expressed by elderly people when they feel threatened by a possible move into residential care, since 'to leave homes which may be inconvenient and difficult . . . would be to relinquish a hold on a base from which personal power can be generated and reinforced' (p. 8). Or, as Steinfeld (1981) explains, housing moves in later life are often linked to negative rather than positive status passages and hence the desire of many to 'stay put'.

However, this argument needs to be balanced against the fact that the consequence for the most frail and impaired people of receiving a multi-agency and multi-professional response to their needs in their own house can have the effect of almost bringing the institution to their home. Gavilan (1992) has argued that the home can take on the features of a total institution because dependence upon home care and other services involves a major intrusion of self and space as illustrated by some of the service users interviewed by Hoyes *et al.* (1994):

> The question I ask is 'who is in control?' . . . I have become totally dependent [on home care] . . . They have meetings in my kitchen, you just don't do that! They treat you like aliens.

However, we support Gavilan's view that what is needed is a transformation in the skills of home care and other health and welfare professionals in terms of their sensitivity to this issue rather than a return to a greater reliance on residential care.

Resettlement and the meaning of home

So far it would appear that not only can Higgins's (1989) typology of home versus institution be accepted, but that the advantages of the former over the latter as the place to receive care is overwhelming. However, we need to ask if the same holds true when we look at the resettlement of many service users, and especially those with learning difficulties, from institutions where they have lived for many years to new homes and hostels in the community. The justification for this has been the characteristics of their institutions, as summarised by Higgins

(1989) and as described in Chapter 2. This policy change has often been supported by individuals with learning difficulties:

> It's a lot better to live on your own. It's important that people with learning disabilities have the right to their own home and their own key and live by themselves. (Quoted in Mental Health Foundation, 1996, p. 50)

However, Saunders (1990) did underline that home for some can be as much a matter of networks and relationships (for council tenants) as of privacy (for owner-occupiers). One danger of the resettlement process is that the hospital-based networks and relationships may be shattered but may not be replaced by equivalent networks in new surroundings. The privacy of the new home or hostel may be experienced by some as a prison of loneliness and despair.

What does the research evidence have to say on this? Cambridge *et al.* (1994) tracked 200 people with learning difficulties from twelve localities over a five-year period from when they left long-stay hospital care. They were thus able to evaluate the quality of life achieved and how this relates to the community care services provided. Their overall conclusion was unambiguous:

> From our involvement with the twelve services included in the evaluation, we know of no reasonable basis on which to challenge the policy of care in the community for people with learning disabilities who would otherwise be long-term hospital residents. In fact, most people are demonstrably better off living in the community than in hospital, over both the short and long term. (p. 105)

Positive outcomes included more choice for most over living environments, and improved support networks. This was despite the fact that they did find 'some community accommodation which was some distance short of ideal in terms of quality, scale or institutional regime' (p. 105).

Emerson and Hatton (1996) reviewed 71 resettlement studies of people with learning difficulties going right back to 1970. The overall message was of improvements in standards of living and quality of life with a wide degree of acceptance by neighbours and local businesses. Above all, people with learning difficulties in nearly all the studies felt that life in the community was superior to life in a hospital, with a key factor in the 'success' or 'failure' of care in the community for individuals often being the quality of staff in their community- based accommodation.

Despite these research findings, a minority of commentators continue to argue that isolation rather than a high quality of life will be the outcome of such aspirations to an 'ordinary life' (see Chapter 4) if the community integration route is pursued, especially for those with severe learning difficulties. New village communities on old hospital sites could provide a much more stimulating environment, at a lower cost (Cox and Pearson, 1993). Such views are dismissed by advocacy organisations such as Values into Action. Poverty level benefits, lack of employment opportunities and a lack of creativity around housing options is what undermines the goal of full integration. Too much community accommodation remains institutional in philosophy (Collins, 1996) rather than providing accommodation and support in a way which enables people with learning difficulties to feel they are living in 'my home' enjoying 'my life' (Simons, 1995).

Supported housing: institution or home?

This last observation points to the question of what is an institution, and how neatly can it be distinguished from a home and ordinary housing. The focus of resettlement studies on supported housing/ community accommodation issues underlines the increasing range of specialist housing available for people with support needs. It is clear that much of this cannot easily be allocated to either the 'institution' category or the 'home' category in the Higgins (1989) typology, although Higgins herself stresses that many care options will contain both home and 'institutional' elements.

Schemes which combine housing with support tend to be referred to as 'special needs' housing or more recently as supported housing. As Hoyes *et al.* (1996) explain:

> Supported housing is a term with broad coverage. It may include sheltered housing, hostels, residential care homes, staffed and unstaffed shared housing and self-contained accommodation with support attached. Its distinguishing feature is that along with the accommodation, services are provided to residents that would not be provided to occupiers of general needs housing. At one end of the spectrum the distinction between hostels that are part of supported housing and institutions that are not classed as housing provision is

sometimes rather fine. At the other end, services can be provided to residents in dwellings that in themselves are part of the mainstream stock, according to need, sometimes through services referred to as 'floating support'. (p. 67)

Sheltered housing is by far the largest element of the supported housing stock. McCafferty (1994) estimated this to be nearly 500,000 units in England of which nearly three-quarters are provided by local authorities. The remaining stock of supported housing was primarily developed by housing associations and other social landlords for a wide variety of people deemed to have 'special' housing needs, including people with mental health problems, people with learning difficulties, physically disabled people, people with HIV/AIDS and people with alcohol and/or drug problems:

> Supported housing forms a significant part of housing associations' business. In 1994/95 some 917 registered housing associations out of a total of 2,200 were recorded as providing 140,800 self-contained dwellings for people with support needs and 63,200 hostel/bedspaces 'occupied by people who require a supported style of housing' (HAR10/1, 1994/95). The NFHA survey 'People First: Housing Associations Caring in the Community, 1995' adopted a broader definition of housing and support than the HAR10/1, and estimated that housing associations are providing housing-based support to approximately 350,000 tenants and non-residential care and support to a further 320,000 service users. 74 per cent and 65 per cent of these respectively were older people, including the frail elderly. (Housing Corporation, 1996, p. 10)

But to what extent does the bulk of this accommodation provide a non-stigmatising home for those who live there? The previous section on resettlement suggested that supported housing schemes varied enormously in terms of this criterion but that overall the research evidence was encouraging. With regard to sheltered housing, high levels of satisfaction amongst most residents continue to be recorded (Riseborough and Niner, 1994), but this has to be balanced against growing evidence that bedsit schemes, schemes in unpopular localities and those with outdated facilities (e.g. shared bathroom) have been rejected by older people and hence are now 'difficult to let' (Tinker *et al.*, 1995).

Some commentators believe the problems of sheltered housing and other forms of supported housing are about much more than just the 'out of date' nature of some schemes. For these critics, many of whom are disabled activists committed to the social model of disability (see Chapter 4), all such schemes should be rejected as inherently stigmatising:

> Segregated provision, whether it is bricks and mortar, care or equipment has adopted and applied the 'special needs' label with regard to disabled people. In terms of 'special needs' housing for disabled people, this . . . includes residential and nursing homes, group homes and hostels, sheltered and very sheltered accommodation and housing association property. This 'special needs' provision is often geographically distinct from ordinary housing, is often inaccessible and denies disabled people the opportunity and right to participate in remunerative employment and fulfilling personal relationships. (Macfarlane and Laurie, 1996, p. 8)

A number of research studies have confirmed this dislike of feeling 'segregated' in 'special schemes'. Thus, a 'special needs'/supported housing survey in Avon found that local groups of service users and disabled people wanted access wherever possible to mainstream housing and mainstream services which should develop the flexibility to respond to individual requirements (Means, 1996a). This should include a recognition of the need for a broad definition of what represents an appropriate housing solution. Thus, the appropriateness of a house or flat for someone might depend on where it was in relation to shops, buses and work, and that rejection of accommodation on these grounds was understandable since an unwise acceptance could lead to extreme isolation. Equally, offers of bedsit or single-bedroom accommodation may be resented if people needed to have friends or relatives staying with them overnight.

In a similar vein, Midgley *et al.* (1997) draw upon separate focus group interviews with older people, their carers and professionals to identify the desired properties of an ideal housing and community care system. They were found to include the following:

- independent living and decent housing should be seen as basic rights;
- choice for older people should be maximised;
- housing should normally be provided to a mixed age group, with the 'special needs' of older people being met as part of this;
- new houses should be built with lifetime needs in mind.

Such criticisms of segregation have had an impact upon policy makers with a growing acceptance from the Housing Corporation that what is needed is more arrangements by which support can be brought to the individual in their ordinary self-contained housing. Where such schemes are run by housing associations or other social landlords this is often referred to as 'floating support', with Morris (1995a) identifying four motivations for their growth:

- to support people moving on from a special needs scheme into general needs accommodation to prevent a breakdown of the tenancy;
- as an alternative to traditional special needs housing schemes;
- for those in general needs accommodation who develop a need for intensive housing management support;
- as part of general diversification as development opportunities for housing associations decrease.

However, floating support schemes have been bedevilled by funding issues relating to the demarcation line between 'what is housing' and 'what is welfare'. Financial support from the Housing Corporation is meant to be a recognition of the extra housing management costs of providing housing for people with support needs rather than to fund welfare activities which are the responsibility of the social services authority. This means that many floating support schemes can only proceed with financial backing from social services, which is unlikely to happen unless the scheme is targeted narrowly at those deemed most at risk.

It is our view that it is wrong to believe that everyone wants to live in general needs housing. The Midgley *et al.* (1997) study argued that some older people wanted 'the choice of going into specialist, segregated accommodation if they prefer' (p. 9). This suggests that there is a rôle for supported housing as one option for some people, but an option which needs to be developed in a way more fully integrated into mainstream housing and other services. This is also recommended by Hudson *et al.* (1996) who interviewed 36 physically disabled people, 22 with a learning difficulty and 19 with mental health problems, about the obstacles they faced in terms of having their care and support needs met. Findings suggested there was a rôle for supported housing for many of these people – for some it offered a route into independence away from the parental home while for others it was a 'halfway' house until the skills and resources had been achieved to enable a 'move on' to fully independent living.

A few commentators go further and, as we saw in Chapter 4, argue for the opportunities offered by collective lifestyles. Dalley (1996) believes this can mean an escape from the oppressions of the nuclear family rather than inevitably having to involve a regimented lifestyle with no personal space. Scepticism has been expressed about the practical relevance of these alternative lifestyles on the grounds that it is unclear 'how these understandings derived from other societies and other periods can directly influence our thinking about the ways care for dependent people in contemporary Britain should be organised' (Baldwin and Twigg, 1991, p. 128). However, recent research by Brenton (1997) has not only demonstrated the growth of co-operative living schemes amongst older women in America, Canada and the Netherlands, but has shown how this might be developed as a policy option in the UK. Although the details of such schemes vary, their essence tends to be self-contained units with some communal support facilities in which each scheme member knew each other prior to moving in. Thus these innovative schemes build upon existing friendships and networks rather than artificially creating a community of strangers.

Perhaps the overall message is that people with support needs require a range of housing and support options to choose from. However, the majority of such people will want to live in mainstream housing and so access to affordable, appropriate and flexible housing within this provision will be pivotal to their quality of life.

Mainstream housing and community care

It can be argued that an emphasis upon 'special needs' housing and supported housing deflects attention away from inadequacies within mainstream housing provision which in turn can lead people to drift into residential care or end up homeless. This section therefore looks at mainstream housing provision in terms of availability, affordability, repair and access, and draws out the implications of our findings for the users of community care services.

The context for doing this is of course Conservative housing policies from 1979 right through to May 1997, particularly as expressed through the Housing Act 1988, the Local Government and Housing Act 1989 and the Housing Act 1996. This has seen a massive emphasis on owner-occupation on the grounds that it is the preferred option of nearly everyone (Department of Environment, 1995). This period saw, amongst other things, the sale of around 2.2 million council houses into owner-occupation from 1980 to 1996 as a result of the 'right to buy' (Office for National Statistics, 1997). There has also been the emergence of housing associations as the preferred developer of new housing for social renting, but in a form which has required them to borrow heavily from the private market. In addition there is an increasing tendency for local authorities to transfer voluntarily part or all of their housing stock to other social landlords. Above all, the period has seen a massive decline in housing investment through public expenditure. Hooton (1996) estimated that 1997/98 housing investment plans meant 'cumulative cuts . . . since 1992/93 now add up to more than £7 billion, or put another way, 220,000 new rented homes and nearly 400,000 renovated homes' (p. 18). Early signs from the 1997 Labour government are that it is far more positive towards social housing than recent Conservative administrations but not much more willing to prioritise it for public investment, despite some release of capital receipts from previous council house sales.

Availability

Whether or not there is a shortage of housing in England and Wales is a more difficult question than it first appears since it requires much more than checking the overall number of units against the overall number of households. To be used by existing or potential households, houses must be affordable, in the right part of the country and of an appropriate design and size, as well as being in good condition. Studies which try to take all these factors into account suggest major housing shortages exist.

Thus, Holmans (1995) has come up with the following figures for England:

- To meet the demand for homes by private owners, and the need for subsidised renting, about 240,000 new homes a year will be required in the two decades 1991–2001 and 2001–11.
- The demand for new homes by owner-occupiers is forecast as 150,000–160,000 in 1991–2001 and 130,000–140,000 in 2001–11.
- The proportion of households that are owner-occupiers will continue to grow, to around 70 per cent; the absolute number of owner-

occupier households will increase by 2.7 million in the two decades together.

- The need for additional 'social' housing will average 90,000 homes a year in 1991–2001 and 100,000 a year in 2001–11 to keep the backlog of unmet need at its 1991 level. These estimates compare with the Department of the Environment's published estimates of 60,000 to 100,000 for 1991–2001.
- The figures rise to an average of about 117,000 homes every year for the 20-year period if the backlog of unmet need for separate homes – between 400,000 and 500,000 in 1991 – is to be eradicated over the two decades.

In terms of the focus of this book, it is interesting to speculate how many people with support needs could manage in mainstream housing if it was available, affordable and in reasonable repair, and if the necessary support services could be brought to such housing. Although numerous attempts have been made to estimate the need for supported housing (McCafferty, 1994; Watson, 1996), all such estimates depend upon assumptions about the rôle of supported housing (see previous section) and its relationship to other housing and support options (Hoyes *et al.*, 1996). However, it is likely that supported housing is often involved in the 'rescue' of homeless people who are suffering from the lack of availability of mainstream housing (Means, 1996a). There is also growing evidence that homelessness due to the non-availability of mainstream affordable housing is now a major cause of mental and physical ill health (Royal Institution of Chartered Surveyors, 1996).

Affordability

In terms of affordability, our main focus is on rented housing. This is not to deny that issues of affordability in owner-occupation do not arise, as the growth of repossessions in the 1990s has served to illustrate. However, elderly owner-occupiers tend to have paid off their mortgage by the time of retirement and hence the major issue for them is often house disrepair (see below). In contrast, younger owners of properties do experience mental health problems; younger physically disabled adults who are owner-occupiers get made redundant; and the house-owning parents of people with learning disabilities die. All three of these situations can raise affordability issues in owner-occupation, which is now the dominant housing tenure in England and Wales.

However, issues of the affordability of housing and community care are most visible in terms of rented property. Both the Housing Act 1988 and the Local Government and Housing Act 1989 had the effect of driving up rents significantly in all types of rented accommodation. The aspiration of central government was to allow markets to determine appropriate rent levels, and then to develop means-tested subsidy systems (housing benefit) to support those on lowest incomes. For example, the 1988 Act established a new funding regime for housing associations which presets the amount of public subsidy prior to scheme commencement and requires them to raise the remainder from banks and building societies. The inevitable result was higher rents for new tenancies:

> Average rents in new lettings rose from £18.16 in the second quarter 1988 to £32.89 by quarter 2 1991, an increase of 81 per cent. Rents for lettings of newly developed homes (new lets) increased by 104 per cent. In comparison, the RPI increased by 26 per cent. Average rents have therefore risen at three times the rate of general inflation. (Randolph, 1993, p. 45)

The consequence of this was to make such tenants highly dependent on the housing benefit system. The main response has been attempts to try and limit rent rises in council and other socially rented housing (*Inside Housing*, 15 August 1997, p. 1).

The Housing Act 1988 also introduced further deregulation of rents in the private sector, a further reduction in security of tenure for some kinds of tenancy, and public subsidy for some types of new private renting schemes. None of this resulted in a major upsurge in the private rented sector. The situation was further complicated in 1996 by changes brought in by an amendment of housing benefit regulations which further restricted the level of housing benefit payable to private renters and altered the payment schedule so that the whole amount would always be paid in arrears. A survey of the likely impact of these changes upon accommodation registers, deposit guarantee schemes and rent in advance schemes suggested the work of such schemes would be seriously undermined (Rugg, 1997).

A new financial regime for local authority housing in England and Wales was introduced by the Local Government and Housing Act 1989. This involved the creation of a housing revenue account ring-fenced from the general funds of the local authority. It has generated some major rent rises, and council rents rose by an average of 30 per cent in England during the first two years of the new system (Malpass, 1993). Again, increased dependency on housing benefit was an inevitable outcome of these trends for low-income people.

As early as 1990, Maclennan *et al.* (1990) were able to demonstrate that almost half of the households in social housing in Britain did not have access to employment and they argued that 'this yawning gap in the sources of income has to be at the forefront of any discussion of the housing benefit system' (p. 36). These words have proved prophetic. The concentration of the unemployed, disabled people, low-income elderly people and people with multiple problems within the socially rented sector has continued to occur, partly because homelessness has become a key route into new tenancies. The London Federation of Housing Associations (1995) estimated that 60 per cent of new tenants housed by their general needs housing associations could be defined as vulnerable.

The vast majority of 'vulnerable' tenants in the public and private sectors are likely to be able to afford their accommodation only because of the housing benefit system. This can be seen in a very positive light:

> Housing Benefit is uniquely adaptable to the accommodation-related needs of people who require support to live in the community. It is cost-effective – payments can be tailored to the type of supported accommodation required as the individual's capacity for community living increases or diminishes over time. (Griffiths, 1997, p. 23)

However, the response of governments has been the opposite of this. Housing benefit costs have grown considerably and hence there have been numerous attempts to limit entitlement. The impact of this upon the standard of living of people with support needs has been substantial. In terms of older people, Marsh and Riseborough (1995) found that 'even where housing costs are paid by housing benefit, tenants find themselves with very limited incomes, often below income support levels' (p. 65).

One reason for the low standard of living of these elderly people, despite housing benefit support, was the high cost of the service charge, and a key area of tension has become the extent to which housing benefit is subsidising the 'support' as well as the 'housing' element of supported accommodation (Oldman *et al.*, 1996). At the time of writing, this whole issue was subject to an inter-departmental government review.

Housing conditions

Leather and Morrison (1997) have recently profiled the appalling state of UK housing. They found that:

- some 1,638,000 occupied dwellings in the UK were either unfit for human habitation or below the Scottish tolerable standard – this represented about 7 per cent or one in 14 dwellings in the UK;
- problems of disrepair are more widespread than unfitness, with almost one in five dwellings in England having urgent repair costs of more than £1,000;
- people on low incomes are the most likely to live in poor housing conditions and this includes many older people especially above the age of 75;
- houses in poor condition are to be found across all tenures (see Table 7.2).

The implications of such poor housing conditions for people with support needs are immense. In terms of council housing and other socially rented estates, a concentration of people with social and health

TABLE 7.2   Dwellings in poor condition by tenure, England and Wales (1991/93)

	Percentage dwellings in each tenure group			
	Owner-occupied	Private rented	LA rented	HA rented
England				
Unfit	5.5	20.5	6.9	6.7
Urgent repairs over £1,000	17.3	41.0	15.1	12.7
Northern Ireland				
Unfit	8.5	27.9	2.0	2.1
Urgent repairs over £1,000	15.5	38.9	5.6	1.4
Wales				
Unfit	11.9	25.6	15.8	6.0
Repairs over £1,500	19.9	34.3	18.7	8.4

Notes: Figures for England are for 1991; figures for Wales are for 1993. Excludes vacant dwellings. Comparisons cannot be made between countries.
Source: Leather and Morrison (1997) p. 32.

difficulties into poor housing has helped to generate almost total environmental and social collapse requiring broad strategies of estate regeneration to tackle the resultant problems rather than just the repair of the housing stock (Stewart and Taylor, 1995). For those in owner-occupied housing, and especially for low-income elderly people, there is a constant pressure about how best to maintain property to a reasonable standard.

With regard to the latter group, Leather and Morrison found that the proportion of households living in unfit housing in England rises from 6.6 per cent for households where the head is aged between 60 and 64 to 13.2 per cent for households where the head is aged over 85. People on low incomes including elderly and disabled people can apply for repair help through the home improvement grant system (see Table 7.3 for more details). However, this system is complex and many elderly and disabled people lack the knowledge, expertise or confidence to apply for a renovation grant or home repair assistance and then to organise the subsequent building work.

An option increasingly used in this situation is for elderly and disabled people to turn to a specialist home improvement agency (HIA) for advice. These are non-profit-making bodies which offer independent advice and support on how to repair, improve and adapt homes (Bradford, Mares and Wilkins, 1994). Such agencies are often called Care and Repair or Staying Put projects although some agencies use other names. There are 200 such agencies in England and they are supported in their work by a national co-ordinating body called Care and Repair (England). A further 25 HIAs are to be found in Wales and these are co-ordinated by Care and Repair (Wales).

HIAs are used extensively by people with support needs. For example, *Poor Housing: Who Cares?* (Care and Repair, 1994) looked at the characteristics of nearly 20,000 clients and discovered that 18 per cent of the single older clients and 28 per cent of the older couples had been in hospital during the last twelve months. These clients also included 6,080 who were registered or registrable as disabled under the Chronically Sick and Disabled Persons Act 1970 with 16 per cent of them being under 60 years of age. This client profile has meant not only an expanding rôle in home adaptation (see next section) as well as home improvement, but also the development of a range of new services such as handyperson, home security and home safety schemes (Smart and Means, 1997).

Owner-occupation in later life will be a boon to many. With the mortgage paid off, housing costs will drop at a time when weekly

TABLE 7.3   Repair and renovation

A. Name of grant	B. Purposes	C. Who eligible?
Renovation Grant	To make fit. To put into good repair. To provide insulation, heating system, safe internal arrangement, means of escape from fire, and radon remedial measures. There is also power for the Secretary of State to specify other measures.	Owner-occupiers or tenants of private landlords.
Home Repair Assistance	To carry out works of repair, improvement or adaptation. Help may be in the form of cash grant, or provision of materials, or both.	Owner-occupiers, all tenants except council tenants and people with the right to occupy for at least 5 years, who, in each case, are aged 18 or over and in receipt of a means-tested benefit. Includes owners or tenants of houseboats or mobile homes if certain conditions are met. Any owner or non-council tenant who is elderly, disabled or infirm – they do not have to be on benefits. Any owner or non-council tenant – they do not have to be on benefits – who needs the work in order to care for someone who is elderly, disabled or infirm.

Note: This table is provided only as a guide. Full details need to be checked in the 1996 Housing Grants, Construction and Regeneration Act, Part I, and in subsequent Circulars.
Source: Means *et al.* (1997), p. 64.

D. Terms	E. Conditions
Discretionary. No limits specified. Test of resources prescribed by the Secretary of State.	Property to be at least 10 years old. Applicant must have owned or (if tenant) lived for at least 3 years in the property (except grant for fire escape – or if property is in a Renewal Area or other exceptions). Grant to be repaid if house sold within 5 years of date of grant approval (with exemption in certain circumstances). Local authority has discretion to disregard all these conditions.
Discretionary. Applicant or partner must be in receipt of Income Support, Family Credit, Housing Benefit, Council Tax Benefit or Disability Working Allowance unless they are elderly, disabled or infirm, or the grant is to care for someone who is elderly, disabled or infirm. No further means test. Maximum £2,000 per grant or £4,000 in 3-year period (may be altered by the Secretary of State).	Applicant must have lived in property for at least 3 years unless assistance is for fire escape, or to enable elderly, disabled or infirm person to be cared for or property is in a Renewal Area.

income is reduced, thus avoiding a major decline in living standards. For many, there is the prospect of a move from a family home to a smaller property, thus releasing equity to be used in a variety of ways, including meeting future care needs. But others will be trapped in poorly repaired property of limited value with few assets with which to develop a maintenance and repair strategy in later life. The housing dimension of community care needs to include a strategy for offering support to elderly and disabled people facing these kinds of repair problems.

Access (new build and adaptation)

In discussing issues of access, it is important to distinguish between wheelchair and mobility standard housing. Mobility housing is housing suitable for ambulant disabled people, while wheelchair housing is housing suitable for the permanent accommodation of people who are wheelchair users. The late 1980s saw a decline in new-build housing meeting either of these standards despite the rhetoric of central government about the importance of independent living. The Rowe Report (1992, p. 14) drew upon previous research to suggest a shortfall of 330,000 dwellings suitable to accommodate wheelchair users.

Earlier, the impact of the Housing Act 1988 and the Local Government and Housing Act 1989 was discussed in terms of affordability issues. However, these Acts have also had a major influence on the reduction in building housing to mobility and wheelchair standard. The decline in local authority starts reflects the general discouragement and opposition of central government to all new build by local authorities. However, the poor performance of housing associations in recent years with regard to mobility and wheelchair standard housing has a more complex explanation. Morris (1990b) has argued that

> The new finance system for housing associations is squeezing the small 'special needs' housing associations and threatening their very existence. At the same time, the larger general needs housing associations, and particularly those in the forefront of using private finance, are ignoring the needs of disabled people. (p. 23)

The picture with regard to private sector new–build is even more bleak. Reeves and McCaskie (1995) point out that although 84 per cent of new houses between 1986 and 1993 were built by the private sector, this sector contributed on average only 14 per cent of new wheelchair housing and 13 per cent of mobility housing.

In recent years such attitudes have been challenged with the argument that improved access requirements for new domestic dwellings should be built into planning law and building regulations. The aim is to build houses, flats and bungalows which are flexible, adaptable and accessible, and hence:

> designed either to meet the changing needs occurring throughout one family's lifetime – raising small children, accommodating the teenager with a broken leg, having grandparents to stay, mobility difficulties in old age – or to meet the varying needs of numerous changes of occupier in the same home. (Brewerton and Darton, 1997, p. 4)

More specifically, the concept of lifetime homes has been developed and such homes have 16 design features (see Figure 7.1). A cost–benefit argument is being made that the resultant increased building costs can be offset by savings in terms of wider economic benefits (e.g. reduced home care, health and adaptation costs) as well as major social benefits such as improved quality of life (Cobbold, 1997).

A complementary approach to using new-build schemes to increase mobility and wheelchair access is to emphasise the importance of adaptation to existing properties. The main public subsidy for adaptation work is now through the disabled facilities grant. Table 7.4 outlines the main features of this complex grant which has been criticised on a number of fronts. Many complain that the means-tested element discourages some applicants, especially since major outgoings such as mortgage payments are not taken into account in considering what the applicant can reasonably afford (Sapey, 1995). Second, the complexity of the system is often criticised in terms of the failure to co-ordinate the various professional inputs (Mackintosh and Leather, 1994) in a context in which there is often dispute between housing and social services about the best way to proceed (Heywood, 1994) and how this might best be funded (Heywood with Smart, 1996).

Heywood (1994) talks of 'this kaleidoscope of possible permutations' in which 'getting from "A" (needing an adaptation) to "B" (securing the necessary adaptation) may mean encountering occupational therapists, grants officers, technical officers, agency workers, planners, builders, stairlift companies and work inspectors' (p. 5). A number of studies have stressed the need to develop a culture which Heywood

Access

1. Where car parking is adjacent to the home, it should be capable of enlargement to attain 3.3 metres width.
2. The distance from the car parking space to the home should be kept to a minimum and should be level or gently sloping.
3. The approach to all entrances should be level or gently sloping. (Gradients for paths should be the same as for public buildings in the Building Regulations.)
4. All entrances should be illuminated and have level access over the threshold, and the main entrance should be covered.
5. Where homes are reached by a lift, it should be wheelchair accessible.

Inside the home

6. The width of the doorways and hallways should accord with the Access Committee for England's standards.
7. There should be space for the turning of wheelchairs in kitchens, dining areas and sitting rooms and adequate circulation space for wheelchair users elsewhere.
8. The sitting room (or family room) should be at entrance level.
9. In houses of two or more storeys, there should be space on the ground floor that could be used as a convenient bed space.
10. There should be a downstairs toilet which should be wheelchair accessible, with drainage and service provision enabling a shower to be fitted at any time.
11. Walls in bathrooms and toilets should be capable of taking adaptations such as handrails.
12. The design should incorporate provision for a future stairlift and a suitably identified space for potential installation of a house lift (through-the-floor lift) from the ground to the first floor, for example to a bedroom next to the bathroom.
13. The bath/bedroom ceiling should be strong enough, or capable of being made strong enough, to support a hoist at a later date. Within the bath/bedroom wall, provision should be made for a future floor-to-ceiling door, to connect the two rooms by a hoist.
14. The bathroom layout should be designed to incorporate ease of access, probably from a side approach, to the bath and WC. The wash basins should also be accessible.

Fixtures and fittings

15. The living room window glazing should begin at 800mm or lower, and windows should be easy to open/operate.
16. Switches, sockets and service controls should be at a height usable by all (i.e. between 600mm and 1,200mm from the floor).

Source: Cobbold (1997) p. 2.

FIGURE 7.1   The lifetime homes standards

calls 'finding ways to say yes'. Thus Pieda Plc (1996) outlined a range of options for improved liaison:

- The creation of joint teams.
- Regular liaison meetings between social services staff and grants staff. This probably needs to occur both at a senior level to discuss policy, and at a lower level to discuss particular cases.
- Many authorities have found it useful to undertake joint training so that both social services authority and housing authority staff understand the responsibilities of staff in the other authority and the way in which that authority operates.
- Joint visits where the adaptations to be provided are likely to be complex and require a technical input. The contacts that such visits afford also help to build up personal relationships between staff.
- Common information systems. Authorities could examine establishing common information systems (databases) that would allow staff in one authority, for example, to identify what stages in the enquiry process the client has reached.

A further two possibilities also need to be mentioned. First, the work of home improvement agencies (see previous section) is increasingly focused upon helping elderly and disabled people through the whole process of obtaining an appropriate adaptation (Smart and Means, 1997). A second option relates to developing disabled persons' accommodation agencies. These equally offer expertise in obtaining an adaptation but many of them are also involved in developing comprehensive registers of adapted and mobility housing within their localities (Means *et al.*, 1997).

Towards an integrated response?

This whole chapter has emphasised the importance of the housing dimension of community care, and hence the need to draw housing agencies and housing professionals into the centre of community care at both the strategic and operational levels. However, Chapter 6 emphasised the obstacles to effective joint working because of conflicts over rôles and responsibilities, a lack of knowledge of each other's networks and a tendency for professionals to hold stereotypical images about each other.

TABLE 7.4   Home adaptation

A. Name of grant	B. Purposes	C. Who eligible?
Mandatory disabled facilities grant	To facilitate use by disabled people of their homes. Specifically to provide: • access to building • making dwelling safe for disabled persons or others • access to and provision of living room, bedroom, lavatory, bathroom (including use of bath and/or shower) and wash handbasin • providing suitable cooking facilities and suitable power, lighting and heating controls • improving or providing suitable heating system • movement around dwelling in order to care for someone • other purposes as may be specified by the Secretary of State	Anyone over 18 in any tenure who is either disabled themselves or needs the grant to allow them to adapt the house for a disabled person. The definition of disabled person for purposes of this grant is given at Section 100 of the 1996 Housing Grants, Construction and Regeneration Act. It includes a very broad range of older and disabled people, including disabled children.
Discretionary disabled facilities grant	Either to augment a mandatory grant for purposes described above or to make the building suitable for the 'accommodation, welfare or employment' of the disabled occupant.	As above.

Note: This table is provided only as a guide. Full details need to be checked in the 1996 Housing Grants, Construction and Regeneration Act, Part I, and in subsequent Circulars.
Source: Based on the work of Heywood in Means *et al.* (1997) p. 71.

D. Terms	E. Conditions
Mandatory for the purposes defined in Section 23, a-1 of the 1996 Housing Grants, Construction and Regeneration Act. Maximum grant £20,000 (but NB discretionary grant for mandatory purposes may be added on). Test of resources as prescribed by the Secretary of State. Housing authorities must be satisfied that works are (a) 'necessary and appropriate' and (b) 'reasonable and practicable'. In deciding (a) they shall consult the social services authority if it is a different authority. Payment of grants may in exceptional cases (i.e. where it would not cause hardship to the applicant) be deferred for 12 months from the date of application.	Disabled person (or parent if the disabled person is a child) must complete a test of resources which takes into account their income and that of their partner or spouse. This means test does not take existing outgoings into account, and there are therefore serious problems for people with mortgages or other debts. DoE Circular 4/97 provides for a test of resources to be applied to people over 16 and under 19, in receipt of Income Support and no longer at school, in their own right, even if they are living with their parents.
Discretionary. Test of resources as above.	As above.

Many of these difficulties exist with regard to housing and social services. Thus, housing professionals have been described as seeing social workers in the following terms:

> There is a stereotyped image of the social worker as young and freshly qualified, straight from school via college, without any practical experience who would be entirely subjective and idealistic about clients and will seek all manner of handouts and special treatments for them without ever expecting them to stand on their own two feet. (Institute of Housing report, quoted in BASW, 1985)

Social workers, in their turn, have characterised housing workers as follows:

> I am not saying that they are a lot of heartless villains. I just think they are conditioned and they have little scope to do anything other than reach their targets in terms of rent arrears. (quoted in Clapham and Franklin, 1994)

In terms of rôles and responsibilities there are clear tensions at both the strategic and operational levels especially in areas such as homelessness and funding for supported housing. At the centre of this tension lies the issue of who should provide the care and fund the care of people whose housing and support difficulties are not so great as to ensure they meet the priority criteria of social services for care management and a care package. Thus, housing may define a single homeless person as in priority need on the grounds of old age, mental health problems, learning difficulties, physical impairment or major health problem. It may be felt that such an individual would fail to retain any offered tenancy and hence drift back into homelessness unless offered additional support. But social services will often feel unable to respond, and hence housing workers and housing agencies feel they are being 'dumped upon'. Such feeling can be especially acute amongst the wardens/managers of sheltered housing schemes as residents become more frail and some develop symptoms of dementia. They can feel great bitterness at the apparent assumption of both health and social services that they should be able to cope (Langan and Means, 1995).

A number of studies have pointed to the extent to which there has been a failure to address these and other issues relating to the integration of housing into the community care agenda. The govern-

ment's own study of community care and housing/homelessness devoted a chapter to joint assessment, and found that

> Although housing agencies are beginning to be engaged in commu-
> nity care implementation, housing solutions for people with 'special'
> needs and homeless people are still being developed in isolation, and
> links between community care and housing assessment procedures
> are rare. (Department of Health, 1994)

Arblaster *et al.* (1996) carried out a national postal survey backed up
by three case studies on inter-agency working to address the housing,
health and social care needs of people in ordinary housing. They found
a lack of effective communication between agencies, caused partly by a
lack of conceptual understanding about the overall functions of each
other combined with a lack of awareness of what each other did in
practice on a day-to-day basis. Lund and Foord (1997) studied the
housing strategies and community care plans of a range of local
authorities and concluded that further progress required an improved
integration of assessment procedures, a systematic recording of need,
and 'robust performance indicators' which are 'relevant to community
care' (p. 47).

Such studies tend to claim that some limited progress has been made
and most are able to offer examples of good practice. Central government has proved willing to encourage the further integration of
housing into the community care agenda through the publication of
strategic and operational guidance which is supported by both the
Department of Environment and the Department of Health. The aim
of *Housing and Community Care: Establishing a Strategic Framework*
(DH/DoE, 1997) was 'to provide a framework to help housing, social
services and health authorities to establish joint strategies for housing
and community care so that at a strategic level, the necessary co-
ordination between housing, social services and health is achieved'
(p.1). The positive message of the guidance was that effective joint
working at the strategic level maximises available resources and can
also enable agencies to meet their own aims as well as joint objectives.

*Making Partnerships Work in Community Care: A Guide for Practi-
tioners in Housing, Health and Social Services* (Means *et al.*, 1997) looks
at many of the same issues from an operational perspective and with an
emphasis on the need for field-level staff to map their localities, because
it is essential for them to have an awareness of how a wide range of
agencies might be able to contribute to meeting the housing, health and

support needs of service users. The guide also argues for a much clearer view of the housing and care management interface than has been attempted in most discussions of the 'failure' of joint assessment. The starting point is to clarify respective rôles:

Why bring in housing?

(i) The care manager is not sure of their client's housing needs and hence wishes to access a specialist housing needs assessment, e.g. of the damp in the house, of their tenancy rights, of their entitlement to a home improvement grant, of whether they are homeless as defined by housing legislation, of whether their housing is inappropriate.

(ii) The care manager wishes to access housing or housing services for their client, e.g. a council house, a housing association property, a housing with support scheme, a home adaptation.

(iii) The care manager needs to work with the housing professional to address issues of, for example, rent arrears, housing repair and maintenance or conflict with neighbours, etc.

Why bring in social services?

(i) The housing professional is not sure of the care and support needs of their client and hence wishes to access a specialist community care assessment.

(ii) The housing professional wishes to access services provided or funded by social services such as home care, respite care or a place in a residential or nursing home.

(iii) The housing professional needs to work with the care manager to sort out her/his tenant's existing care package, to address issues relating to the distressing behaviour of neighbours known to social services or to assess whether the housing situation is exacerbating his/her social care needs, etc.

(Means *et al.*, 1997, pp. 38–9)

The guide argues that it might be more helpful to think in terms of the complementary assessment rôles of both housing and social services staff. It also underlines that joint working between housing and social services raises issues throughout the care management process and not just in relation to assessment. From such a perspective, the key task is to clarify the basic knowledge about housing that should be held by social services staff and the basic knowledge about community care

Housing staff need to have the following skills and knowledge:

- awareness of how social services and health are organised locally, what their priorities are and what they might realistically be likely to provide;
- knowledge of how to make appropriate referrals to health and social services, including information required by social services;
- knowledge of signs of possible dementia and when to seek further advice;
- ability to recognise possible signs of crisis and vulnerability;
- alternative sources of help and advice (advocacy groups, organisations of service users/disabled people, specialist voluntary agencies, etc.);
- a commitment to work in partnership with the tenant, housing applicant or their advocate.

Housing staff cannot demand that health and social services provide services, but they can encourage a specialist assessment to be made where they have concerns about a client or tenant.

Social services staff need to have the following skills and knowledge:

- awareness of how housing is organised locally, what their priorities are and what housing agencies might realistically be likely to provide (NB: housing authorities must provide free copies of a summary of their housing allocation schemes);
- this awareness to include an understanding of both options for homeless people and vulnerable tenants, together with options for those seeking advice on home improvement and/or adaptation;
- knowledge of how to make appropriate referrals to housing agencies;
- knowledge of how to respond appropriately to referrals from housing agencies;
- awareness of alternative sources of help and advice (advocacy groups, organisations of service users/disabled people, specialist voluntary agencies, etc.);
- commitment to work in partnership with service users and their advocates.

Social services staff cannot demand a response from housing agencies but they can encourage a (re)assessment to be made where they have concerns about their client's housing situation.

Source: Means *et al.* (1997).

FIGURE 7.2 Housing and social services staff: key knowledge and skills

that is needed by housing workers (see Figure 7.2). From such an agreed base, it becomes possible for each to know when to refer on for more specialist assessment and support.

Conclusion

The publication in 1997 of these documents is encouraging in terms of improving the robustness of the housing dimension of community care at the local level, and elsewhere one of us has referred to an emerging agreed vision for housing and community care (Means, 1996b) in terms of a commitment to independent living and a growing recognition that 'nobody . . . should be expected to change their permanent residence simply in order to obtain the services which they need' (Wagner Report, 1988, p. 114).

However, the inadequacy of what has been achieved needs to be recognised in terms of the limitations of the overall housing stock of this country and the resultant knock-on consequences of this for the quality of life for many people with support needs. The result is homelessness and misery for more and more (Bines, 1994; Crane, 1997). But it also leads to misery for many others because of expensive, poorly repaired and inflexible housing. From such a perspective, joint working and integrated responses are still to be encouraged as the way to make best use of inadequate resources, but they are no substitute for also tackling the 'bricks and mortar' issues raised by this chapter. People with support needs deserve good-quality houses, flats and bungalows which help them develop a sense of home, security and independence.

8 European Perspectives on Community Care

The forces which have influenced the development of community care policy and practice have not been confined to the UK. The governments of other countries in Western Europe have also had to address the consequences of demographic changes, high levels of unemployment, deep recession and public expenditure pressures on the rôle of the family in caring, on the costs of institutional care, on the notion of the mixed economy of welfare, on the problems of inter-agency collaboration and on the voice of the service user or carer (Tester, 1996).

Whilst the pressures on social welfare policies have not recognised national boundaries, the responses of individual West European states have varied, reflecting the differences in welfare traditions and regimes. There are several typologies of European welfare states but the categorisation used in this chapter is that employed by Abrahamson (1991a). Four types of welfare state are identified, each reflecting a particular kind of welfare regime. The *rudimentary* welfare state (or Catholic social policy) is associated with Latin Rim countries, such as Spain and Portugal. This tradition emphasises philanthropic solutions to welfare provision by traditional institutions such as the church, family and private charity, with limited public welfare institutions and policies developing alongside. The *residual* welfare state (or liberal social policy) has been associated in recent years with the UK. As outlined earlier in this book, this is characterised by rolling back the boundaries of the welfare state and by public services being contracted out to the independent sector. The state is a safety-net rather than a primary provider. The *institutional* welfare state (or corporatist social policy in the Bismarckian tradition) has been linked in particular to Germany. This tradition puts emphasis on labour market solutions to social issues, such as unemployment, sickness or old age. Those outside the labour market are likely to be dependent on local charity. The *modern* welfare state (or social democratic policy) is associated with Scandinavian countries. This is characterised by wide provision of good-quality publicly provided services, with the private and voluntary sectors becoming increasingly involved in the welfare mix.

These four broad categories may in themselves not be robust enough to withstand the societal and economic pressures impinging on Western European countries in the late twentieth century, but they provide a vehicle for examining the core elements of community care in different European countries. The residual model is not, however, considered below, as it is the focus of most of this book. The European perspectives on community care have been drawn from a small number of European countries, principally Greece, Germany and Denmark, representing three different kinds of welfare regime. Some material has also been drawn from Italy, Spain and Portugal. Ireland has been excluded, for good or ill, because its welfare arrangements are seen as part of the Anglo-Saxon tradition. Austria, Belgium, the Netherlands and Luxembourg are linked to the corporatist social tradition of Germany; Sweden and Finland are not unlike Denmark. Of the EU countries this leaves France, which has been described as a hybrid between the Bismarckian, Anglo-Saxon and the rudimentary welfare regimes of the Latin Rim countries (Walker, 1992, p. 3).

The rôle of the family in caring

The family remains the main supporter of those needing care across the European Union. According to a 1992 Eurobarometer Survey, adult children were the most frequently mentioned carers of older people (40 per cent), followed by spouses (32 per cent) and other relatives (14 per cent). The other sources of care were public social services (13 per cent), private paid help (11 per cent), friends and neighbours (6 per cent each) and voluntary bodies (3 per cent). There were, unsurprisingly, major variations between individual countries. In-house care by adult children was most common in Greece (39 per cent) and much less common in Denmark (4 per cent). In Greece, 47 per cent of those receiving care were supported by a spouse, compared with 19 per cent in Denmark (The Netherlands reported even lower percentages) (Walker and Maltby, 1997, p. 101).

National attitudes, behaviour and policy towards caring for adults were examined in a 16-country cross-national study on family obligations undertaken in 1994 covering the then twelve member states of the European Union and the four applicant countries of Austria, Finland,

Norway and Sweden. Millar and Warman (1996) distinguish between those countries where there are legal obligations on the family to provide care (e.g. Germany and Greece) and those where there are no such obligations (e.g. Denmark). They also categorise the sixteen countries into those where service provision is locally organised (such as Germany); those where it is locally organised under national regulation (Denmark); and those where it is nationally organised (Greece). Systems of care payments were divided into those made to care givers (Denmark), those made to care receivers (Germany and Greece), and those made to both (the United Kingdom). The adequacy of payments was, however, another matter. In other words, the picture was one of great variety. The rôle of the family in caring covered a wide spectrum ranging from systems 'where the family provides virtually all the support to situations where family care is an optional extra to state services' (p. 43) and there was no trend towards a common pattern of provision.

The family continues to hold a central position in Catholic and Orthodox social policy. In countries like Portugal and Spain the supply of domiciliary and day care is generally inadequate and dependence on care provided by women in the family system is high. Such community care services as are provided are designed to supplement family care, enabling dependent people to remain at home. As Anderson (1992) explains: 'In Greece, the Church and voluntary organisations particularly the Greek Red Cross, dominate provision of welfare services. . . This means that the distribution of such services is related to the presence of voluntary agencies and private benefactors rather than to any assessments of need' (p. 77).

Whilst the family may be central to social policy in the rudimentary welfare states, it is less than clear that this is reflected in everyday experience in Latin Rim countries. Potter and Zill (1992) argue that older people regard the informal care from family members as insufficient, as a burden on the carers which can lead to conflict in the household. In countries like Greece and Spain, value systems are changing more rapidly among younger people, creating the danger 'that the traditional informal support networks of the family are breaking down before these countries acquire the prosperity to be able to fund effective formal care services for older people' (pp. 124–5). It is the case that families are perceived by older people to be less willing to care than in the past. Table 8.1 shows the responses to this issue by older people in a survey carried out in the then twelve member states of the European Community in April–May 1992. The EC average showed

TABLE 8.1   'Families are less willing to care for older relatives than they used to be' (older people only) (percentages)

	EC12	Greece	Italy	Portugal	Spain	UK	Germany	Denmark
Agree strongly	33.4	36.0	39.4	42.9	45.2	26.4	24.0	32.7
Agree slightly	34.0	35.5	34.6	36.2	34.8	31.8	37.2	26.6
Disagree slightly	18.2	15.1	17.1	12.6	10.5	18.9	24.8	19.4
Disagree strongly	10.4	7.8	5.1	4.9	5.5	18.3	10.2	16.4
Don't know	4.1	5.4	3.8	3.5	4.1	5.3	3.7	4.8

Source: Eurobarometer Survey (1993) p. 29.

that about two-thirds of older people agreed that families were less willing to care than in the past, whereas the proportion for Greece and Italy was over 70 per cent and for Spain and Portugal approaching 80 per cent.

The family is also expected to play a central rôle in the institutional welfare state, particularly for those outside the labour market, creating a major responsibility and strain on relatives, where they exist (Evers and Olk, 1991, p. 66; Dieck, 1994, p. 253). In Germany the provision of income support can be made only after a comprehensive examination of the circumstances of family members. As stressed by Jamieson (1990a), the ideology of family responsibility is stated very explicitly in the principle of subsidiarity which guides social service provision. Although family members are not compelled by the state to provide care for a needy person, nevertheless the state provides financial incentives only to those who are willing and able to provide care. One of the consequences of this is that many adult children in Germany are struggling to mobilise the resources necessary to carry out caring tasks. Tester (1994) blames subsidiarity for the extensive fragmentation of services.

The modern welfare state (or social democratic social policy) is also under pressure (Daatland, 1992), but here the thrust is to involve the voluntary and private sectors more, rather than require the family to take on the caring rôle. In Denmark, compared with Southern European countries, older people are less likely to argue that families are less willing to care (see Table 8.1). The argument in Denmark is that the family is not in a position to provide care. Munday (1996) draws on the 1992 Danish report to the European Commission Observatory on Social Exclusion to point out that the institution of the family had weakened substantially in the last thirty years so care functions were taken over by the state. The relatively high level of social care provision 'is partly explained by the rapidly rising female participation rate in the labour market' (p. 34), leading to 'shrinkage of the female caretaker potential' (Alber, 1993, p.104 quoted in Hantrais, 1995, p. 140). However, children do care about their older relatives; this takes the form of advocacy and pressure on the professionals. The main burden of informal care in Denmark falls upon spouses or partners, and Jamieson (1991) argues that 'perhaps these are the ones who pay the highest price for a welfare system which is geared towards state-provided professional solutions to health and social problems' (p. 120).

This conclusion is supported by the results of the study in the early 1990s of family carers in eleven member states of the EU:

> Virtually all social policies actually count on, or entirely depend on the family – yet few member states have taken any practical steps to provide that primary pillar with any real support. There is an urgent need for practices and policies to improve family carers' living and working conditions – because caring for an old person is work. (Jani-Le Bris, 1993, pp. 10–11)

Based on this range of reports, Salvage (1995) examined future prospects for the family care of older people in the EU over the next twenty years. She concluded that governments needed to make urgent plans based on the recognition of the current overdependence on informal care. Four options were put forward (pp. 68–76):

1. reducing demand for care by improving older people's health and independence;
2. stimulating supply by making it easier for families to support older relatives;
3. developing new ways of providing support, including surrogate families and intergenerational housing schemes;
4. improving the image and experience of residential care.

The place of institutional care

In a number of northern European countries the policy trend since the mid-1970s has been away from institutional provision, particularly for elderly people (Alber, Guillemard and Walker, 1991, p.37). The prime reason for this policy shift has been the cost to the public purse, supported by what were seen as inappropriate admissions of people who could live in (cheaper) non-institutional settings. Another factor has been the preferences of disabled and older people themselves. These preferences were shared by the vast majority of the general public in the European Community who thought that older people should be helped to stay in their own homes. This consensus extended across virtually the whole of the age group and is shared by both sexes (Eurobarometer Survey, 1993, p. 29).

Italy, as a southern European country, has engaged in a policy debate about the need to run down large institutions for frail elderly people, but it is far better known for its radical experiments to close its psychiatric institutions, based on legislation passed in 1978 (Ramon and Giannichedda, 1991). Under this law, new admissions to psychiatric hospitals were to cease after 31 December 1979 and there were to be no readmissions after 31 December 1980. No new building in the psychiatric sector was to be permitted from the date the law was put into effect (1 May 1978). Community mental health centres were to be established by the regions throughout Italy. Compulsory admissions (for only 48 hours in the first instance) had to be based on an order proposed by a psychiatrist, and agreed by the local mayor. It could be renewed for a further seven days if approved by a judge. This law was the product of a range of local experiments in deinstitutionalisation in the 1970s and the movement known as Psichiatria Democratica, which involved left-wing political parties, radical psychiatrists and progressive jurists. It will come as no surprise to learn that there have been major implementation difficulties, and revisions of the law began to emerge in the 1980s.

It is not reasonable to class Italy as a rudimentary welfare state (partly because of the enormous regional variation) but Greece is not untypical of such a regime in having only a small minority of elderly people living in residential homes. In the early 1980s there were just under 6,000 residents in just over 100 non-profit-making homes mostly run by the Greek Orthodox Church. This total of residents amounted to about 0.5 per cent of the elderly population in Greece (Ziomas, 1991, p. 68). As outlined in the previous section, care for elderly people in

Greece is mainly a family affair. There is concern that changes in Greek society may reduce the availability of family carers, because of fewer children in the family, greater participation of women in the formal labour market, greater geographic mobility of younger people and increasing divorce rates. Some private sector for-profit homes have been established, mainly in and near Athens, to respond to demand from more affluent frail elderly people (or their families) and some day centres have been developed on the initiative of the state.

It is anticipated that the cost to the public purse of supporting frail people in non-profit-making residential homes will be such that policies for alternative non-institutional services, such as the day centres (see Amira, 1990, p. 73) will be further developed. This financial argument is underpinned by a view that residential care reflects a paternalistic ideology of protection, a logic of dependence and division between age groups (Ziomas, p. 70). Such an outlook accords with the results of the Eurobarometer survey summarised at the beginning of this section, but contrasts with the view from the EC Observatory on Older People that, 'since community services can only complement but not substitute care rendered in the family system, the twin process of a growing number of elderly people who need support and of a shrinking pool of voluntary female carers – who provided the bulk of support in the past – will invariably lead to a growing demand for institutionalised care in specialised geriatric hospitals or in residential homes for older people' (Alber, Guillemard and Walker, 1991, p. 38).

In the institutional welfare state, represented in this section by Germany, the policy trend in the 1980s, fuelled by the need to cut costs, has been to increase day care and domiciliary services at the expense of residential services. In 1984 the social assistance law gave community services priority over care in institutions (Tester, 1996, p. 18).

One of the major assumptions of various social reformers during the 1970s was that residential institutions, both for young people at risk and for the physically and/or mentally ill, should be avoided in favour of out-patient or counselling approaches, which respected as much as possible the home environment of the client/patient. Such reforms, which were soon applied to hospitals and homes for the elderly as well, initially encountered a good deal of institutional resistance from the residential lobby, but then found increasing support from decidedly non-reform-minded quarters during the years of austerity. (Brauns and Kramer, 1989, p. 144)

Residential care for elderly people is in the main provided by the non-statutory sector and in 1990 provided for about 5 per cent of the older population of the former West Germany (Landwehr and Wolff, 1992, p. 26). This is because the principle of subsidiarity applies not only to the responsibilities of families for their needy members but also to the relationship between statutory and voluntary bodies. Conditional priority is given to voluntary non-profit organisations which wish to provide such social help. Public social assistance bodies are obliged to support the voluntary welfare organisations, such support including means-tested financial help (Jarre, 1991).

The financial responsibility of the family to support an elderly relative often means that the parent moves in with the children rather than entering residential care. However, as in Greece and elsewhere, there is concern that the capability of the family to provide care is lessening because of changes in society and the increasing numbers of older people. Alber (1991) has argued that increases in home and day care services need to be accompanied by an increase in the supply of nursing homes and hospices for frail older people, though progress in providing them is slow. It is also reported that about 30 per cent of all beds in acute hospitals are occupied by elderly patients with an average length of stay as high as forty days. The extent of hospital care is related to a shortage of domiciliary and day care services. It has been officially estimated that some 20–30 per cent of hospital patients over the age of 65 are long-term patients who could be better supported through day clinics, rehabilitation centres or nursing homes. The problem is made more acute by the social insurance system in Germany which draws a distinction between sickness (covered by insurance) and general frailty (perceived as a personal risk). Alber explains how this means that 'prolongation of the stay in acute hospitals is the only way to prevent older patients from having to foot the bill for delivery into nursing homes which they can rarely afford' (p. 25). Dieck (1990) points out that this creates a large gap between policy and practice in that 'whilst it is the official goal of social policy to encourage nursing at home and to stop the trend towards institutionalisation, institutions receive full cost-coverage and ambulant services do not' (p. 115). The lack of mainstream home, day and respite care services 'can mean unnecessary institutional care for those without family carers' (Tester, 1994, p. 260).

Following widespread public debate, major reforms of the German health insurance scheme were introduced in 1993, covering the risk of needing long-term community-based care:

People in need of long-term domiciliary care are assessed and allocated to a hierarchy of need categories. These entitle them to choose between payments for care . . . and services in kind . . . bought on their behalf by the insurance funds. . . The monetary value of the hours of help is greater than the alternative cash payment so as to discourage misuse of funds. (Baldock and Ely, 1996, p. 211)

This scheme is expected to become fully operational by the year 2000.

It is of interest to note that Denmark, with its emphasis on universality, prevention and the protection of living standards, core characteristics of social democratic social policy, has had a comparatively high rate of institutional care for older people in the European Union – 14.7 per cent of the 75-plus age group (Walker, 1992) – although this is the lowest volume for the four Nordic countries (Daatland, 1992). The principle of universality covers both health and social care (unlike the case of Germany) and is based on citizenship rather than insurance rights. The services are both financed and provided by the public sector, leaving the voluntary sector to provide advocacy and act as pressure groups. The home help service has been merged with domiciliary health care to overcome the conflicts between health and social care staff (Walker and Maltby, 1997, p. 94).

In the 1960s, both domiciliary and residential care services for older people were expanded, and there was no intention to replace institutional care. Rather, the range of services was to relieve families of the caring rôle and attempt to improve the quality of life for older people. However, in the 1980s there was a growing critique of institutional care, which resulted in major legislative reform in 1987. In brief, the principle underpinning the legislation was that the care available to people should not be linked to the kind of accommodation they were living in:

There is no longer to be a dichotomy between nursing homes/ residential homes on the one hand, and home care on the other. . . In short, the concept of nursing homes has been abolished by law. In practice this means that no new nursing homes can be built. From now on there are only to be elderly dwellings. (Jamieson, 1991, p. 119)

The point of the reform was that every older person, whatever kind of care he or she needs, has the right to independent housing and care according to his/her needs. Just as the radical mental health legislation in Italy ran into implementation problems, so the impact of these legal changes was affected by professional resistance, local politics and the economic disruption caused by the recession (Abrahamson, 1991b, p. 56).

The mixed economy of welfare

Evers and Olk (1991, p. 77) point to the useful distinction between the terms 'welfare mix' and 'welfare pluralism'. The former refers to the empirical issue of the proportion of investment in goods and services provided by the state, by the not-for-profit sector, by the private-profit making sector and by the informal sector. In this respect, all welfare states have a mix of this kind, though the proportions may vary between them and over time (Baldock, 1993) and the degree of interaction between the sectors is also likely to differ. The latter term, 'welfare pluralism', addresses the issue of the *preferred* mix in the mixed economy of welfare. What are the values that lie behind the recent arguments about the mixed economy of welfare? Chapter 3 outlined how proponents of welfare pluralism were claiming that the perceived predominance of the state sector was unsatisfactory and that the voluntary, commercial and informal sectors should have a greater rôle. It is now recognised that, in all welfare regimes, the informal sector has played the dominant, albeit often invisible, rôle (Tester, 1996, p. 8). In the *rudimentary* welfare states, the case is being made for increased state support in response to the changes in society affecting the capability of family and local community to provide the level of care taken for granted in the past. In addition, the amount of community-based care is increasing to fill the gap.

In the *modern* welfare state, the argument is for increasing the rôle of the non-statutory sector, although not necessarily taken as far as the 'compulsory voluntarism' suggested by the Swedish Secretariat for Future Studies who put forward the idea of community care conscription along the lines of military conscription (quoted in N. Johnson, 1987, p. 58). For Denmark, Abrahamson (1991b) argues for what he calls new concepts in social policy, which for disabled and elderly people would mean 'they should have the opportunity – to a much greater degree than beforehand – to purchase services on the market (privatization); to be serviced by a neighbourhood activity center (decentralization); and to be encouraged to obtain help from voluntary and self-help institutions (de-professionalization)' (p. 49).

In the corporatist social policy context, the notion of the mixed economy of welfare has been central to the ideology of the *institutional* welfare state, embedded as it is in the principle of subsidiarity in which non-state institutions play a constitutionally independent rôle, even where there is extensive support from the public sector. This traditional rôle of the voluntary sector is being challenged by both new-style, that is radical, non-profit-making and private sector initiatives, which include, for example, the development in Germany of profit-oriented home nursing and of family-type care for frail older people who have no families of their own (Dieck, 1990). In the 1990s, legislation has been put forward to underpin long-term care for vulnerable older people through extending the coverage of health insurance so that 'for the first time in the history of care policy, health insurance funding had been extended to care services' (Dieck, 1994, p. 260). In their commentary on new welfare mixes for elderly people in Germany, Evers and Olk (1991, pp. 78–9) argue for

a changing welfare mix in care services which allows for more pluralism of organisations and concepts on the side of the providers, more individual arrangements on the side of the users, and more specific help and general support for them in making their decisions on both how to share their own contributions and how to use services . . . this leaves the state less impact as a provider but more for its regulative and redistributive rôle, in order to enable it to balance the new potentials for individual choice and participation with the need of guaranteeing basically equal rights in care and access to the system.

In order to achieve this new kind of mix, new forms of networking and co-ordination are required, both of a top-down kind to integrate strategies and a bottom-up kind to facilitate packages of services influenced by user and carer preferences. Collaboration and the rôles of the service user and carer are the concern of the next two sections of this chapter.

Collaboration

Problems of collaboration and co-operation between health services and community social services are a central theme in accounts of home care almost everywhere. (Baldock and Ely, 1996, p. 198)

In her review of community care developments for older people in France, Germany, Italy, the Netherlands, the United Kingdom and the United States, Tester (1996) concluded that, whilst the need for better co-ordination was widely recognised, implementation was equally widely inhibited:

> Despite the policy initiatives and processes implemented to promote co-ordination, there is little evidence that co-ordinated community care has been achieved. Reports of poor co-ordination, gaps and overlaps in services and lack of information in the countries studied continued to appear in the early 1990s. (p. 170)

One of those reports was by Alber, Guillemard and Walker (1991) who highlighted the problem of fragmentation of responsibility for providing community care services. They argued that 'there seems to be insufficient co-operation between the nursing and social support staff of the community services supplied by the various associations and the local government social workers, or between nursing, social support and the other personnel within the community services' (p. 40). They pointed to differing systems of finance and administration for health and social care in different countries and concluded that, 'since community care for persons living in private households often requires the co-ordination of services provided by various public and voluntary agencies, whereas residential care provides most services under one common organisational roof, there continues to be an administrative incentive to admit elderly people to residential care' (p. 37).

This problem appears to be less acute in Denmark, where all home care services are organised by the local authority and where the modern welfare state principle of universality implies comprehensive provision based on citizenship rather than insurance rights. However, problems remain over the co-ordination between hospitals and primary health care and social services since 'the separation of the community care budget (the communes) from the hospital budget (the county) hardly provides any financial incentive for the communes to take over patients ready for discharge from hospital as early as possible' (Holstein *et al.*, 1991, p. 60).

The principle of subsidiarity in the context of corporatist social policy requires partnership between the statutory and the non-statutory sectors, but the diversity of local supply, which is intended to offer choice of services to the individual, does not usually promote collaborative endeavour. In Germany, there may be close links between the state and the non-statutory welfare agencies over matters such as finance and the law but the fragmentation of responsibility for service delivery makes effective co-operation to support particular individuals problematic. Alber (1991) complained that 'although the goal of expanding the supply of ambulatory services was successfully promoted, the plurality of religious, secular and public . . . agencies and the dominance of professional nurses rather than social workers and volunteers within the services still bring forth serious problems of co-ordination in planning and implementation' (p. 31). Tester identified serious obstacles to co-ordinated community care 'in the strong divisions in organisation and funding between hospital and ambulatory services, health and social care' (1996, p. 179).

In the rudimentary welfare state of Spain one of the key concerns has been the co-ordination of the public and private sectors in providing personal social services. The rôle of the public sector increased after the end of the Franco regime but economic difficulties have since led to demands for reductions in public expenditure plus a more flexible, less bureaucratic management style. The outcome has been a very uneven distribution of supply with traditionally provided services not being linked to more recent developments, particularly for specific groups of people (Rossell and Rimbau, 1989, pp. 118–19).

One of the responses to the lack of collaboration because of the variety of providers and funding arrangements has been the attempt to introduce case (or care) management. The UK experience is addressed elsewhere in this book (see Chapter 5) but it is worth noting that one of the main conclusions of a comparative study of innovations in care in the Netherlands, Sweden and England and Wales was the need to invest in the management of care.

> [The] central issue and problem is one of management – the intelligent, consistent, informed organisation of care. . . This problem of management exists at two levels: the level of the individual client and the level of the care system as a whole. . . It is no accident that case management at the level of the individual client is more developed in the United Kingdom. It is a solution of later resort, typical of systems where resources are in chronically short supply. (Baldock and Evers, 1991, pp. 193, 196)

It was this pressure to make effective use of scarce resources in an ideological context of consumer choice that made the idea of case management as developed in the United States attractive to the British government struggling to pursue a coherent policy and practice on community care. Residual welfare state systems were perhaps influencing each other's liberal social policies, though with increasing pressures on public expenditure in the late 1980s and early 1990s countries like the Netherlands and France were beginning to undertake case management experiments or at least to debate the means of integrating social care services. Baldock and Ely (1996) conclude that the provision of social care is in practice inherently complex and call it the 'paradox of complex mundaneity' (pp. 202–3), or, less grandly, the complexity of everyday life. In particular, the unpredictability of need at the individual level distinguishes people with mental health problems and frail elderly people on the one hand from people with learning difficulties and physically disabled people on the other.

User empowerment

The notion of 'consumer choice' underlies the debate about empowerment in the residual welfare state. The individual consumer can 'exit' by choosing an alternative source of supply rather than attempt to influence that source of supply by 'voice' or engagement in the process of planning, resourcing, managing and delivering services (see Chapter 4). Empowerment is a slippery term, but it does connote more than the provision of information to allow individuals to exercise choice. It is to do with involvement, with active participation, co-decision-making or even control. In some circumstances, the difficulties faced by frail individuals require the presence of an advocate. Alber, Guillemard and Walker (1991, p. 42), for instance, suggest in their European Observatory report that there should be an elected ombudsman of frail older people on the administrative boards of community care agencies. Whilst family and neighbourly care remain central to the support of frail older people in Greece, the government has provided funding for the development of open-access day centres (KAPI), which provide health and social care as well as being community centres mainly in urban areas. There were 278 of these opened by 1994 (Millar and Warman, 1996). They are administered by a council of representatives from the local municipality, local citizens, and older people themselves (Amira, 1990), and so in principle older people have a say in the running of the centres. However, the centres tend to cater for the less frail, and those who are homebound are not well served through this initiative (Ziomas, 1991, p. 75; Hugman, 1994, pp. 163–6).

Turning to the corporatist social policy of the institutional welfare state, Evers and Olk (1991) have concluded that for elderly people in Germany there was a strong dominance of producers' over consumers' interests and power. However, they have contrasted this with the debate held by organisations of disabled people who have argued that the power of decision-making should be turned upside down to create a user-centred culture of care. In addition, the 'exit' rather than 'voice' strategy was introduced for certain categories of very dependent elderly people living in their homes under reforms initiated in 1989 and 1991. 'Since 1991, those in need of extensive or intensive care who live at home can choose either 25 hours of professional care per month, not exceeding the value of DM 750, or DM 400 in cash, usually for care provided by relatives' (p. 73). As already noted in relation to the 1993 health insurance scheme, the cash total is less than the maximum value of professional care that can be secured to avoid the misuse of funds. This level of difference has taken on greater significance because of the influence of disabled people who are beginning to assert that 'they know best how to use money for help and care services; they therefore opt for a system which is based on attendance allowances granted to the elderly and to people with disabilities in need of care' (p. 81). For frail, older people and others who could face difficulties in deciding between care or cash, and in deciding what to purchase if the cash option is preferred, the development of independent non-profit-making advocacy and advice centres has been an important innovation in Germany. Baldock and Ely (1996) report that many more people are choosing to receive monthly payments than are accepting the higher value service in kind (p. 213).

The debate on empowerment has been muted in modern welfare states like Denmark and Sweden. Because access to both benefits and services is open to all as a citizen's right, most provision is not seen as stigmatising and is not conditional upon insurance contributions. The main rôle of pensioners' organisations has been to demand the right to negotiate the amount of pensions and to struggle against the exclusion by professionals of, for instance, elderly people participating in decision-making in domiciliary or institutional care (Jamieson, 1990b, p. 13). Sixty-five per cent of homes for elderly people had residents' councils as long ago as 1965 (Munday, 1996, p. 35). An attempt to form a Grey Panthers party in Denmark in 1989 came to nothing.

The reason for the lack of political movement among . . . older people might be ascribed to the fact that the existing political parties all give high priority to old age issues. And another explanation might be that the income of . . . pensioners has grown more than income in general during the last decade. (Bertelsen and Platz, 1991, para.5.6)

However, Walker and Maltby (1997) report that in Denmark a recently formed pressure group called the 'C Team' has called for mass protests in Copenhagen to try to stop proposed cuts in social care for elderly people.

Whilst the 1992 Eurobarometer Survey reported very low levels of involvement in political or pressure group activities, Wilson (1993) has argued that the ageing of the electorate across the EU (and beyond) could increase the pressures on politicians and policy makers to adjust policies even if there is no sign of the development of a powerful elderly voting bloc. In particular, older women, who will by the year 2020 make up between 26 and 29 per cent of the electorate in fourteen of the fifteen EU countries (Ireland will be the exception), could have an increasing influence on the social policy debate, not least if they combined with younger women to improve the situation of both service users and care givers.

The institutions of the European Union and policy

Examination of certain features of community care policy in a selection of Western European countries may throw some light on our domestic concerns in the UK. But the European Union itself, as a supranational institution, is also not without influence on the policies of the member states. The second part of this chapter therefore examines the impact of European Union policies and practices on community care strategies in the UK. It begins with a brief description of the institutions of the EU and the process of policy-making, and then examines the impact of its policies for older people, for disabled people and for the providers of community care.

In one sentence, the EU policy process can be summarised as 'The Commission proposes; the Council of Ministers disposes.' Needless to say, it is rather more complicated than that. However, the Commission, the civil service or executive arm of the EU, is the body that has the duty to initiate legislation, amongst its other responsibilities. It is not a large bureaucracy, having about 18,350 operational staff in all, of whom 1,700 are language staff (Watson, 1996, p. 18). It is divided into twenty-four directorates, covering a range of policy areas, such as agriculture, transport, energy, regional policy and the environment. Directorate-General V covers social and employment issues and is therefore the part of the Commission most closely associated with social and community care.

Policy proposals are developed within, and sometimes between, the directorates of the Commission and, usually after much debate, are formally presented to the twenty Commissioners. Once a policy proposal is approved by the Commissioners by a simple majority vote it is forwarded to the Council of Ministers for consideration. The Council of Ministers is made up of ministers from member state governments, with the actual composition of the Council depending on the subject under discussion. When a proposal arrives from the Commission, it is passed on to the Committee of the Permanent Representatives of the Member States (COREPER). This comprises civil servants from the governments of the fifteen member states and one of their key tasks is to take an initial close scrutiny of the proposal forwarded from the Commission.

As well as forwarding proposals to the Council of Ministers, the Commission sends them to the European Parliament. In 1997, the Parliament comprised 626 members from all fifteen member states, 87 of them from the UK. Unlike Westminster, the European Parliament does not propose and pass legislation; rather, it examines and debates the proposals and passes opinions. The mechanism for doing this is by consideration in one of the committees of the Parliament which broadly reflect the Directorates-General of the Commission. The committees are in turn supported by a secretariat, paid officials of the Parliament, who undertake the detailed work. Typically, one MEP from the committee is nominated as a rapporteur to produce a draft report. When this has been approved by the committee, it goes to the full Parliament for debate, adoption or rejection. Its opinion is then communicated to the Council of Ministers. The Parliament also has about 50 inter-groups. These comprise interested members of the European Parliament from different political parties who examine particular issues in great detail, including ageing, disabled people and the family.

The opinions of the European Parliament are considered by both COREPER and the secretariat to the Council of Ministers and a common position is adopted either at official level or, in areas of major difficulty, by the appropriate Council of Ministers. For some policy issues the European Parliament gets a second chance to comment on the proposed legislation, but the final decision is that of the Council of Ministers, which formally adopts the legislation. The outcome is published in the *Official Journal of the European Communities*. The legislation can take different forms. A regulation applies directly from the day it comes into force; a directive requires domestic legislation in member states if appropriate legislation does not already exist; decisions usually apply to specific problems rather than to the EU as a whole, and are binding on those to whom they are addressed. Where there is a failure to agree on legislation in the Council of Ministers, a recommendation or an opinion may emerge. These have no legislative force, though they are not necessarily without influence. Some legislative proposals can be adopted by a majority vote (known as qualified majority voting) with voting weighted according to the population of the member state; other legislation requires unanimity.

The formal process of policy-making has been described, but the informal processes are just as important. First of all, the Commission officials do not just sit behind their desks in Brussels and think up new legislation. They are lobbied from every quarter, including other institutions of the EU, such as the Council of Ministers who can ask them to focus their minds on a particular issue, or the European Parliament which can issue its own views on subjects as well as pass opinions on draft legislation. The Commission follows the progress of legislation through the system very closely and is in frequent contact with COREPER working groups. Meanwhile, it is lobbied by a wide range of interests. Individual members of the European Parliament may press for meetings to be arranged with delegations from a particular region or a particular sector of industry. A substantial number of regional and local authorities have opened offices in Brussels to be able to hear about and influence the policy debate at very early stages, even before a directive is initially drafted within the Commission.

As well as regional authorities and industrial interests, voluntary organisations have also developed a lobbying base in Brussels, some focusing on environmental or consumer issues and others on the 'social dimension' of the European Union. Examples include COFACE (Confederation of Family Organisations in the European Community), Eurolink Age, European Women's Lobby and the European Anti-Poverty Network. They have been prominent in pressing for EU recognition of the massive social implications of its agricultural, economic and industrial policies, and for implementation in member states of EU legislation on equal pay and equal opportunities.

Against this backcloth of the main institutions of the EU, the policy process and the way interest groups have organised to influence legislative outcomes, we can now turn to the impact of EU policies, practices and procedures on community care in the UK.

The impact of EU policies on community care

Much of social policy is seen as a domestic issue for individual member states of the European Union, as the legal base for intervention by the EU is very restricted. 'Adherence to (the) policy of subsidiarity has made the EC reluctant to override national sovereignty by introducing any radical action in the social field' (Swithinbank, 1991, p. 4). The Commission tends to limit its rôle to the encouragement of convergence of different member state policies, information exchange, support for innovation, the designation of special years and good practice through networking and co-funding of cross-national projects.

The EU focus has in the main been on economic, industrial and trade policies. It does, however, recognise that strategies such as the completion of the internal market, the free movement of goods, services, capital and labour and other measures of economic integration do cause problems for particular regions or particular groups of people. Discriminatory effects are addressed, though perhaps not adequately, by special support for disadvantaged regions and by special measures to help groups such as disabled people, migrant workers and women to secure employment in the open labour market (Swithinbank, 1996, p. 68).

This was particularly reflected in the 1994 White Paper on European social policy (European Commission, 1994). It recognised the adverse consequences of competing more effectively in the global market and called for an 'active society for all'. But it did not lay out a specific programme of action, apart from reaffirming existing programmes addressing problems of urban and rural deprivation and marginalisation of groups in the population, such as disabled people (see below) and promising further targeted action to tackle poverty.

This action has been blocked by Germany with tacit support from other member states, including the UK, on the grounds that anti-poverty strategies should be seen as a domestic rather than a European concern. The European Commission has, as a consequence, used one of the strands of its Employment Community Initiative to address problems of disadvantage, at least in the labour market. Between

1994 and 1997, the HORIZON programme supported transnational projects to improve the employment possibilities of disabled people and other disadvantaged groups. For the 1997–9 period, the HORIZON programme has focused solely on disabled people (see below), and a new programme, INTEGRA, was introduced to provide financial support for innovative projects aimed at improving access to jobs or to (pre) vocational training schemes.

The 1994 White Paper was followed in April 1995 by another three-year Social Action Programme which had little by way of legislative proposals and rather more by way of studies and debates. One of the debates was the first European Social Policy Forum held in March 1996 in Brussels and attended by over a thousand people from the voluntary sector, academe, professional interests and the social partners. The key themes were employment, equal opportunities, the future of working life and social protection. The main feature of this Forum was the presentation of a report by the Comité des Sages which, *inter alia*, argued for a Bill of Rights to be included in the revision of the EU Treaty following the 1996–7 Intergovernmental Conference, including a right not to be discriminated against. An anti-discrimination clause was included in the revised Treaty signed in Amsterdam in October 1997. However, the proposal to permit programmes targeted at older and disabled people to be established through qualified majority voting was removed, yet again at the insistence of Germany, from the draft text of the Amsterdam Treaty. Commentators have suggested that these two decisions conflict with each other:

> While member states seem to have ruled out taking any positive action to help the physically impaired, the treaty boasts a brand new 'anti-discrimination' clause which specifically mentions both the disabled and the elderly. (Coss, 1997)

Whilst there was no direct reference in the 1994 White Paper, in the three-year programme, the report of the Comité des Sages or the Treaty of Amsterdam to social care services, the EU has over time nevertheless made an impact. The following sections look at a range of EU policies affecting older people, disabled people and the providers of community care.

Older people

The Social Charter, adopted by all member states, except the UK, in December 1989 referred to the rights of workers rather than citizens.

From this perspective, it asserted that elderly people, at the time of retirement, should have resources sufficient to provide a decent standard of living, as well as medical and social assistance suited to their needs. Retirement pensions are thus seen as deferred income, so the quality of life for older people did become a concern of the European Union. A three-year EU social action programme for older people was launched at a conference in Brussels in September 1991, with the aim of encouraging the transfer between member states of knowledge, ideas and experience on ageing and elderly people. It included the creation in 1992 of an Observatory on Ageing and Older People, which was charged to focus on four areas:

> living standards and way of life, employment and the labour market, health and social care, and the social integration of older people in both formal and informal settings. (Walker, 1993, p. 9)

The work of this Observatory and the results of two 1992 Eurobarometer Surveys (see earlier in this chapter) have been usefully brought together by Walker and Maltby (1997). The main social care issues highlighted by the Observatory included:

- consensus that community care was the most appropriate policy for older people;
- overall severe under-supply of community care services;
- need for new incentives for the development of community care. (Walker and Maltby, 1997, p. 91)

Most member states of the EU supported the inclusion of the ideas outlined in the 1989 Social Charter, including the protection of pensioners, in the provisions of the Maastricht Treaty formally signed in 1992. However, the UK government objected to the notion that social affairs could be agreed by qualified majority voting rather than unanimity, and so the then eleven other EU countries agreed to a social policy protocol appended to but not officially part of the Maastricht Treaty. The UK Labour government elected in 1997 is committed to signing up to the Social Chapter so that it can be incorporated into the Treaty arrangements underpinning the EU.

In March 1992 a European Seniors Parliament was held in Luxembourg with representatives from all twelve member states. A European Senior Citizens Charter was voted through, which emphasised the rights, individual and social, of older people.

It further stresses the rights to dignity, autonomy and security of income; to housing; to safe environments; to residential, health and community services; the right to pursue leisure, cultural and educational activities and to responsible citizenship through effective participation in decision-making processes. (Walker and Maltby, 1997, p. 114)

The 1991–3 social action programme culminated in the designation of 1993 as European Year of Older People and Solidarity between the Generations. The emphasis was on the contribution that older people make to the community, and the healthy and active life enjoyed by most older people, rather than focusing on the need of some for care and support.

In the same year, the European Commission (1993) published a Green Paper on future options for European social policy. As well as commenting on the financial challenges to the level of official welfare support that would be provided, it also noted the demographic pressures resulting from an increasing number of older people relying on the support of a shrinking number of economically active people. The ensuing White Paper (see above) further emphasised the importance of economic wellbeing for underpinning state support of welfare services. 'Levels of spending on social protection and social services will be affected by countries' costs of addressing the unemployment problem' (Munday, 1996, p. 27). The strategy for tackling unemployment has remained high on the European agenda and EU policies for older people have not progressed as much as their advocates hoped. However, the lobbying has continued.

The European Parliament formed an Intergroup on Ageing, which meets about four times a year and is serviced by the transnational interest group on behalf of older people, Eurolink Age, which was formed in 1981. The Parliament has pressed the Commission to put forward, through the social action programme that followed the acceptance (except by the UK) of the Social Charter, 'specific solutions at Community level' to challenges posed by an ageing population. Citing the Treaty of Rome provision to improve the living conditions of European Community citizens, the European Parliament called for a directive on the right to home care and better provision of home help and health care.

The main concerns of the Intergroup in the current Parliament (elected in 1994) have been the age limits in recruitment to EU institutions, issues faced by older women, the place of older people in the 1996 European Year of Lifelong Learning and the 1997 European Year Against Racism, Xenophobia and Anti-Semitism, the continued blockage of a new social action programme on older people, the organisation of a second European Seniors Parliament in the autumn of 1998 and the inclusion of age in the anti-discrimination clause in the revised EU Treaty formally signed in Amsterdam in October 1997. (At the time of writing, this Treaty awaits ratification by individual member states, by no means a forgone conclusion.)

There has been growing awareness in the last decade that the community care implications of completing the single market could be far-reaching. Chapman (1989) argued that the removal of trade barriers in 1992 would create an internal market for social services as well as in industry and commerce. She pointed out that 'some home care organisations are looking at the potential of expanding their services across national boundaries' and 'sources of funding are expected to change as the market for home care opens up' (p. 19). Munday (1996) describes the creation of a Danish social care export/consultation agency called DANSOC: 'The agency existed to make Danish expertise and excellence in child care and services for disabled and elderly people available to interested organisations in other countries' (p. 35).

There are also possible community care implications of international retirement migration, particularly to the coastal areas of Portugal and Spain (Williams, King and Warnes, 1997). Over the years these elderly migrants will grow 'increasingly frail and dependent in a situation where there is little established structure for collaboration in the personal social services field' (Bongers, 1990, p. 58). What is likely to happen?

> When, for example, older people from Northern Europe migrate to the south but then fall ill, will they be flown back to their countries of origin as soon as their personal resources run out, or their demands on personal and health services intensify, in a sort of new law of settlement? Or will Member States develop schemes for charging the country of origin for such care? (Room, 1991, p. 4)

Alternatively, might social services agencies combine to establish care services in these retirement areas, or offer consultancy services to the care authorities in these localities? A vivid picture of the language problems faced by older British migrants on the Costa del Sol is provided by Betty (1997). The 1992 Eurobarometer Survey reported that a quarter of older people wanted information about services, benefits and facilities available in EU countries other than their own (Walker and Maltby, 1997, p. 119).

The 1993 European Year of Older People and Solidarity between the Generations covered an enormously wide range of activities and was reported as having been very successful, even though only one in ten adults surveyed in the UK in February 1994 said they had been aware of the Year (Department of Health, 1995e). A five-year follow-on programme was proposed by the Commission and the scope was broadened to cover not only active elderly people but also those approaching retirement and the very old. However, this programme had by the middle of 1997 still not been implemented as the UK government had challenged the legality of European Commission spending on these kinds of activities and the European Court of Justice's final judgement was not expected until well into 1998. (An interim ruling supported the case brought by the UK government.) Meanwhile, the Commission is preparing a document on older people's issues in the medium to long term, which is due for publication in 1998 in time for the second European Social Policy Forum and the European Seniors' Parliament. It is likely to form part of the Commission's strategy towards the UN International Year of Older Persons in 1999.

Despite the block on the programme following the 1993 year, funds have been made available (i) to support the exchange of information and best practice in relation to people suffering from Alzheimer's disease and their carers; (ii) to underpin the transnational activities of charitable bodies and non-governmental organisations dealing with the interests of elderly people; and (iii) to fund pilot projects for the development of rehabilitation technology to help elderly and disabled people (known as TIDE).

Disabled people

The first action programme to promote the social integration of disabled people was a response to the 1981 International Year of Disabled People and ran from 1984 to 1987. A Bureau for Action in Favour of the Disabled was established in Directorate-General V (Social Affairs) of the Commission. One of the main features of this programme was to create a network of local projects across the Community, funded 50 per cent from the European Social Fund. The second action programme aimed at both vocational and social integration and independent living. It was called HELIOS (Handicapped People in the European Community Living Independently in an Open Society) and ran from 1988 to 1992. The programme covered a large number of initiatives and outlined key policy guidelines. General initiatives included (i) further development of HANDYNET, a multi-national, multilingual computerised database of information on disability questions; (ii) a focus on occupational rehabilitation of disabled women; and (iii) encouragement of integration of disabled people in mainstream education. In 1993 a European Disabled People's Parliament was held to mark the first European Day of Disabled Persons. One of the resolutions was a call for a general anti-discrimination clause to be included in any amendment to the Treaty on European Union.

A third programme, called HELIOS II, ran between 1993 and 1996 and comprised four themes, which built on earlier programmes: social integration and independent living; functional rehabilitation and economic integration; vocational training and employment rehabilitation; and educational integration. The modest funds were to support transnational conferences, visits and training. It also introduced the idea of a European Disability Forum, and the unit in the European Commission responsible for disabled people changed its name from Measures for the Disabled to Integration of the Disabled (Hantrais, 1995, p. 126). The 1994 Social Policy White Paper reinforced the theme of integration and suggested that measures should be brought in to counter discrimination against disabled people in the labour market. The argument is summarised in Waddington (1997).

Organisations of disabled people were critical of the third HELIOS programme (Wilson, 1996, p. 186). The proposed European Disability Forum first met in March 1997 and one of its key priorities was to press for a clause on non-discrimination in the revised EU Treaty. This aim was achieved, as noted earlier. The possibility of an Observatory on disability issues is also on the agenda.

In 1990, the European Community formally agreed three new crossnational grant aid initiatives to improve education and training facilities and to provide new employment opportunities. One of these initiatives, called HORIZON, was aimed at people with physical or mental disabilities, those who work with them, and other disadvantaged individuals. As well as focusing on employment issues, including long-term unemployed people or 'women returners' to the labour market becoming carers of older, frail people, the programme covered the adaptation of public infrastructure to improve access and mobility. Funding for the HORIZON programme (1990 to 1993) amounted to

180 million ecus. For the 1992–3 period (known as HORIZON II) one-third of the funds was reserved for projects linked to disabled people, a reduced emphasis compared with the earlier years of the programme. In 1994 the HORIZON programme was subsumed under a broad employment/human resources initiative and 730 million ecus was allocated for the 1994–9 period to support two main kinds of activities: improving the quality of training and creating jobs through new types of work organisation for both disabled and disadvantaged people. At least half of the resources was reserved for projects involving disabled people. The UK was allocated just over 60 million ecus and the programme was formally approved in the late summer of 1995. Sixty-five per cent of funds were to be allocated to projects involving people with disabilities (Harris, 1995, p. 35). In July 1996 the European Commission published revised guidelines for Community Initiatives to cover the 1997–9 period. One of the proposals was to separate support for disadvantaged people from support for disabled people. The latter were still covered by the HORIZON initiative and the emphasis on training and job creation remained. The UK budget for this three-year period was just over 20 million ecus.

Providing care in the community

The focus so far has been on groups in the population likely to be users of community care. EU policies also impinge on the providers of care, as the emphasis on the single market and labour market issues would lead one to expect. The completion of the single market, embodying the principle of freedom of movement of people and services, provides opportunities for businesses, voluntary bodies and self-employed individuals from mainland Europe to establish services in the social care field, including community care. It also offers opportunities for statutory, voluntary and private sector community care providers to export their expertise to continental Europe.

> Organisations which have been established by local authorities at arm's length, such as housing trusts, training agencies or occupational therapy and other bureaux, may wish to expand into the European market. (Swithinbank, 1996, p. 76)

On the labour market side, UK doctors and nurses have since 1977 and 1979, respectively, been able to work in any member state of the EU, provided they have the appropriate language skills and are prepared to undertake some locally based training. This has not led to major cross-boundary migrations, but the implications are clear. Skills shortages in community health services could be overcome by a recruitment campaign in other member states, while health workers unable to find suitable jobs after completing their training in the UK may look for work elsewhere. On a sceptical note, richer member states may attract workers trained in poorer member states, since 'partners may very easily become poachers' (Harris and Lavan, 1992, p. 13). The legislation on the mutual recognition of professional qualifications came into force in January 1991. Rather than looking at each individual profession, a long and laborious process, the position was adopted that a qualification based on three or more years' study at higher education level (whatever that means) in one member state has to be recognised in all member states. This is not without its problems, not least for social work, since expectations of relevant language skills and training in local procedures remain. It has been reported that small but significant numbers of social workers have moved from France, Germany and the Netherlands to work in the UK (Hill, 1991).

Concern has been expressed in the UK that (i) social work has no formal regulatory body as required by the mutual recognition directive; and (ii) the professional qualification does not fit the three-year criterion. However, in June 1992 a second directive on the mutual recognition of qualifications was adopted. This covered post-secondary level diplomas or certificates gained after a period of less than three years and also applied to people without qualifications but with relevant professional experience. UK social workers wanting to work in mainland Europe have been advised to 'keep note of the courses, assessed work and placements they successfully completed during training and they should even gather their course material, reports and references together into a portfolio' (Lyons, 1992, p. iii). As with doctors and nurses, major cross-boundary moves are not anticipated, but there is an oversupply of social workers in some member states, and private, voluntary or statutory sector providers of community care in the UK could decide to mount a recruitment campaign, if they were severely understaffed and had the resources to recruit. Recruiters would need to develop some understanding of the training and professional qualifications in social care, social work and social assistance in other member states of the European Union. Likewise, welfare rights advisers need to recognise that people who move between EU countries carry their entitlements with them based on their contributions to the country of origin's social security system.

Over the years the European Union has also been concerned to develop an equal opportunities programme, with the primary aim of countering discrimination in the labour market, though with a much greater emphasis on sex equality than race equality (see Buckley and Anderson, 1988; Meehan and Whitting, 1989). The designation of 1997 as the European Year Against Racism, Xenophobia and Anti-Semitism may begin to redress this imbalance. EU legislation has covered equal pay for equal work, equal access to employment and training, equal treatment in pensions and social security schemes and for self-employed women, and prohibition of discrimination at work. One British case, with implications for community care, was the European Court of Justice decision that married women should receive the same payments as other people for caring for severely disabled people. Previously, they had not been eligible.

The NOW strand of the Employment Community Initiative (New Opportunities for Women) is intended to encourage women to enter or re-enter the formal labour market either by finding a job (probably after training) or by setting up a small business. All projects have to have transnational partners. Swithinbank (1996, p. 84) reports that social services have used the NOW programme to retrain traditional care workers or heads of residential homes to become care managers or managers of new business-style enterprises.

Many of the proposals in the EU 1995–7 social action programme were uncontroversial, particularly in the field of health and safety at work. However, some of the proposals on working hours or those that affected part-time or temporary workers were resisted by the Conservative government in the UK. The implications of the UK Labour government's acceptance of the Social Chapter are not inconsiderable for the delivery of community care:

> European legislation has included a minimum daily rest period (eleven hours), a maximum working week (forty-eight hours), a ban on individuals working two consecutive shifts, a ban on night work for people under the age of eighteen and pregnant women, and a maximum working night time of eighteen hours. As social care work requires people to provide round-the-clock cover, social services agencies will have to ensure adequate rest periods and limited hours. This applies especially to residential care staff, after-hours and emergency staff cover and attendance at evening meetings. Any junior staff or pregnant women will be unable to provide night care or be on call. Social services departments in Britain will need to

ensure that contracted private and voluntary residential homes abide by these requirements. (Swithinbank, 1996, p. 74)

One of the features of the Social Chapter is to bring opportunities for non-casual part-time workers into line with those of full-time workers. By 1999 this agreement on part-time work will be applied in Britain. It has been calculated that it will affect half a million people who work part-time in social services departments and nearly 300,000 working part-time in the independent social care sector. Most of those affected are women. However, it does not apply to the large numbers of agency staff used by local authorities or in the independent sector (Thompson, 1997).

Finally, the 1977 acquired rights directive may well have major implications for the transfer of staff from one employer to another, for instance from a local authority to a company responsible for the provision of community care. This directive overrules any domestic legislation with which it is in conflict. There has been some uncertainty whether the directive and Britain's Transfer of Undertakings (Protection of Employment) Regulations 1981 (TUPE) applied, for instance, to compulsory competitive tendering, which, it has been argued, tended to cut the terms and conditions of local authority workers. In February 1997, the European Commission issued a revised proposal to amend the 1977 directive in which it was made clear that the proposed directive would apply to both private and public undertakings. One leading local authority lawyer said, in the light of recent judgements by the European Court of Justice, that one 'might be forgiven for thinking that EU law on transfers of undertakings seems to have the steadiness of a weather-vane' (Dobson, 1996). Rose and Cooke (1997a, 1997b) concluded that contractors have little guidance on how to bid for contracts, local authorities have a difficult choice to make on how to advertise for tenders and employees do not know for how long their jobs are secure. They called for legislation to clear up the confusion and in the summer of 1997 the new Labour government announced a major review of TUPE led by the Department of Trade and Industry.

Concluding comments

The impact of EU policies on community care developments in the UK has been in the main indirect and, where direct, modest. What is unambiguous is the increased investment by the European Union in social policy issues in recent years. There is major concern for the social integration of people seen to have special needs. The implications of moves towards the completion of the internal market have highlighted the social responses needed to address likely problems of dislocation. The debate on political union has brought into focus the position of residents, not only of workers in the European Union. External migratory pressures demand a social policy as well as a border control response. The increasing rôle of women in the formal labour market has added considerably to the force of the argument that the European Union is much more than a common market. The European Charter of Fundamental Social Rights refers to older people, people with disabilities and women among its concerns and these references have not diminished in more recent debate, despite the application of the principle of subsidiarity.

This internationalisation of the policy debate may not lead to a high proportion of social (as opposed to economic) legislation being of EU origin, but it will enable campaigners and policy-makers in the UK to become more aware and make use of illuminating policies, practices and procedures in community care in other countries.

9 Community Care: Achievements, Failures and Challenges for the Future

The community care reforms outlined in the 1990 Act have been in operation since April 1993. It might be expected, therefore, that it is possible to come to clear conclusions about their impact upon the quality and range of services available at the local level and how this relates to the emphasis of the reforms on stimulating a quasi-market in social care.

Bartlett and Le Grand (1993) have argued that such quasi-markets should be judged in terms of the extent to which they do or do not encourage efficiency, responsiveness, choice and equity in terms of their impact upon service users. However, Chapter 1 of this book indicated that a growing number of authors were highly critical of the reforms as having created 'care in chaos' (Hadley and Clough, 1996) and, as such, these authors can be interpreted as dismissing them as inefficient, unresponsive, offering no choice and inequitable. However, even if their pessimism is justified at this present point in time, such apparent policy failure is open to numerous interpretations in terms of the arguments for and against introducing markets into social care:

- the reforms ushered in a system which was no better, and possibly worse, than the previous more bureaucratic systems of resource allocation;
- the reforms were an excellent idea, but they received little understanding or commitment from social services as the lead agency in community care;
- the missionary zeal of the local authority was undermined by vested professional interests, low-quality staff or the service legacy of the last forty years;
- the reforms were undermined through chronic underfunding by central government;

- the full extent of the implementation challenge generated by these reforms was not appreciated and it is still too early to make a full assessment of their impact.

One message of this book is that it is still too early to judge the extent to which quasi-markets are or are not a superior system to more bureaucratic systems of resource allocation, although we argue in Chapter 3 that turning the clock back to 1978 is not an option for Tony Blair's Labour government. Chapter 5 suggested that managers and field-level staff are gradually beginning to understand how to operate quasi-markets but that they are doing this in a situation of considerable underfunding. The whole book has illustrated the extent of the implementation challenge generated by these reforms.

In any case, it is probably impossible to come to a definitive 'success' or 'failure' judgement on quasi-markets in terms suggested by Bartlett and Le Grand (1993). We still know relatively little about outcomes in social care and how these relate to services received. Growing interest in the need to change this situation dramatically can be identified (Nocon and Qureshi, 1996) but even if this was achieved there would still be great difficulty in isolating the impact of the reforms from the community care system more generally.

The resettlement of people with learning difficulties from long-stay mental handicap hospitals is a good example of this. This policy influenced the reforms through the key Audit Commission report (1986), *Making a Reality of Community Care*, but it has also remained a policy in its own right, with its own logic and its own strengths and weaknesses.

The impact of the community care reforms: a stakeholder perspective

Having made these important caveats, it is still possible to carry out a 'half-time' audit on the community care reforms in terms of the main stakeholders affected by their implementation, namely central government, local authorities and above all service users and carers. In terms of *central government* objectives, the implementation of the reforms has been largely successful. Chapter 3 stressed that the overriding objective was to cap public expenditure on independent sector residential and nursing-home care. This has been achieved in that local authorities are now responsible not only for operating a needs-based yet cash-limited system but also for the rationing consequences of trying to combine both elements. Second, there was a clear agenda about developing a quasi-market in terms of stimulating a mixed economy of providers. Chapter 5 illustrated that mixed economy provision in residential and nursing-home care has been maintained despite the capping of the social security budget and that many more independent sector providers of domiciliary services are beginning to become established. However, the last Conservative government was clearly unhappy with the progress being made on this front and its White Paper flagged a desire to speed up the process by which local authorities withdraw as major service providers (Department of Health, 1997a). The next section will consider the likelihood of a major reversal of these policies under a Labour government.

It can be argued that a third objective of central government was to redraw the boundaries of NHS continuing care so that a great deal of previous NHS provision would be defined as within the funding responsibilities of local authorities, the great advantage of this being, that NHS patients receive free care on the whole while social services clients can be charged.

At first glance, this appears another area of 'success' for past Conservative governments in that continuing care boundaries have been redrawn, as we saw in Chapter 6. However, continuing care has also become an explosive political issue as older people and their relatives begin to complain that they should be entitled to free care under the NHS rather than be expected to pay all, or part, of their residential and nursing-home care fees. To make matters worse, it was becoming clear that demographic projections of an ageing population suggested public expenditure costs would continue to rise despite the capping of the social security budget. Commentators began to ask 'Who will look after granny?' (*Guardian Society*, 6 March 1996, p. 6) and to talk of 'Grim time for the greyheads' (*The Guardian*, 29 March 1995, p. 22).

A key aspect of this grim time was that older people and their relatives became angry at having to pay for long-term care in residential and nursing homes through the sale of their owner-occupied houses. As Harding *et al.* (1996) explain:

> The heavy reliance (as at present) on assets and housing equity to fund long-term care costs results in very high costs to those who need such care and who also have assets or higher incomes. Their resources may be quickly exhausted and the system could act as a disincentive to saving. Moreover, the state of the housing market

bears little relationship to demand for long-term care; it may be difficult for people to realise their assets on demand. (p. 18)

The search began for a new system of funding long-term care that is seen as affordable in terms of public expenditure and more equitable than present arrangements. The preference of the previous government was for private insurance schemes subsidised in various ways by central government (Chancellor of the Exchequer *et al.*, 1996). Others have argued for a partial home equity release insurance scheme (Richards *et al.*, 1996), while the Joseph Rowntree Foundation Inquiry on *Meeting the Costs of Continuing Care* (Barclay Report, 1996) called for a public/private partnership system based on the following key elements:

- a national entitlement to an agreed minimum level of good quality care;
- the removal of the distinction, at the point of delivery, between health care and social care, both being provided without a means test;
- no change to the principle of NHS care, free at the point of delivery;
- the continuation of means-testing for the accommodation costs of residential and nursing homes;
- a new compulsory insurance scheme to ensure that those with sufficient income put money into a fund to pay for their future care;
- management of these funds in the independent/private sector, at arm's length from government;
- a National Care Council as the regulatory body to oversee contributions, entitlements and other financial arrangements.

Given the controversial nature of this issue, it was perhaps not surprising that the Labour Party included in its manifesto a commitment to establish a Royal Commission to work out a fair system for funding long-term care (see next section).

'Achievements' and 'failures' from the point of view of *local authorities* since April 1993 is a very mixed picture, as seen in previous chapters. There are some positive points. Social services and other key agencies have managed to cope with enormous change under conditions of considerable financial stringency without allowing their basic capacity to deliver services to collapse. Relations between social services managers and health managers are probably better in most localities than they were prior to the reforms. A mixed economy of social care is being developed and care managers and senior managers are gradually learning how to make and regulate the resultant (quasi) markets. The emphasis of the 1990 Act on user involvement and empowerment legitimised the voice of the user, carer and disability movements in a way that was not the case previously, so that Hoyes *et al.* (1993) felt able to claim that

> On the whole, and given the difficult resource climate and the lack of experience local authorities have in consulting and involving users and carers, we feel that they are taking the challenge seriously and are open to learning how to succeed. . . Examples of good practice include: supporting users with learning difficulties on planning groups; purchasing advocacy services; funding transport for people to attend user group meetings; enabling HIV service users to switch to an alternative home care provider; and piloting 'cash for care' through an Independent Living Scheme.

The obvious challenge was to turn such pockets of innovation systematically into good practice within their organisations. However, it is not really possible to claim that this has happened. Limited further progress may have been made but the focus of many local authorities on this issue has been deflected by such factors as local government restructuring, budget cutbacks and the impact of health authority withdrawal from continuing care. As we saw in Chapter 5, a key response to these pressures has been for social services authorities to develop priority and targeting systems which concentrate upon those assessed as most 'in need'. However, one consequence of this has been to deny services to people assessed as having low priority need and to leave other professionals, and especially housing workers, to deal with the consequences of this. This is an especially explosive issue in terms of inter-agency working when housing professionals feel people with mental health and other problems have been 'dumped' on their estates and that social services do not want to know.

Overall the biggest obstacle faced by local authorities in terms of making a success of quasi-markets in social care is the lack of what Bartlett and Le Grand (1993) called conditions for market success. These five conditions were discussed in Chapter 4 and are also laid out in Figure 9.1. This book has repeatedly underlined how difficult local authorities have found and will continue to find the achievement of these conditions.

For example, progress may have been made with regard to market structure and motivation, since Chapter 5 stressed the growing number

---

1. **Market structure:** This condition requires that, to avoid monopoly, there should be many service providers. Entry by new providers should be relatively costless; and unsuccessful providers should be allowed to go out of business. Also, to avoid monopolistic purchasing power, there should be many purchasing agents.

2. **Information:** Providers must be able to cost and price their activities properly. Purchasers must have accurate and independent information about the quantity and particularly the quality of the service being provided, so as to prevent opportunistic behaviour.

3. **Transaction costs and uncertainty:** Where transactions are multidimensional and outcomes depend upon an uncertain environment, the associated contracts . . . may be difficult to write, implement and enforce, and the associated transaction costs may be high. Markets will have failed if these transaction costs are greater than the efficiency gains achieved through moving to a more market-oriented system.

4. **Motivation:** On the purchaser side it is important that purchasers are motivated to fulfil the needs and wants of users. It would appear that this is more likely to be the case the closer purchasers are to users. Providers need to be profit maximisers for a normal market to be efficient (and in a quasi-market they may need to be constrained by a budget to at least avoid a deficit).

5. **Cream-skimming:** Service providers may attempt to maximise their 'profits' by trying to restrict the service to users with relatively straightforward service requirements. Purchasers need to avoid this happening.

Source: Based on Le Grand and Bartlett (1993).

FIGURE 9.1   Conditions of market success

of independent providers in the mixed economy of social care. However, this chapter also stressed how complex is the balance of power between purchasers and providers, while Chapter 6 illustrated how difficult it is for health and social services purchasers to work together within the (quasi) market. Chapter 7 provided examples of how problematic it can be for new providers to enter and leave the market when very large capital costs are tied up in such developments as supported and sheltered housing.

Major problems have been identified in previous chapters with regard to information and transaction costs. In terms of information, it has been shown how most social services authorities lack adequate computer-based information systems, mechanisms for costing services or approaches to evaluating the impact of care packages upon individuals. With regard to transaction costs, there is a real danger that contract specification, the administrative and financial responsibilities of care managers and the costs associated with the assessment and collection of charges will impose additional demands upon purchasers and providers which could offset and just possibly overwhelm the efficiency gains delivered through increased provider competition.

Finally, there is the issue of what Le Grand and Bartlett refer to as 'cream-skimming'. It is one thing for social services to develop a priority matrix relating to those who should receive services, and another for the resultant criteria to be applied in practice. The reluctance of some residential homes and sheltered housing schemes to support service users if they develop dementia is a good example of this type of dilemma.

In many ways, the biggest issue cuts across 'information' and 'cream-skimming' and relates to how purchasers can regulate for quality within a market of multiple providers. How can they be sure they are obtaining what they paid for? How can they be certain that high-quality services are being provided? How can they ensure services are being provided to those in greatest need? And how can they ensure that neither residential staff, nursing home staff nor home care staff are involved in the exploitation and/or abuse of their vulnerable clients? Skills in monitoring of contracts remain in their infancy while formal systems of registration and inspection relate only to residential care and nursing-home care and not to domiciliary care providers. And even the regulation systems for institutional care are presently split between social services and health, and in any case focus more on bricks-and-mortar issues such as space standards rather than the quality of care provided to service users (Hoyes and Johnson, 1997).

This may appear a rather bleak assessment, and yet we need to remember the Audit Commission's (1992) stress on the cascade of change implications of the 1990 reforms. It will take a long time for the conditions for quasi-market success to be established and considerable progress has been made. Later in this chapter we consider whether the Labour government is likely to continue down this difficult path or seek an entirely different route.

Finally, in this section we need to consider the impact of the 1990 reforms from the perspective of the most important stakeholders of all, namely *service users and carers*. At first glance, the picture is quite encouraging from research findings. Thus the Department of Health and the Audit Commission (1997) have published their first joint review report which covers the social services performance of five authorities. Drawing on information from over 1,000 service users and carers, they found that

> Most people are pleased with their social services. Overall, 71 per cent of people responding rate services as excellent or good. Only 5 per cent think services are very poor.
>
> There is some variation across authorities; the lowest percentage for excellent or good is 62 per cent and the highest 83 per cent. The range for poor is between 1 per cent and 10 per cent. Overall, social services are better thought of by women and older people and less well regarded by younger users and men.
>
> Among users who felt that recognition of their race or culture was a factor in service quality 40 per cent reported that social services had taken account of this. (p. 7)

However, as we stressed at the start of this chapter, it is hard, if not impossible, to relate such comments to the quasi-market reforms of the 1990 Act rather than to the strengths and weaknesses of the community care system in general and individual field-level staff in particular. The judgement of clients about services is likely to be more closely related to the personal qualities of the staff which deliver them rather than to whether they are underpinned by a quasi-market or bureaucratic system of service delivery.

More clearly linked to the 1990 Act has been the way in which organisations of carers, disabled people and service users have all been able to use the rhetoric of user empowerment and user-centred services to push central and local government towards more progressive and imaginative forms of consultation, assessment and service delivery. In addition, carers winning the right to a separate assessment and local authorities being allowed to run their own direct payment schemes are two examples of subsequent legislative change being fostered by the emphasis in the 1990 Act on the need to be user-centred.

The overall situation, however, is far from positive, for a number of reasons. First, the community care changes do seem to have encouraged what is sometimes called a 'Rolls Royce' service for the few, but this has been at the expense of withdrawing or reducing the availability of support services for those deemed at only medium or low risk. The tensions created in this in terms of inter-agency collaboration were drawn out in Chapters 6 and 7.

Second, some of the most glaring failures and weaknesses of community care policy and practice relate to continuities of assumptions rather than to the negative impact of radical change. Perhaps the most obvious of these concerns attitudes to carers (see Chapter 2). Despite the rhetoric of the 1989 White Paper, *Caring for People,* and the subsequent Carers (Recognition and Services) Act 1995, it is clear that the government sees this in terms of supporting carers to care and assist others physically, rather than in terms of enabling them to make real choices about whether or not they wish to do this by offering high-quality alternatives. Indeed, access to public subsidy for people to live in independent sector residential and nursing homes is now through care managers, and so it can be argued that it has become easier for the state to discourage people from giving up their caring responsibilities. The main sadness of any failure to offer alternatives and choices is that it encourages an element of hostility between user and carer groups, because some users feel they have an enforced dependency on carers and some carers feel that their personal assistance rôles have not been taken on by choice. We remain as far away as ever from the model outlined by Morris (1991) in which users and carers are offered high-quality non-stigmatising alternatives, which are based on independent living principles.

Third, the 1990 Act did offer up a number of opportunities for service users to be consulted but it is less clear how often this has resulted in users and carers having a real influence. How often does the input of user and carer groups into community care planning have a real impact on purchasing decisions? How often are service users offered a real choice over the components of their care package? Chapters 4 and 5 suggested there is still a long way to go.

Fourth, the joint reviews of social services (Department of Health/ Audit Commission, 1997) may have generated positive views from most service users but other studies show that service users and carers often feel muddled by what they continue to see as a confusing and incoherent system of community care (Baldock and Ungerson, 1994). Most service users do not understand the differing roles and responsibilities of health, housing and social services. They are often confused about who is their key worker and which agency they come from.

And, finally, most of the community care reform studies (Hoyes *et al.*, 1994; Lewis and Glennerster, 1996; Wistow *et al.*, 1996) have been very broad-based in approach. They have not been very helpful in enabling us to see whether or not the policy and practice of community care in the late 1990s is leading to improved assessment and service delivery to such groups as elderly people with dementia, people with severe head injuries, people with severe learning disabilities, and so on. We need more studies, such as the work of Moriarty and Webb (1997) on people with dementia, which focus down upon specific types of client and which go on to try and understand the impact of community care planning, care management and a mixed economy of care upon the quality of services being received.

Chapter 2 outlined why community care provision was often referred to as 'the cinderella services'. The community care reforms did not herald a new age in which the 'Cinderella' tag could be abandoned for ever. But we would claim some progress has been made, although the credit for that almost certainly lies with the disability and user movements demanding a better and more appropriate service from professionals rather than from the desire of Conservative governments to shake up local authorities through the introduction of market principles and provider competition. But what are the prospects for the future of community care with the election of a Labour government in May 1997?

New Labour? New vision?

On 1 May 1997 a Labour government was elected to power with a large majority of 179 seats. Writing in autumn 1997, it is still very early to understand the details of the direction in which a Labour administration will decide to steer community care policy and practice. However, most of the key issues and questions they face are already clear and this section will consider whether or not their response to these is likely to add up to a new vision for community care.

This book has illustrated the complexity of these challenges. As a society, we remain ambiguous about the degree to which community care provision should be underpinned by public expenditure and to what extent the better-off should be expected to pay for their own care. We want extensive public services for the 'needy' combined with low taxation for ourselves (Parker and Clarke, 1997). Even when this dilemma is resolved, the Labour government will need to decide on the best mechanisms for ensuring that appropriate support is received:

- To what extent should we move to a 'cash in hand' approach in which people arrange for their own support needs (integration into the labour market, improved benefits, direct payment schemes, etc.)?

- Should the above strategy include a growing reliance on private insurance, probably subsidised by the state through tax-forgone allowances for those who take out policies?
- What should be the respective purchasing/planning roles of health and social services?
- What is the best balance of service delivery between the state, private and voluntary sectors?

The end result of such thinking needs to be gathered into a single Community Care Act which draws together and updates the present mishmash of legislation along the lines achieved by the Children Act 1989. The government needs to ensure the chosen approach is developed in such a way as to be genuinely user-driven.

Despite this enormous agenda, manifesto commitments relating to community care were quite limited but did include the following:

- a long-term care charter will be introduced which will define the standards of services people are entitled to receive from health, housing and social services;
- a Royal Commission will be set up to work out a fair system for funding long-term care for elderly people;
- independent inspection and regulation service for residential and domiciliary care;
- local authorities will be free to develop a mix of public and private residential care;
- comprehensive civil rights will be developed for disabled people;
- there will be a fairer distribution of government grants to local authorities.

At first glance, the emphasis on agreed standards of care, a fair system for funding long-term care and civil rights for disabled people are all very exciting and seem to imply something of a rights-based approach to future community care provision. However, such optimism has to be tempered by the fact that the two biggest manifesto commitments of all were not to raise the basic rate of income tax and not to exceed the public expenditure plans of the previous administration for the next two years. This has led some commentators such as Andrew Dilnot, Director of the Institute of Fiscal Studies, to claim that 'Britain's middle classes are poised to opt out of state health and education in droves over the next few years in revolt against the Government's squeeze on public expenditure' (*The Guardian*, 26 June 1997, p. 3).

In terms of community care policy and practice, such financial restrictions are likely to mean that the policy agenda will continue to be dominated by rationing rather than rights, and that guaranteed standards of service will only apply to those who are deemed most at risk and thus qualifying for a care package. Paul Boateng, the junior health minister with responsibility for community care, has already confirmed this. When asked about national standards in community care, he made a distinction between national guidelines on quality and the issue of eligibility since, with regard to the latter, 'of course there is the issue of resources' (quoted in Downey, 1997, p. 11).

Equally, civil rights for disabled people are likely to be restricted to those with only limited public expenditure implications. Thus the co-director of the National Centre for Integrated Living may tell the government:

> How we pay for long-term maintenance of people with long-term support needs is the question of the hour. Any answer needs to break away from the disabled–dependent burden that dominates conventional thinking on welfare, and to plan instead for independence and inclusion. (Hasler, 1997, p. 22)

We agree on the importance of this question but have doubts about the likelihood of getting an adequate answer. Those unable to work are likely to remain dependent on poverty benefits. Equally the proposed system for the funding of long-term/continuing care from the Royal Commission is likely to place a higher emphasis on self-provisioning and private insurance than on public expenditure.

Having said this, some real changes will be taking place, especially in terms of attitudes to local government and its rôle as a provider of social care services. As Boateng explains:

> We don't have the same ideological hang-ups of the last government where . . . it was a question of private good, public bad. What we are concerned about is quality, value for money, what the user, what the citizen gets out of it and I don't mind if it is in the public sector or the private sector. The important thing is that we deliver to the service user and the wider community. (Downey, 1997, p. 11)

In such comments there is no suggestion of a reversal to the local authority as the sole provider but rather the concept of a mixed economy in which provider rôles are 'given' on the basis of what the government increasingly refers to as 'best value'.

The difficulty faced by the government is how to assess 'best value', especially if there is a reluctance to accept that this should be judged through competition in a (quasi) market. The approach by Boateng seems to be to revert back to the concept of rational planning, and hence there is an enormous stress on the need for much improved statistics on service delivery and outcomes:

> There's one thing I'd like to leave behind . . . that at least my successor and the local authorities and the Treasury . . . have a better way of measuring the cost of what we are doing and how effective it is. (Downey, p. 11)

The other logical consequence to a hostility to social care markets is an even greater emphasis than previously upon the virtues of working together. Thus, Boateng is keen on pooled budgets between health and social services, especially where this can foster the planning of services across the health and social care divide at the locality level. In terms of the delivery of operational services, Alan Milburn as the then Labour shadow junior health minister, had called for a one-stop care approach based upon multi-agency working at the operational level (Powell, 1996). Such sentiments are fine but there is as yet little concrete idea of how the obstacles to joint working are to be overcome in a context of continuing major resource shortfalls and a mixed economy of social care.

What has been said so far seems to add up to rather less than a new vision for community care. Sadly, it seems true that the Labour government has no such vision – their main thinking has been directed to health care and the NHS, partly because of its great cost but also because of the attachment of the general public to a universal health care system, free at the point of delivery. Community care for frail elderly people and for disabled people does not generate the same response and hence is far lower down the political agenda.

Towards a new vision after all?

Field-level and managerial staff working in community care agencies have a responsibility to service users not to allow the difficulties outlined above to undermine their determination to improve community care policy and practice at the local level in the coming years. In this respect, we want to conclude the second edition of our book on a positive note.

Local authorities have a far greater capacity to meet community care objectives within given resources than is presently being achieved (and this is in *no* way intended to imply that they do not need more resources). However, this requires them to take a far broader view of community care than they presently do. The justification for a narrow approach is that resource shortages mean that only those that are most 'at risk' can be responded to. However, Langan *et al.* (1996) studied the meaning of home and independence in a sample of elderly people whom social services would be likely to assess as having only low or medium dependency needs. Overall, these older people wanted only modest forms of help and what they wanted was often outside the confines of traditional community care services. The help required related to housing, transport and mobility issues, while another major concern was the importance of companionship, the need for social relationships and involvement in meaningful activities (Means, 1997a). This can be generalised across nearly all people with support needs. And yet a failure to respond to such needs can cause a decline in health leading to a need for expensive crisis intervention (Wistow and Lewis, 1996).

In many ways, this calls not only for a refocusing on the importance of prevention and quality of life issues but also a combination of this with a much more creative use of existing resources which looks beyond traditional community care budgets and services. Here are just two examples. Barnes (1997) has described the activities of 'Ecoworks' in Nottingham, which

> promotes the development of small-scale, local activities which can enable people experiencing emotional distress, and other unemployed people in the locality, to take on work which not only contributes to their own personal empowerment but also to the achievement of ecological objectives. (p. 157)

Such projects draw upon the capacity of communities to support local disabled people and people with mental health problems. It also shows how such communities can positively gain from their presence. There is great scope for developing such initiatives through urban regeneration and other initiatives.

The second example relates to the enormous potential to empower people through participation in the arts. Drawing upon a wide range of arts projects, Matarasso (1997) has felt able to argue:

> Participation in the arts does bring benefits to individuals and communities. On a personal level these touch people's confidence, creative and transferable skills and human growth, as well as their social lives through friendships, involvement in the community and enjoyment. Individual benefits translate into wider social impact by building the confidence of minority and marginalised groups, promoting contact and contributing to social cohesion. New skills and confidence can be empowering as community groups become more (and more equitably) involved in local affairs. (p. 79)

Yet it is rare for social services to see such arts projects as central to their own community care concerns.

What is badly needed is for social services authorities to take a broad view of their responsibilities as the lead agency in community care. To begin with, social services need to encourage a corporate approach from the whole local authority along the lines advocated over ten years ago in *Councils of Care: Planning a Local Government Strategy for Older People* (Norton *et al.*, 1986). This called for a consideration of transport, planning, leisure and environmental issues by local authorities as well as narrowly defined community care services, an emphasis also to be found in the much more recent work by Leat and Perri 6 (1997) in their study of how Britain can grow old better in the twenty-first century. The provider rôle of local authorities may have declined since the 1986 report was written but they still have a major rôle in the provision of library and leisure facilities and retain considerable responsibility for transport issues. With regard to the latter, safe walking environments can be crucial to the quality of life of many people with support needs yet the quality of most pavements is a disgrace, causing Plowden (1997) to remark that this makes even a short walk an ordeal for physically disabled, blind and partially sighted people. He argues that

> Local authorities should turn the intermittent pavements of today into level and uninterrupted walking networks linking key destinations and public transport services, as is happening in York and Edinburgh. (p. 3)

Local authorities have enormous scope to tackle these issues and social services need to exert much more pressure to ensure they do so rather than seeing such environmental and transport issues as worthy but irrelevant to their own community care concerns.

Nevertheless, the power and the potential of local authorities no longer relates solely to the services it provides. As Corrigan (1997) explains:

> In the past local government had a clear view that power lay in the town hall and in its capacity to run services. . . Now local government has recognised that power – real power to change and influence the social problems of locality – is found not in the town hall but in civil society beyond its walls. (p. 12)

Local authorities have developed their skills at facilitating joint ventures and partnerships in civil society not only with the voluntary sector through arts and employment initiatives but also with the private sector (Hutchinson, 1994). These skills need to be applied to encouraging the private sector to see elderly and disabled people as important consumers. For example, ways could be explored by which village shops could survive through diversification (Piachaud and Webb, 1996). But equally, there could be discussions with new supermarkets at the planning stage about how design and other arrangements could enable older and disabled people to continue to use their services (wider alleys, free bus services with high access standards, home shopping facilities, etc.)

The Langan *et al.* (1996) study showed that many people with support needs require very simple services from the private sector, such as plumbing, carpentry, gardening or electrical work, while help with keeping the car on the road was a concern to many others. Fletcher and Herbert (1996) have argued that this situation requires the establishment of local services networks which would offer

> a local access point to which enquiries could be made about available support to assist with practical and personal care needs. The access point could provide simple information about accredited providers of services in the locality. Independence-supporting services (meals, gardening, household maintenance, adaptations, shopping, technology) as well as more traditional services . . . would be accredited. (p. 19)

Such a network would be run by paid staff so as to enable local people to access services with confidence. Most of these services would need to be paid for either directly by the elderly or disabled person or through some form of grant or subsidy.

This does create a dilemma. The better-off would be able to use the network to meet their needs through paying for such services, but others may be forced to wait until a crisis ensured that they became eligible for help from social services. One alternative is to explore options by which elderly and disabled people can exchange services on a reciprocal rather than a fee payment basis, the assumption being that most people with support needs have skills and abilities as well as a need for services. How might this work in practice? Local exchange trading schemes (LETS) enable people, especially in low-income communities, to exchange goods and services without having to use money as the currency of exchange. To do this

> a group of people set up an association and create a local unit of exchange (e.g. bobbins in Manchester, favours in Calderdale, solents in Southampton). They then offer goods and services to each other priced in these units. Each member makes a list offering various kinds of work, along with a list of requests of what s/he wants doing, which are entered on a directory circulated to all members. . . Individuals then contact each other to buy or sell their goods or services. The price for any transaction is arrived at through reciprocal agreement between the buyer and seller. (Williams, 1996, p. 260)

Williams has indicated that 64 per cent of local authorities have expressed an intention to help develop LETS schemes in their area. Figure 9.2 provides an example from the Bradford scheme of some of the goods and services available through such schemes, and this underlines their relevance to a wide range of people with support needs, as both potential contributors and receivers of services. But again the same issue arises. Local authorities are interested in LETS schemes as contributors to community development and urban regeneration, but do social services authorities appreciate their potential as a contributor to the implementation of a broad vision of community care?

Conclusion

The comparative perspective offered in Chapter 8 underlined the fact that issues such as the respective responsibilities of the family and the

1. Building and home improvement
  – electrical work
  – painting (interior)
  – general DIY/repairs
  – decorating
  – minor plumbing
  – carpentry
2. Lifts, cars and bikes
  – lifts (shopping, hospital visits)
  – car maintenance
3. Babysitting
	4. Child minding
	5. Animals
	  – cat sitting
	  – dog sitting
	6. Cleaning
	7. Clothes
	  – use of washing machine
	  – sewing alterations
	  – knitting
	8. Gardening
	9. Food and catering
	10. Arts and craft

FIGURE 9.2   Examples of services available from Bradford LETS

state towards people with health and social care needs are debated in nearly all countries, as is the question of what the state can afford. Chapter 8 also illustrated the wide variations of policy approaches which might be available, but also the extent to which systems based upon service delivery by large welfare bureaucracies were being rejected by all countries. There is no way of returning to the 'golden age' of the early 1970s, when incremental growth through ever-expanding social services departments, housing departments and health authorities seemed the best approach. Continued radical change is inevitable because, as Chapter 3 argued, we have learnt how to harness information technology to the development of new types of organisation and new approaches to management. However, the values which should underlie such innovation are not given, nor is the amount of public subsidy which should be invested in their development. That debate will continue and creates the space for us to judge the emerging reforms in terms of whether or not they make a sufficient contribution to enabling older people and people with physical impairments, mental health problems and learning difficulties to remain or become full citizens of the society in which they live. It is not until that occurs that the 'Cinderella' tag for community care services will have finally been removed.

Guide to Further Reading

Chapter 1 Introducing Community Care

Readers seeking an introduction to the key debates in community care will find the reader edited by Bornat *et al.* (1993) is an excellent starting point. The White Paper on community care (Department of Health, 1989a) and the subsequent policy guidance (Department of Health, 1990) are both worth a read. Both Lewis and Glennerster (1996) and Wistow (1995) also provide good introductions to the main issues in community care.

Chapter 2 From Institutions to Care in the Community: The History of Neglect

Some readers may wish to learn more about the general development of the British welfare state as well as the more specific history of community care policy. Fraser (1984), Lowe (1993) and Hill (1993) all provide clear introductions. More detailed service histories can be found in Means and Smith (1998) for elderly people, Leat (1988) for physically disabled people, Kathleen Jones (1993) for people with mental health problems and Wright and Digby (1996) for people with learning difficulties. Political economy perspectives on service neglect are well covered by Phillipson (1982) and Oliver (1990, 1996), while the rôle of institutions in society is well summarised by Parker (1988). Both Dalley (1996) and Morris (1996) provide useful discussions of feminism and community care. Cultural assumptions about disability and ageing are explored by Barton (1996) and Wilson (1991).

Chapter 3 Community Care and the Restructuring of Welfare

Making a Reality of Community Care (Audit Commission, 1986) outlines the slow progress in resettling people from long-stay hospitals, and was the report which sparked off the Griffiths Report (1988) on community care provision and the subsequent White Paper on community care (Department of Health, 1989a). Chapter one of Lewis and Glennerster (1996) provides a useful summary of the various critiques of the community care reforms.

The aim of the chapter is to set the community care reforms within broader debates and trends in welfare provision. Le Grand and Bartlett (1993) outline the quasi-market perspective while Hoggett (1991, 1996) provides an introduction to the post-Fordist and public sector management debate. For those wishing to explore welfare change in this period across policy areas, Sullivan (1994), Clarke and Newman (1997) and Bartlett *et al.* (1994) provide useful starting points.

Chapter 4   Towards User and Carer Empowerment?

Lukes (1974) provides the classic discussion of power, while more general reviews of empowerment and community care are to be found in Servian (1996) and Jack (1995). Oliver (1996) and Campbell and Oliver (1996) provide excellent introductions to the development of the disability movement and its demand for adequate income, personal assistance and independent living based upon the rights of disabled people to be full citizens of society. The extensive carer literature is well summarised by Nolan *et al.* (1996).

Le Grand and Bartlett (1993) discuss 'exit' and quasi-market approaches to empowerment, while many of the chapters in Jack (1995) are very good on voice perspectives. Campbell and Oliver (1996) are excellent on both rights and struggle approaches to empowerment.

Chapter 5   Leaders at Last: The Changing Rôle of Social Services

The history of arguments about whether or not local authority social services departments should be the lead agency in community care is covered in detail by Means and Smith (1985). A number of studies look at how local authorities are tackling the implementation of the reforms and the best of these include Hoyes *et al.* (1994), Lewis and Glennerster (1996) and Wistow *et al.* (1996). Forder *et al.* (1996) provide a fascinating discussion of making markets in community care, while Bewley and Glendinning (1994) take a detailed look at community care planning. The weekly journal *Community Care* is an excellent guide to what is happening on the ground.

Chapter 6   The Health Dimension of Community Care: Towards Collaborative Working?

This chapter looks at joint working between health and social services. For those wishing to learn more about policy making in the NHS, Ham (1994) is essential reading. The theory of collaborative working and the reasons why it is so problematic to develop are specified clearly by Hudson (1987) and Huxham (1996), while Means *et al.* (1997) describe useful, practical examples of collaborative working in action. One reason why 'working together' has been particularly difficult in this area is that there has always been a debate going on about what is health care and what is social care, an issue addressed in detail by Means and Smith (1985). Clark *et al.* (1996) provide interesting insights into hospital discharge, while Wistow (1996) offers important observations on the continuing care debate. *Building Bridges* (Department of Health, 1995b) is a crucial document in terms of the delivery of services for people with severe mental health problems, while Hudson (1995) is excellent on issues around joint commissioning.

Chapter 7 Housing and Community Care

A useful overview of housing policy is provided by Malpass and Murie (1994). Gurney and Means (1993) offer an introduction to issues around the meaning of home, while Higgins (1989) remains the classic discussion of home versus institution. Emerson and Hatton (1996) offer a useful review of a wide range of resettlement studies, while Watson (1997) has recently produced an excellent review of Rowntree Foundation funded research on housing and community care. Department of Health/Department of Environment (1997) looks at joint working at the strategic level across housing, health and social services, while Means *et al.* (1997) look at this issue from the perspective of practitioners. Heywood with Smart (1996) is a must for those interested in adaptation issues.

Chapter 8 European Perspectives on Community Care

Useful publications on European welfare traditions and regimes include Esping-Andersen (1990), Abrahamson (1991a) and Leibfried and Pierson (1995), and analyses of welfare states in Europe can be found in C. Jones (1993) and George and Taylor-Gooby (1996). Overviews of family policy in European Union countries are provided in Hantrais (1995) and Millar and Warman (1996). Profiles of and policies for older people in Europe are covered in Hugman (1994), Tester (1996) and Walker and Maltby (1997). Disabled people are addressed in Wilson (1996) and Waddington (1997). The institutions of the European Union and the process of policy-making in the EU are described in many recent publications for students of public administration and government. Among the more readable are Archer and Butler (1996), Richardson (1996) and Wallace and Wallace (1996). The impact of the EU on local government in the UK is addressed by Bongers (1992) and Goldsmith and Klausen (1997).

Chapter 9 Community Care in the 1990s: Achievements, Failures and Challenges for the Future

Reading recommended for Chapter 5, such as Lewis and Glennerster (1996) and Wistow *et al.* (1996), is also very useful in terms of considering achievements, failures and challenges, as is Hadley and Clough (1996). Harding, Meredith and Wistow (1996) are excellent on the specific issue of options for long-term care. Barnes (1997), Leat and Perri 6 (1997) and Means (1997b) all offer a broad vision for the future of community care.

Bibliography

Abberley, P. (1991) 'The significance of the OPCS disability surveys', pp. 156–76 in M. Oliver (ed), *Social Work, Disabled People and Disabling Environments* (London: Jessica Kingsley).

Abbott, P. and Sapsford, R. (1987) *Community Care for Mentally Handicapped Children* (Milton Keynes: Open University Press).

Abel-Smith, B. and Titmuss, K. (eds) (1987) *The Philosophy of Welfare: Selected Writings of Richard M. Titmuss* (London: Allen & Unwin).

Abrahamson, P. (1991a) 'Welfare and poverty in the Europe of the 1990s: social progress or social dumping?', *International Journal of Health Services*, vol. 21, no. 2, pp. 237–64.

Abrahamson, P. (1991b) 'Welfare for the elderly in Denmark: from institutionalization to self-reliance', pp. 35–61 in A. Evers and I. Svetlik (eds), *New Welfare Mixes in Care for the Elderly, Vol.2, Austria, Denmark, Finland, Israel, Netherlands* (Vienna: European Centre for Social Welfare Policy and Research).

Abrams, P. (1977) 'Community care: some research problems and priorities', *Policy and Politics*, vol. 6, no. 2, pp. 125–51.

Ahmad, W. and Atkin, K. (eds) (1996) *'Race' and Community Care* (Buckingham: Open University Press).

Alber, J. (1991) *The Impact of Public Policies on Older People in the Federal Republic of Germany*, Konstanz, Spring (submission to the EC Observatory on Older People).

Alber, J. (1993) 'Health and social services', pp. 100–33 in A. Walker, J. Alber and A.M. Guillemard (eds), *Older People in Europe: Social and Economic Policies – the 1993 Report of the European Observatory* (Brussels: Commission of the European Communities).

Alber, J., Guillemard, A.M. and Walker, A. (1991) *The Impact of Social and Economic Policies on Older People in the European Community: An Initial Overview*, EC Observatory on Older People, First Report, Commission of the European Communities, Directorate General V, Employment, Social Affairs, Industrial Relations, June.

Allen, I., Dalley, G. and Leat, D. (1992) *Monitoring Change in Social Services Departments* (London: Policy Studies Institute for the Association of Directors of Social Services).

Amira, A. (1990) 'Family care in Greece', pp. 72–9 in A. Jamieson and R. Illsley (eds), *Contrasting European Policies for the Care of Older People* (Aldershot: Avebury).

Amulree, Lord (1951) *Adding Life to Years* (London: National Council of Social Service).

Anderson, R. (1992) 'Health and community care', pp. 63–84 in L. Davies (ed.), *The Coming of Age in Europe: Older People in the European Community* (London: Age Concern England (ACE) Books).

Anderson Report (1947) *The Care and Treatment of the Elderly and Infirm* (London: British Medical Association).

Arber, S. and Ginn, J. (1991) *Gender and Later Life: A Sociological Analysis of Resources and Constraints* (London: Sage).

Arber, S. and Ginn, J. (1995) *Connecting Gender and Ageing: A Sociological Approach* (Buckingham: Open University Press).

Arblaster, L., Conway, J., Foreman, A. and Hawtin, M. (1996) *Asking the Impossible? Inter-Agency Working to Address Housing, Health and Social Care Needs of People in Ordinary Housing* (Bristol: Policy Press).

Archer, C. and Butler, F. (1996) *The European Union: Structure and Process*, 2nd edition (London: Pinter).

Askham, J., Henshaw, L. and Tarpey, M. (1995) *Social and Health Services for Elderly People from Black and Minority Ethnic Communities* (London: HMSO).

Atkin, K. (1996) 'An opportunity for change: voluntary sector provision in a mixed economy of care', pp. 144–60 in W. Ahmad and K. Atkin (eds), *'Race' and Community Care* (Buckingham: Open University Press).

Atkinson, D. (1988) 'Residential care for children and adults with mental handicap', pp. 125–56 in I. Sinclair (ed.), *Residential Care: The Research Reviewed* (London: HMSO).

Audit Commission (1985) *Managing Social Services for the Elderly More Effectively* (London: HMSO).

Audit Commission (1986) *Making a Reality of Community Care* (London: HMSO).

Audit Commission (1992) *Community Care: Managing the Cascade of Change* (London: HMSO).

Audit Commission (1994) *Finding a Place: A Review of Mental Health Services for Adults* (London: HMSO).

Audit Commission (1996a) *Balancing the Care Equation: Progress with Community Care* (London: HMSO).

Audit Commission (1996b) *What the Doctor Ordered: A Study of GP Fundholders in England and Wales* (London: HMSO).

Aves, G. (1964) 'The relationship between homes and other forms of care', pp. 11–17 in K. Slack (ed.), *Some Aspects of Residential Care of the Elderly* (London: National Council of Social Service).

Bailey, R. and Brake, M. (1975) *Radical Social Work* (London: Edward Arnold).

Baldock, J. (1993) 'Patterns of change in the delivery of welfare in Europe', pp. 24–37 in P. Taylor-Gooby and R. Lawson (eds), *Markets and Managers: New Issues in the Delivery of Welfare* (Buckingham: Open University Press).

Baldock, J. and Ely, P. (1996) 'Social care for elderly people in Europe: the central problem of home care', pp. 195–225 in B. Munday and P. Ely (eds), *Social Care in Europe* (Hemel Hempstead: Prentice Hall).

Baldock, J. and Evers, A. (1991) 'Concluding remarks on the significance of the innovations reviewed – their implications for social change', pp. 186–202 in R.J. Kraan, J. Baldock, B. Davies, A. Evers, L. Johansson, M. Knapen, M. Thorslund and C. Tunissen (eds), *Care for the Elderly: Significant Innovations in Three European Countries* (Boulder, Colorado: Westview Press).

Baldock, J. and Ungerson, C. (1994) *Becoming Consumers of Community Care* (York: Joseph Rowntree Foundation).

Baldwin, S. and Lunt, N. (1996) *Charging Ahead: The Development of Local Authority Charging Policies for Community Care* (Bristol: Policy Press).

Baldwin, S. and Parker, G. (1989) 'The Griffiths report on community care', pp. 143–65 in M. Brenton and C. Ungerson (eds), *Social Policy Review, 1988–89* (London: Longman).

Baldwin, S. and Twigg, J. (1991) 'Women and community care – reflections on a debate', pp. 117–35 in M. Maclean and D. Groves (eds), *Women's Issues in Social Policy* (London: Routledge).

Barclay Report (1996) *Meeting the Costs of Continuing Care: Report and Recommendations* (York: Joseph Rowntree Foundation).

Barnes, C. (1996) 'Theories of disability and the origins of the oppression of disabled people in western society', pp. 43–60 in L. Barton (ed.), *Disability and Society: Emerging Issues and Insights* (Harlow: Longman).

Barnes, M. (1997) *Care, Communities and Citizens* (London: Longman).

Barnes, M. and Walker, A. (1996) 'Consumerism versus empowerment: a principled approach to the involvement of older service users', *Policy and Politics*, vol. 24, no. 4, pp. 375–94.

Barnes, M., Prior, D. and Thomas, N. (1990) 'Social services', pp. 103–53 in N. Deakin and A. Wright (eds), *Consuming Public Services* (London: Routledge).

Baron, S. and Haldane, J. (eds) (1992) *Community, Normality and Difference: Meeting Social Needs* (Aberdeen: Aberdeen University Press).

Barrett, S. and Hill, M. (1984) 'Policy, bargaining and structure in implementation theory: towards an integrated perspective', *Policy and Politics*, vol. 12, no. 3, pp. 219–40.

Bartlett, W. and Le Grand, J. (1993) 'The theory of quasi-markets', pp. 13–34 in J. Le Grand and W. Bartlett (eds), *Quasi-markets and Social Policy* (Basingstoke: Macmillan).

Bartlett, W., Propper, C., Wilson, D. and Le Grand, J. (eds) (1994) *Quasi-Markets in the Welfare State*, SAUS Study No.14 (Bristol: School for Advanced Urban Studies).

Barton, L. (ed.) (1996) *Disability and Society: Emerging Issues and Insights* (Harlow: Longman).

BASW (1985) *Housing and Social Work* (Birmingham: British Association of Social Workers).

Baxter, C., Poonia, K., Ward, L. and Nadirshaw, Z. (1990) *Double Discrimination: Issues and Services for People with Learning Difficulties from Black and Ethnic Minority Communities* (London: King's Fund Centre/Commission for Racial Equality).

Becker, S. (1996) 'Juggling people's lives', *Community Care*, 3–9 October, pp. i–iii.

Begum, N., Hill, M. and Stevens, A. (eds) (1994) *Reflections: Views of Black Disabled People on their Lives and Community Care* (London: Central Council for Education and Training in Social Work).

Beresford, P. and Trevillion, S. (1995) *Developing Skills for Community Care: A Collaborative Approach* (Aldershot: Arena).

Bernard, M. and Meade, K. (eds) (1993) *Women Come of Age* (London: Edward Arnold).

Bertelsen, O. and Platz, M. (1991) *The Impact of Social and Economic Policies on Older People in Denmark*, Danish National Institute of Social Research, April (submission to the EC Observatory on Older People).

Betty, C. (1997) 'Language problems of older British migrants on the Costa del Sol', *Generations Review*, vol. 7, no. 2, June, pp. 10–11.

Beveridge Report (1942) *Social Insurance and Allied Services* (London: HMSO).

Bewley, C. and Glendinning, C. (1994) *Involving Disabled People in Community Care* (York: Joseph Rowntree Foundation).

Biggs, S. (1990/91) 'Consumers, care management and inspection: obscuring social deprivation and need', *Critical Social Policy*, issue 30, pp. 23–8.

Biggs, S., Phillipson, C. and Kingston, P. (1995) *Elder Abuse in Perspective* (Buckingham: Open University Press).

Bines, W. (1994) *The Health of Single Homeless People*, Discussion Paper No.9 (Centre for Housing Policy, University of York).

Boddy, M. and Fudge, C. (eds) (1984) *Local Socialism? Labour Councils and New Left Alternatives* (London: Macmillan).

Bone, M. and Meltzer, H. (1989) *The Prevalence of Disability Among Children*, OPCS Surveys (London: HMSO).

Bongers, P. (1990) *Local Government and 1992* (Harlow: Longman).

Bongers, P. (1992) *Local Government and the Single European Market* (Harlow: Longman).

Bornat, J., Pereira, C., Pilgrim, D. and Williams, F. (eds) (1993) *Community Care: A Reader* (Basingstoke: Macmillan).

Bosanquet, N. (1978) *A Future for Old Age* (London: Temple Smith).

Bosanquet, N. and Propper, C. (1991) 'Charting the grey economy in the 1990s', *Policy and Politics*, vol. 19, no. 4, pp. 269–82.

Boucher Report (1957) *Survey of Services Available to the Chronic Sick and Elderly 1954–55*, Reports on Public Health and Medical Subjects No.98 (London: HMSO).

Bovell, V., Lewis, J. and Wookey, F. (1997) 'The implications for social services departments of the information task in the social care market', *Health and Social Care in the Community*, vol. 5, no. 2, pp. 94–105.

Bowl, R. (1986) 'Social work with old people', pp. 128–45 in C. Phillipson and A. Walker (eds), *Ageing and Social Policy* (Aldershot: Gower).

Bradford, I., Mares, P. and Wilkins, N. (1994) *Home for Good: Making Homes Fit for Community Care* (Nottingham: Care & Repair (England)).

Brauns, H.-J. and Kramer, D. (1989) 'West Germany – the break up of consensus and the demographic threat', pp. 124–54 in B. Munday (ed.), *The Crisis in Welfare: An International Perspective on Social Services and Social Work* (Hemel Hempstead: Harvester Wheatsheaf).

Braye, S. and Preston-Shoot, M. (1995) *Empowering Practice in Social Care* (Buckingham: Open University Press).

Brenton, M. (1997) 'Choice, mutual support and autonomy in old age: older women's co-operative living arrangements', unpublished paper delivered to 'Elder Power in the 21st Century', annual conference of the British Society of Gerontology, 19–21 September, at the University of Bristol.

Brewerton, J. and Darton, D. (eds) (1997) *Designing Lifetime Homes* (York: Joseph Rowntree Foundation).

British Medical Association (1992) *Priorities for Community Care* (London: British Medical Association).

Brockington, R. (1963) 'A community health authority', *Hospital and Social Services Journal*, 20 September, pp. 1145–6.

Brown, M. (1972) 'The development of local authority welfare services from 1948–1965 under Part III of the National Assistance Act 1948', PhD thesis, University of Manchester.

Brown, R. (1979) *Reorganising the National Health Service* (Oxford: Blackwell).

Buckley, M. and Anderson, M. (eds) (1988) *Women, Equality and Europe* (Basingstoke: Macmillan).

Burrows, R. and Loader, B. (eds) (1994) *Towards a Post-Fordist Welfare State?* (London: Routledge).

Cambridge, P. (1992) 'Case management in community services: organisational responses', *British Journal of Social Work*, vol. 22, no. 5, pp. 495–517.

Cambridge, P., Hayes, L. and Knapp, M. with Gould, E. and Fenyo, A. (1994) *Care in the Community: Five Years On* (Canterbury: Personal Social Services Research Unit, University of Kent).

Campbell, J. and Oliver, M. (1996) *Disability Politics: Understanding our Past, Changing our Future* (London: Routledge).

Care and Repair (1994) *Poor Housing – Who Cares? The Housing Circumstances of Home Improvement Clients* (Nottingham: Care and Repair (England))

Carter, T. and Nash, C. (1995) 'Pensioners' forums – a voice for older people', pp. 157–69 in R. Jack (ed.), *Empowerment in Community Care* (London: Chapman & Hall).

Cervi, B. (1996) 'Cut to fit', *Community Care*, 18–24 April, pp. 18–19.

Challis, D., Chessum, R., Chesterman, J., Luckett, R. and Woods, R. (1988) 'Community care for the frail elderly: an urban experiment', *British Journal of Social Work*, vol. 18 (supplement), pp. 13–42.

Challis, L. (1990) *Organising Public Social Services* (London: Longman).

Chancellor of the Exchequer *et al.* (1996) *A New Partnership for Care in Old Age* (London: HMSO).

Chapman, K. (1989) 'Trends of home care provision into the 1990s', *Eurolink Age Bulletin*, September.

Chappell, A. (1992) 'Towards a sociological critique of the normalisation principle', *Disability, Handicap and Society*, vol. 7, no. 1, pp. 35–52.

Chetwynd, M., Ritchie, J., Reith, L. and Howard, M. (1996) *The Cost of Care: The Impact of Changing Policy on the Lives of Disabled People* (Bristol: Policy Press).

Clapham, D. and Franklin, B. (1994) *The Housing Management Contribution to Community Care* (Glasgow: Centre for Housing Research and Urban Studies, University of Glasgow).

Clark, H., Dyer, S. and Hartman, L. (1996) *Going Home: Older People Leaving Hospital* (Bristol: Policy Press).

Clarke, J. and Newman, J. (1997) *The Managerial State* (London: Sage).

Clarke, L. (1984) *Domiciliary Services for the Elderly* (London: Croom Helm).

Clegg, S. (1989) *Frameworks of Power* (London: Sage).

Clough, R. (1990) *Practice, Politics and Power in Social Services Departments* (Aldershot: Avebury).

Cobbold, C. (1997) *A Cost Benefit Analysis of Lifetime Homes* (York: Joseph Rowntree Foundation).

Cohen, S. (1985) *Visions of Social Control: Crime, Punishment and Classification* (Cambridge: Polity Press).

Collins, J. (1996) *What's Choice Got to Do With It?* (London: Values into Action).

Coote, A. (ed.) (1992) *The Welfare of Citizens: Developing New Social Rights* (London: Institute of Public Policy Research/Rivers Oram Press).

Corrigan, P. (1997) 'The halls of change', *Municipal Journal*, 4 April, pp. 12–13.

Coss, S. (1997) 'Anger at treatment of elderly and disabled', *European Voice*, vol. 3, no. 25, 26 June–2 July, p. 4.

Cox, C. and Pearson, M. (1993) *Made to Care* (The Rannoch Trust).

Craig, G. and Manthorpe, J. (1996) *Wiped Off the Map – Local Government Reorganisation and Community Care*, Papers in Social Research No.5 (Hull: University of Lincolnshire and Humberside).

Crane, M. (1997) *Homeless Truths: Challenging the Myths about Older Homeless People* (London: Help the Aged and London: Crisis).

Cranston, M. (1976) 'Human rights: real and supposed', pp. 133–44 in N. Timms and D. Watson (eds), *Talking about Welfare* (London: Routledge & Kegan Paul).

Crowther, M. (1981) *The Workhouse System, 1834–1929: The History of an English Social Institution* (London: Methuen).

Daatland, S.O. (1992) 'Ideals lost? Current trends in Scandinavian welfare policies on ageing', *Journal of European Social Policy*, vol. 2, no. 1, pp. 33–42.

Dalley, G. (1996 edition) *Ideologies of Caring: Rethinking Community and Collectivism* (Basingstoke: Macmillan).

Dant, T., Carley, M., Gearing, B. and Johnson, M. (1987) *Dependency and Old Age: Theoretical Accounts and Practical Understandings*, Care of Elderly People at Home Project Paper No.3 (Milton Keynes: Open University Press/ London: Policy Studies Institute).

Davey, J. (1996) *Equity Release: An Option for Older Home Owners* (York: Centre for Housing Policy, University of York).

Davies Report (1995) *Report of the Inquiry into the Circumstances Leading to the Death of Jonathan Newby (A Volunteer Worker) on 9th October 1993 in Oxford* (Oxford: Oxfordshire Health Authority).

Davies, B. (1992) 'On breeding the best chameleons', *Generations Review*, vol. 2, no. 2, pp. 18–21.

Davies, B. and Challis, D. (1986) *Matching Needs to Resources* (Aldershot: Gower).

Davison, B., Kendig, H., Stephens, F. and Merrill, V. (1993) *It's My Place: Older People Talk about their Homes* (Canberra: Australian Government Publishing Service).

Deakin, N. (1987) *The Politics of Welfare* (London: Methuen).

Deakin, N. (1995) 'The perils of partnership: the voluntary sector and the state, 1945–1992', pp. 40–65 in J. Davis Smith, C. Rochester and R. Hedley (eds), *An Introduction to the Voluntary Sector* (London: Routledge).

Deakin, N. and Walsh, K. (1996) 'The enabling state: the role of markets and contracts', *Public Administration*, vol. 74, Spring, pp. 33–48.

De Jasay, A. (1991) Choice, Contract, Consent: A Restatement of Liberalism (London: Institute of Economic Affairs).

Department of the Environment (1995) *Our Future Homes – Opportunity, Choice, Responsibility* (London: HMSO).

Department of the Environment/Department of Health (1992) *Housing and Community Care*, Circular 10/92 and LAC (92) 12 (London: HMSO).

Department of Health (1989a) *Caring for People: Community Care in the Next Decade and Beyond* (London: HMSO).

Department of Health (1989b) *Working for Patients* (London: HMSO).

Department of Health (1990) *Community Care in the Next Decade and Beyond: Policy Guidance* (London: HMSO).

Department of Health (1993) *Training for the Future* (London: HMSO).

Department of Health (1994) *Implementing Caring for People: Housing and Homelessness* (London: Department of Health).

Department of Health (1995a) *NHS Responsibilities for Meeting Continuing Health Care Needs* (London: Department of Health).

Department of Health (1995b) *Building Bridges: A Guide to Arrangements for Inter-Agency Working for the Care and Protection of Severely Disabled People* (London: Department of Health).

Department of Health (1995c) *An Introduction to Joint Commissioning* (London: Department of Health).

Department of Health (1995d) *Practical Guidance on Joint Commissioning* (London: Department of Health).

Department of Health (1995e) *European Year: A Historical Report and Evaluation* (London: Department of Health).

Department of Health (1997a) *Social Services: Achievement and Challenge* (London: The Stationery Office).

Department of Health (1997b) *Developing Partnerships in Mental Health* (London: The Stationery Office).

Department of Health/Audit Commission (1997) *Reviewing Social Services* (London: Department of Health and London: Audit Commission).

Department of Health/Department of the Environment (1997) *Housing and Community Care: Establishing a Strategic Framework* (London: Department of Health).

Department of Health and Social Security (1971) *Better Services for the Mentally Handicapped* (London: HMSO).

Department of Health and Social Security (1975) *Better Services for the Mentally Ill* (London: HMSO).

Department of Health and Social Security (1978) A *Happier Old Age* (London: HMSO).

Department of Health and Social Security (1981a) *Care in the Community: A Consultative Document on Moving Resources for Care in England* (London: Department of Health and Social Security).

Department of Health and Social Security (1981b) *Growing Older* (London: HMSO).

Department of Health and Social Security (1983) *Care in the Community and Joint Finance*, Health Circular (83)6 and Local Authority Circular (83)5, March (London: Department of Health and Social Security).

Department of Health/Social Services Inspectorate (1990) *Training for Community Care: A Strategy* (London: Department of Health).

Department of Health/Social Services Inspectorate (1991) *Care Management and Assessment: Summary of Practice Guidance* (London: HMSO).

Department of Health/Social Services Inspectorate (1993) *No Longer Afraid: The Safeguard of Older People in Domestic Settings* (London: HMSO).

Dieck, M. (1990) 'Politics for elderly people in the FRG', pp. 95–119 in A. Jamieson and R. Illsley (eds), *Contrasting European Policies for the Care of Older People* (Aldershot: Avebury).

Dieck, M. (1994) 'Reforming against the grain: long-term care in Germany', pp. 253–66 in R. Page and J. Baldock (eds), *Social Policy Review 6* (Canterbury: Social Policy Association).

Digby, A. (1978) *Pauper Palaces* (London: Routledge & Kegan Paul).

Dobson, N. (1996) 'Loose cannon', *Municipal Journal*, 8 November, p. 18.

Dominelli, L. and Hoogvelt, A. (1996) 'Globalization and the technocratization of social work', *Critical Social Policy*, vol. 16, no. 2, pp. 45–62.

Downey, R. (1997) 'Minister's counsel for care', *Community Care*, 12–18 June, pp. 10–11.

Drake, R. (1996) 'A critique of the role of the traditional charities', pp. 147–66 in L. Barton (ed.), *Disability and Society: Emerging Issues and Insights* (Harlow: Longman).

Eaton, L. (1997) 'Vital signs are poor', *Community Care*, 17–23 April, pp. 18–19.

Edelman, M. (1971) *Politics as Symbolic Action* (Chicago: Markham).

Edwards, P. and Kenny, D. (1997) *Community Care Trends 1997 Report* (Luton: The Local Government Management Board).

Emerson, E. (1992) 'What is normalisation?', pp. 1–18 in H. Brown and H. Smith (eds), *Normalisation: A Reader for the Nineties* (London: Tavistock/ Routledge).

Emerson, E. and Hatton, C. (1996) *Moving Out: The Impact of Relocation from Hospital to Community on the Quality of Life of People with Learning Disabilities* (London: HMSO).

Esping-Andersen, G. (1990) *The Three Worlds of Welfare Capitalism* (Oxford: Polity Press).

Eurobarometer Survey (1993) *Age and Attitudes: Main Results from a Eurobarometer Survey* (Brussels: Commission of the European Communities, Directorate-General V, Employment, Industrial Relations and Social Affairs).

European Commission (1993) *European Social Policy: Options for the Union* (Luxembourg: Office for Official Publications of the European Communities).

European Commission (1994) *European Social Policy: A Way Forward for the Union* (Luxembourg: Office for Official Publications of the European Communities).

Evers, A. and Olk, T. (1991) 'The mix of care provisions for the frail elderly in the Federal Republic of Germany', pp. 59–100 in A. Evers and I. Svetlik (eds), *New Welfare Mixes in Care for the Elderly, Vol.3, Canada, France, Germany, Italy, United Kingdom* (Vienna: European Centre for Social Welfare Policy and Research).

Eyden, J. (1965) 'The physically handicapped', pp. 161–74 in D. Marsh (ed.), *An Introduction to the Study of Social Administration* (London: Routledge & Kegan Paul).

Finch, J. (1984) 'Community care: developing non-sexist alternatives', *Critical Social Policy*, issue no. 9, pp. 6–18.

Finch, J. (1989) *Family Obligations and Social Change* (Cambridge: Polity Press).

Finch, J. and Groves, D. (eds) (1983) *A Labour of Love: Women, Work and Caring* (London: Routledge & Kegan Paul).

Finkelstein, V. (1993) 'Disability: a social challenge or an administrative responsibility?', pp. 34–43 in J. Swain, V. Finkelstein, S. French and M. Oliver (eds), *Disabling Barriers – Enabling Environments* (London: Sage).

Firth Report (1987) *Public Support for Residential Care*, Joint Central and Local Government Working Party (London: Department of Health and Social Security).

Fisher, M. (1990–1) 'Defining the practice content of care management', *Social Work and Social Services Review*, vol. 2, no. 3, pp. 204–30.

Fisher, M. (1994) 'Man-made care: community care and older male carers', *British Journal of Social Work*, vol. 24, no. 6, pp. 659–80.

Fletcher, P. and Herbert, G. (1996) 'Trapped in care', *Community Care*, 4 January, p. 19.

Flynn, N. (1989) 'The "new right" and social policy', *Policy and Politics*, vol. 17, no. 2, pp. 97–110.

Forder, J., Knapp, M. and Wistow, G. (1996) 'Competition in the mixed economy of care', *Journal of Social Policy*, vol. 25, Part 2, pp. 201–22.

Forrest, R., Kennett, P. and Leather, P. (1994) *Home Owners with Negative Equity* (Bristol: SAUS Publications).

Foucault, M. (1967) *Madness and Civilisation* (London: Tavistock).

Foucault, M. (1979) *Discipline and Punish: The Birth of the Prison* (Harmondsworth: Penguin).

Fraser, D. (1984) *The Evolution of the Welfare State*, second edition (London: Macmillan).

Friend, J., Power, J. and Yewlett, C. (1974) *Public Planning: The Intercorporate Dimension* (London: Tavistock).

Fulcher, G. (1996) 'Beyond normalisation but not utopia', pp. 167–90 in L. Barton (ed.), *Disability and Society: Emerging Issues and Insights* (Harlow: Longman).

Gavilan, H. (1992) 'Taking control from the frail', *The Guardian*, 17 June.

George, V. and Taylor-Gooby, P. (eds) (1996) *European Welfare Policy: Squaring the Welfare Circle* (Basingstoke: Macmillan).

Gibbins, J. (1988) 'Residential care for mentally ill adults', pp. 157–97 in I. Sinclair (ed.), *Residential Care: The Research Reviewed* (London: HMSO).

Gillie Report (1963) *The Field of Work of the Family Doctor* (London: HMSO).

Gladstone, D. (1996) 'The changing dynamic of institutional care', pp. 134–61 in D. Wright and A. Digby (eds), *From Idiocy to Mental Deficiency* (London: Routledge).

Glendinning, C. and Bewley, C. (1992) *Involving Disabled People in Community Care Planning – the First Steps* (Manchester: Department of Social Policy and Social Work, University of Manchester).

Glennerster, H., Falkingham, J. and Evandrou, M. (1990) 'How much do we care?', *Social Policy and Administration*, vol. 24, no. 2, pp. 93–103.

Godlove, C. and Mann, A. (1980) 'Thirty years of the welfare state: current issues in British social policy for the aged', *Aged Care and Services Review*, vol. 2, no. 1, pp. 1–12.

Goffman, E. (1968) *Asylums: Essays on the Social Situation of Mental Patients and Other Inmates* (Harmondsworth: Penguin).

Goldsmith, M. and Klausen, K. (eds) (1997) *European Integration and Local Government* (Cheltenham: Edward Elgar).

Goodwin, S. (1990) *Community Care and the Future of Mental Health Service Provision* (Aldershot: Avebury).

Green, H. (1988) *Informal Carers: General Household Survey, 1985* (London: HMSO).

Griffiths Report (1988) *Community Care: An Agenda for Action* (London: HMSO).

Griffiths, S. (1997) 'Bringing the house down', *Community Care*, 29 May–4 June, pp. 22–3.

Groves, D. (1995) 'Costing a fortune? Pensioners' financial resources in the context of community care', pp. 141–62 in I. Allen and E. Perkins (eds), *The Future of Family Care for Older People* (London: HMSO).

Guillebaud Report (1956) *Committee of Enquiry into the Cost of the National Health Service* (London: HMSO).

Gurney, C. (1990) *The Meaning of Home in the Decade of Owner Occupation* (Bristol: School for Advanced Urban Studies).

Gurney, C. and Means, R. (1993) 'The meaning of home in later life', pp. 119–31 in S. Arber and M Evandrou (eds), *Ageing, Independence and the Life Course* (London: Jessica Kingsley).

Haber, C. (1983) *Beyond Sixty-Five: The Dilemma of Old Age in America's Past* (Cambridge: Cambridge University Press).

Hadley, R. and Clough, R. (1996) *Care in Chaos: Frustration and Challenge in Community Care* (London: Cassell).

Hadley, R. and Hatch, S. (1981) *Social Welfare and the Failure of the State: Centralised Social Services and Participatory Alternatives* (London: Allen & Unwin).

Ham, C. (1994) *Management and Competition in the New NHS* (Oxford: Radcliffe Medical Press).

Ham, C. and Hill, M. (1993 edition) *The Policy Process in the Modern Capitalist State* (Brighton: Wheatsheaf).

Hambleton, R. and Hoggett, P. (eds) (1984) *The Politics of Decentralisation: Theory and Practice of a Radical Local Government Initiative*, Working Paper No.46 (Bristol: School for Advanced Urban Studies).

Hamnett, C. (1995) 'Housing equity release and inheritance', pp. 163–80 in I. Allen and E. Perkins (eds), *The Future of Family Care for Older People* (London: HMSO).

Hantrais, L. (1995) *Social Policy in the European Union* (Basingstoke: Macmillan).

Harding, T., Meredith, B. and Wistow, G. (1996) 'Options for long-term care: economic, social and ethical choices', pp. 7–26 in T. Harding, B. Meredith and G. Wistow (eds), *Options for Long-Term Care* (London: HMSO).

Harris, A. (1961) *Meals on Wheels for Old People* (London: National Corporation for the Care of Old People).

Harris, L. (1995) 'Employment initiatives – what next?', *European Information Service*, no. 158, March, p. 35.

Harris, R. and Lavan, A. (1992) 'Professional mobility in the new Europe: the case of social work', *Journal of European Social Policy*, vol. 2, no. 1, pp. 1–15.

Harrison, F. (1986) *The Young Disabled Adult, the Use of Residential Homes and Hospital Units for the Age Group, 16–64* (London: Royal College of Physicians).

Harrison, L. and Means, R. (1990) *Housing: The Essential Element in Community Care* (Oxford: Anchor Housing Trust/SHAC).

Hasler, F. (1997) 'Disability: something old, something new', *Community Care*, 22–28 May, p. 22.

Hayward, D. (1976) 'Dimensions of home', in S. Weidemann and J. Anderson (eds), *Priorities for Environmental Design Research* (Washington, DC: EDRA).

Health Advisory Service (1983) *The Rising Tide: Developing Services for Mental Illness in Old Age* (London: HMSO).

Henwood, M. (1992) 'Twilight zone', *Health Services Journal*, 5 November, pp. 28–30.

Henwood, M. (1994) *Hospital Discharge Workbook: A Manual on Hospital Discharge* (London: Department of Health).

Herbert Report (1960) *Royal Commission on Local Government in Greater London 1957–1960* (London: HMSO).

Heywood, F. (1994) *Adaptations: Finding Ways to Say Yes* (Bristol: SAUS Publications).

Heywood, F. with Smart, G. (1996) *Funding Adaptations: The Need to Co-operate* (Bristol: Policy Press).

Higgins, J. (1989) 'Defining community care: realities and myths', *Social Policy and Administration*, vol. 23, no. 1, pp. 3–16.

Hill, M. (ed.) (1991) *Social Work and the European Community: The Social Policy and Practice Context*, Research Highlights in Social Work 23 (London: Jessica Kingsley).

Hill, M. (1993) *Understanding Social Policy*, fourth edition (Oxford: Blackwell).

Hills, J. (ed.) (1990) *The State of Welfare* (Oxford: Oxford University Press).

Hirschman, A. (1970) *Exit, Voice and Loyalty: Responses to Decline in Firms, Organisations and States* (Cambridge, Mass: Harvard University Press).

Hoggett, P. (1990) *Modernisation, Political Strategy and the Welfare State: An Organisational Perspective*, DQM Paper No.2 (Bristol: School for Advanced Urban Studies).

Hoggett, P. (1991) 'The new public sector management', *Policy and Politics*, vol. 19, no. 4, pp. 243–56.

Hoggett, P. (1992) 'The politics of empowerment', *Going Local*, no. 19, pp. 18–19.

Hoggett, P. (1996) 'New modes of control in the public sector', *Public Administration*, vol. 74, Spring, pp. 9–32.

Hoggett, P. and Hambleton, R. (1987) *Decentralisation and Democracy*, Occasional Paper No.28 (Bristol: School for Advanced Urban Studies).

Holmans, A. (1995) *Housing Demand and Need in England, 1991 to 2011* (York: York Publishing Services).

Holstein, B.E., Due, P., Almind, G. and Holst, E. (1991) 'The home help service in Denmark', pp. 38–62 in A. Jamieson (ed.), *Home Care for Older People in Europe: A Comparison of Policies and Practices* (Oxford: Oxford University Press).

Hooton, S. (1996) 'Nightmare on Clarke Street', *Inside Housing*, 6 December, pp. 18–19.

House of Lords Library (1995) *Community Care (Direct Payments) Bill: Library Notes* (London: House of Lords).

Housing Corporation (1996) *Supported Housing: Discussion Paper* (London: Housing Corporation).

Hoyes, L. and Harrison, L. (1987) 'An ordinary private life', *Community Care*, 12 February, pp. 20–1.

Hoyes, L. and Johnson, M. (1997) 'Under the same roof', *Community Care*, 8–14 May, pp. 30–1.

Hoyes, L. and Le Grand, J. (1991) *Markets in Social Care Services: A Resource Pack* (Bristol: School for Advanced Urban Studies).

Hoyes, L. and Means, R. (1993a) 'Markets, contracts and social care services: prospects and problems', pp. 287–95 in J. Bornat *et al.* (eds), *Community Care: A Reader* (Basingstoke: Macmillan).

Hoyes, L. and Means, R. (1993b) 'Quasi-markets and the reform of community care', pp. 93–124 in J. Le Grand and W. Bartlett (eds), *Quasi-Markets and Social Policy* (Basingstoke: Macmillan).

Hoyes, L. and Means, R. (1993c) 'Making changes', *Community Care*, 30 May, p. 22.

Hoyes, L. and Means, R. (1994) 'Open plan', *Health Services Journal*, 4 August, p. 23.

Hoyes, L. and Means, R. with Hawes, D., Smart, G. and Smith, R. (1996) *Supported Housing and Community Care* (London: Housing Corporation).

Hoyes, L., Means, R. and Le Grand, J. (1992) *Made to Measure? Performance Measurement and Community Care*, Occasional Paper 39 (Bristol: School for Advanced Urban Studies).

Hoyes, L., Jeffers, S., Lart, R., Means, R. and Taylor, M. (1993) *User Empowerment and the Reform of Community Care: An Interim Assessment* (Bristol: School for Advanced Urban Studies).

Hoyes, L., Lart, R., Means, R. and Taylor, M. (1994) *Community Care in Transition* (York: Joseph Rowntree Foundation and London: Community Care).

Hudson, B. (1987) 'Collaboration in social welfare: a framework for analysis', *Policy and Politics*, vol. 15, no. 3, pp. 175–82.

Hudson, B. (1990) 'Social policy and the new right – the strange case of the community care White Paper', *Local Government Studies*, vol. 16, no. 6, pp. 15–34.

Hudson, B. (1992) 'All dressed up – but nowhere to go?, *Health Services Journal*, 22 October, pp. 22–4.

Hudson, B. (1993) *The Busy Person's Guide to Care Management* (Sheffield: Joint Unit for Social Services Research, University of Sheffield).

Hudson, B. (1995) 'Joint commissioning: organisational revolution or misplaced enthusiasm?', *Policy and Politics*, vol. 23, no. 3, pp. 233–49.

Hudson, B. (1996) 'Community care plans: a new agenda?', *Local Government Policy Making*, vol. 23, no. 1, pp. 19–27.

Hudson, J., Watson, L. and Allan, G. (1996) *Moving Obstacles: Housing Choices and Community Care* (Bristol: Policy Press).

Hugman, R. (1994) *Ageing and the Care of Older People in Europe* (Basingstoke: Macmillan).

Hutchinson, J. (1994) 'The practice of partnership in local economic partnership', *Local Government Studies*, vol. 20, no. 3, pp. 335–44.

Huws Jones, R. (1952) 'Old people's welfare – successes and failures', *Social Service Quarterly*, vol. 26, no. 1, pp. 19–22.

Huxham, C. (ed.) (1996) *Creating Collaborative Advantage* (London: Sage).

Irvine, E. (1950) 'The place of the Health Department in the care of the aged', *The Medical Officer*, 12 August, p. 74.

Jack, R. (ed.) (1995) *Empowerment in Community Care* (London: Chapman & Hall).

Jamieson, A. (1990a) 'Care of older people in the European Community', pp. 32–45 in L. Hantrais, S. Mangen and M. O'Brien (eds), *Caring and the Welfare State in the 1990s*, Cross-National Research Paper 2 (Birmingham: The Cross-National Research Group, Aston University).

Jamieson, A. (1990b) 'Informal care in Europe', pp. 3–21 in A. Jamieson and R. Illsley (eds), *Contrasting European Policies for the Care of Older People* (Aldershot: Avebury).

Jamieson, A. (1991) 'Community care for older people', pp. 107–26 in G. Room (ed.), *Towards a European Welfare State?* (Bristol: SAUS Publications).

Jani-Le Bris, H. (1993) *Family Care of Dependent Older People in the European Community* (Dublin: European Foundation for the Improvement of Living and Working Conditions).

Jarre, D. (1991) 'Subsidiarity in social services in Germany', *Social Policy and Administration*, vol. 25, no. 3, pp. 211–17.

Jenkins, G. (1996) *Residents' Money: A Guide to Good Practice in Care Homes* (London: Age Concern).

Johnson, M. (1990) 'Dependency and interdependency', pp. 209–28, in J. Bond and P. Coleman (eds), *Ageing in Society: An Introduction to Social Gerontology* (London: Sage).

Johnson, N. (1987) *The Welfare State in Transition: The Theory and Practice of Welfare Pluralism* (Brighton: Wheatsheaf).

Johnson, P. (1987) *Structured Dependency of the Elderly: A Critical Note* (London: Centre for Economic Policy Research).

Jones, C. (ed.) (1993) *New Perspectives on the Welfare State in Europe* (London: Routledge).

Jones, K. (1972) *A History of the Mental Health Services* (London: Routledge & Kegan Paul).

Jones, K. (1993) *Asylums and After* (London: Athlone).

Jones, K. and Fowles, A. (1984) *Ideas on Institutions* (London: Routledge & Kegan Paul).

Kestenbaum, A. (1992) *Cash for Care* (Nottingham: Independent Living Fund).

King's Fund Centre (1980) *An Ordinary Life: Comprehensive Locally-based Residential Services for Mentally Handicapped People*, King's Fund Project Paper No.24 (London: King's Fund Centre).

Knapp, M., Wistow, T. and Jones, N. (1992) 'Smart moves', *Health Services Journal*, 29 October, pp. 28–30.

Knapp, M., Wistow, G., Forder, J. and Hardy, B. (1993) *Markets for Social Care: Opportunities, Barriers and Implications*, PSSRU Discussion Paper 919 (Canterbury: Personal Social Services Research Unit, University of Kent).

Laing and Buisson (1992) *Laing's Review of Private Health Care, 1992* (London: Laing and Buisson).

Land, H. (1978) 'Who cares for the family?', *Journal of Social Policy*, vol. 7, no. 3, pp. 257–84.

Landwehr, R. and Wolff R. (1992) 'The Federal Republic of Germany', in B. Munday (ed.), *Social Services in the Member States of the European Community: A Handbook of Information and Data* (Canterbury: European Institute of Social Services, University of Kent).

Langan, J. and Means, R. (1995) *Personal Finances, Elderly People with Dementia and the 'New' Community Care* (Oxford: Anchor Housing Trust).

Langan, J., Means, R. and Rolfe, S. (1996) *Maintaining Independence in Later Life: Older People Speaking* (Oxford: Anchor Trust).

Langan, M. (1990) 'Community care in the 1990s: the community care White Paper: "Caring for People" ', *Critical Social Policy*, issue 29, pp. 58–70.

Lart, R. (1997) *Crossing Boundaries: Accessing Community Mental Health Services for Prisoners on Release* (Bristol: Policy Press).

Lavery, R. and Lundy, L. (1994) 'The social security appointee system', *Journal of Social Welfare and Family Law*, pp. 313–27.

Leat, D. (1988) 'Residential care for younger physically disabled adults', pp. 199–239 in I. Sinclair (ed.), *Residential Care: The Research Reviewed* (London: HMSO).

Leat, D. and Perri 6 (1997) *Holding Back the Years: How Britain Can Grow Old Better in the Twenty First Century* (London: DEMOS).

Leather, P. and Morrison, T. (1997) *The State of UK Housing* (Bristol: Policy Press).

Leedham, I. and Wistow, G. (1992) *Community Care and General Practitioners* (Leeds: Nuffield Institute for Health Services Studies, University of Leeds).

Le Grand, J. and Bartlett, W. (eds) (1993) *Quasi-Markets and Social Policy* (Basingstoke: Macmillan).

Leibfried, S. and Pierson, P. (eds) (1995) *European Social Policy: Between Fragmentation and Integration* (Washington, DC: Brookings Institution).

Lewis, J. and Glennerster, H. (1996) *Implementing the New Community Care* (Buckingham: Open University Press).

Lewis, J., Bernstock, P., Bovell, V. and Wookey, F. (1996) 'The purchaser–provider split in social care: is it working?', *Social Policy and Administration*, vol. 30, no. 1, pp. 1–19.

Lipsky, M. (1980) *Street Level Bureaucracy* (New York: Russell Sage).

London Federation of Housing Associations (1995) *Managing Vulnerability: The Challenge for Managers of Independent Housing* (London: London Federation of Housing Associations).

Lowe, R. (1993) *The Welfare State in Britain Since 1945* (Basingstoke: Macmillan).

Lukes, S. (1974) *Power: A Radical View* (London: Macmillan).

Lund, B. and Foord, M. (1997) *Housing Strategies and Community Care: Towards Integrated Living?* (Bristol: Policy Press).

Lunt, N., Mannion, R. and Smith, P. (1996) 'The finance of community care', pp. 78–96 in N. Lunt and D. Coyle (eds), *Welfare and Policy: Research Agendas and Issues* (London: Taylor & Francis).

Lyons, K. (1992) 'The mobile profession?', *Inside Community Care*, no. 913, 30 April, pp. ii–iii.

McCafferty, P. (1994) *Living Independently: A Study of the Housing Needs of Elderly and Disabled People* (London: HMSO).

McEwan, P. and Laverty, S. (1949) *The Chronic Sick and Elderly in Hospital* (Bradford: Bradford (B) Hospital Management Committee).

Macfarlane, A. and Laurie, L. (1996) *Demolishing 'Special Needs': Fundamental Principles of Non-Discriminatory Housing* (Derby: British Council of Organisations of Disabled People).

McGrath, M. and Grant, G. (1992) 'Supporting "needs-led" services: implications for planning and management systems', *Journal of Social Policy*, vol. 21, part 1, pp. 71–98.

Mackintosh, S. and Leather, P. (1994) 'Funding and managing the adaptation of owner occupied homes for people with physical disabilities', *Health and Social Care in the Community*, vol. 2, no. 4, pp. 229–39.

Maclennan, D., Gibb, K. and More, A. (1990) *Paying for Britain's Housing* (York: Joseph Rowntree Foundation)

Malin, N., Race, D. and Jones, G. (1980) *Services for the Mentally Handicapped in Britain* (London: Croom Helm).

Malpass, P. (1993) 'Housing policy and the housing system since 1979', pp. 23–38 in P. Malpass and R. Means (eds), *Implementing Housing Policy* (Milton Keynes: Open University Press).

Malpass, P. and Means, R. (eds) (1993) *Implementing Housing Policy* (Milton Keynes: Open University Press).

Malpass, P. and Murie, A. (1994 edition) *Housing Policy and Practice* (Basingstoke: Macmillan).

Manthorpe, J. and Stanley, N. (1997) 'A serious failure of vision', *The Guardian Society*, 26 March, pp. 6–7.

Marsh, A. and Riseborough, M. (1995) *Making Ends Meet: Older People, Housing Association Costs and the Affordability of Rented Housing* (London: National Federation of Housing Associations).

Martin, J., Meltzer, H. and Elliot, D. (1988) *The Prevalence of Disability Among Adults*, OPCS Surveys (London: HMSO).

Martin J., White, A. and Meltzer, H. (1989) *Disabled Adults: Services, Transport and Employment*, OPCS Surveys (London: HMSO).

Martin, L. and Gaster, L. (1993) 'Community care planning in Wolverhampton, involving the voluntary sector and black and minority ethnic groups', pp. 15–52 in R. Smith, L. Gaster, L. Harrison, R. Means and P. Thistlethwaite, *Working Together for Better Community Care* (Bristol: SAUS Publications).

Martin, M. (1990) *The Development of Residential Care for Elderly People 1890–1948*, unpublished doctoral thesis, University of Bristol.

Martin, M. (1992) *The Manufacture and Mass Production of the Chronic Sick: A Historical Perspective*, paper delivered to the Annual Conference of the British Society of Gerontology, University of Kent, 18–20 September.

Martin, M. (1995) 'Medical knowledge and medical practice: geriatric knowledge in the 1950s', *Social History of Medicine*, vol. 7, no. 3, pp. 443–61.

Matarasso, F. (1997) *Use or Ornament? The Social Impact of Participation in the Arts* (Stroud: Comedia).

Matthews, O. (undated) *Housing the Infirm*, published by the author and originally distributed through W.H. Smith and Son.

Means, R. (1986) 'The development of social services for elderly people: historical perspectives', pp. 87–108 in C. Phillipson and A. Walker (eds), *Ageing and Social Policy: A Critical Assessment* (Aldershot: Gower).

Means, R. (1996a) 'From "special needs" housing to independent living?', *Housing Studies*, vol. 11, no. 2, pp. 207–31.

Means, R. (1996b) 'Housing and community care for older people – joint working at the local level', *Journal of Interprofessional Care*, vol. 10, no. 3, pp. 273–83.

Means, R. (1997a) 'Home, independence and community care: time for a wider vision?', *Policy and Politics*, vol. 25, no. 4, pp. 409–19.

Means, R. (1997b) 'Housing options in 2020: a suitable home for all?', pp. 142–64 in M. Evandrou (ed.), *Baby Boomers: Ageing in the 21st Century* (London: Age Concern England).

Means, R. and Harrison, L. (1988) *Community Care: Before and After the Griffiths Report* (London: Association of London Authorities).

Means, R. and Langan, J. (1996) 'Charging and quasi-markets in community care: implications for elderly people with dementia', *Social Policy and Administration*, vol. 30, no. 3, pp. 244–62.

Means, R. and Lart, R. (1994) 'Involving older people in community care planning', pp. 25–34 in J. Smith (ed.), *More Power to our Elders* (London: Counsel and Care).

Means, R. and Smith, R. (1985) *The Development of Welfare Services for Elderly People* (London: Croom Helm).

Means, R. and Smith, R. (1988) 'Implementing a pluralistic approach to evaluation in health education', *Policy and Politics*, vol. 16, no. 1, pp. 17–28.

Means, R. and Smith, R. (1998 edition) *From Poor Law to Community Care? The Development of Welfare Services for Elderly People* (Bristol: Policy Press).

Means, R., Smith, R., Harrison, L., Jeffers, S. and Doogan, K. (1990) *Understanding Alcohol: An Evaluation of an Educational Programme* (London: Health Education Authority).

Means, R., Hoyes, L., Lart, R. and Taylor, M. (1994) 'Quasi-markets and community care: towards user empowerment?', pp. 158–83 in W. Bartlett, C. Propper, D. Wilson and J. Le Grand (eds), *Quasi-Markets in the Welfare State*, SAUS Study No.14 (Bristol: School for Advanced Urban Studies).

Means, R., Brenton, M., Harrison, L. and Heywood, F. (1997) *Making Partnerships Work in Community Care: A Guide for Practitioners in Housing, Health and Social Services* (Bristol: Policy Press).

Meehan, E. and Whitting, G. (eds) (1989) 'Gender and public policy: European law and British equal opportunity policies', special issue, *Policy and Politics*, vol. 17, no. 4.

Mental Health Foundation (1993) *Mental Illness: The Facts* (London: Mental Health Foundation).

Mental Health Foundation (1994) *Creating Community Care: Report of the Mental Health Foundation Inquiry into Community Care for People with Severe Mental Illness* (London: Mental Health Foundation).

Mental Health Foundation (1996) *Building Expectations: Opportunities and Services for People with a Learning Disability* (London: Mental Health Foundation).

Midgley, G., Munlo, I. and Brown, M. (1997) *Sharing Power: Integrating User Involvement and Multi-Agency Working to Improve Housing for Older People* (Bristol: Policy Press).

Millar, J. and Warman, A. (1996) *Family Obligations in Europe* (London: Family Policy Studies Centre).

Miller, E. and Gwynne, G. (1972) *A Life Apart* (London: Tavistock).

Ministry of Health (1957) *Local Authority Services for the Chronic Sick and Infirm*, Circular 14/57 (London: HMSO).

Ministry of Health (1966) *Health and Welfare: The Development of Community Care - Revisions to 1975–76* (London: HMSO).

Mishra, R. (1984) *The Welfare State in Crisis: Social Thought and Social Change* (Brighton: Wheatsheaf).

Mishra, R. (1990) *The Welfare State in Capitalist Society: Policies of Retrenchment and Maintenance in Europe, North America and Australia* (Hemel Hempstead: Harvester Wheatsheaf).

Moriarty, J. and Webb, S. (1997) *Part of their Lives: An Evaluation of Community Care Arrangements for Older People with Dementia* (London: National Institution for Social Work Research Unit).

Moroney, R. (1976) *The Family and the State* (London: Longman).

Morris, C. (1940) 'Public health during the first three months of war', *Social Work* (London) January, pp. 186–96.

Morris, J. (1990a) 'Women and disability', *Social Work Today*, 8 November, p. 22.

Morris, J. (1990b) *Our Homes, Our Rights: Housing, Independent Living and Physically Disabled People* (London: Shelter).

Morris, J. (1991) *Pride Against Prejudice: Transforming Attitudes to Disability* (London: The Women's Press).

Morris, J. (1993) *Community Care or Independent Living* (York: Joseph Rowntree Foundation/London: Community Care).

Morris, J. (1995a) *Housing and Floating Support: A Review* (York: York Publishing Services Ltd.).

Morris, J. (1995b) *The Power to Change: Commissioning Health and Social Services with Disabled People* (London: King's Fund Centre).

Morris, J. (ed.) (1996) *Encounters with Strangers – Feminism and Disability* (London: The Women's Press).

Morris, P. (1969) *Put Away: A Sociological Study of Institutions for the Mentally Retarded* (London: Routledge & Kegan Paul).

Munday, B. (1996) 'Social care in the member states of the European Union: contexts and overview', pp. 21–66 in B. Munday and P. Ely (eds), *Social Care in Europe* (Hemel Hempstead: Prentice Hall).

Munday, B. and Ely, P. (eds) (1996) *Social Care in Europe* (Hemel Hempstead: Prentice Hall).

Murphy, E. (1991) *After the Asylums: Community Care for People with Mental Illness* (London: Faber & Faber).

Neill, J. and Williams, J. (1992) *Leaving Hospital: Elderly People and their Discharge to Community Care* (London: HMSO).

Newton, J., Ryan, P., Carman, A., Clarke, K., Coombs, M., Walsh, K. and Muijen, M. (1996) *Care Management: Is It Working?* (London: Sainsbury Centre for Mental Health).

Nocon, A. and Qureshi, H. (1996) *Outcomes of Community Care for Users and Carers* (Buckingham: Open University Press).

Nolan, M. and Caldock, K. (1996) 'Assessment: identifying the barriers to good practice', *Health and Social Care in the Community*, vol. 4, no. 2, pp. 77–85.

Nolan, M., Grant, G. and Keady, J. (1996) *Understanding Family Care* (Buckingham: Open University Press).

Norton, A., Stoten, B. and Taylor, H. (1986) *Councils of Care: Planning a Local Government Strategy for Older People* (London: Centre for Policy on Ageing).

Nuffield Provincial Hospitals Trust (1946) *The Hospital Surveys: The Domesday Book of the Hospital Services* (Oxford: Oxford University Press).

Office for National Statistics (1997) *Social Trends 27* (London: HMSO).

Oldman, C., Quilgars, D. and Oldfield, N. (1996) *Housing Benefit and Service Charges*, Research Report No.55 (London: Department of Social Security).

Oliver, M. (1990) *The Politics of Disablement* (Basingstoke: Macmillan).

Oliver, M. (1996) *Understanding Disability: From Theory to Practice* (Basingstoke: Macmillan).

Owens, P., Carrier, J. and Horder, J. (eds) (1995) *Interprofessional Issues in Community and Primary Health Care* (Basingstoke: Macmillan).

Pahl, R. (1984) Divisions of Labour (Oxford: Blackwell).

Parker, G. and Clarke, H. (1997) 'Will you still need me, will you still feed me? – paying for care in old age', *Social Policy and Administration*, vol. 31, no. 2, pp. 119–35.

Parker, J. (1965) *Local Health and Welfare Services* (London: Allen & Unwin).

Parker, R. (1988) 'An historical background', pp. 1–38 in I. Sinclair (ed.), *Residential Care: The Research Reviewed* (London: HMSO).

Parker, R. (1990) 'Care and the private sector', pp. 293–361 in I. Sinclair, R. Parker, D. Leat and J. Williams, *The Kaleidoscope of Care* (London: HMSO).

Parton, N. (1983) *The Politics of Child Abuse* (Basingstoke: Macmillan).

Peters, T. and Waterman, R. (1982) *In Search of Excellence* (New York: Harper & Row).

Phillips, J. (1996) 'The future of social work with older people in a changing world', pp. 135–51 in N. Parton (ed.), *Social Theory, Social Change and Social Work* (London: Routledge).

Phillipson, C. (1982) *Capitalism and the Construction of Old Age* (Basingstoke: Macmillan).

Piachaud, D. and Webb, J. (1996) 'Crumbling cornerstone', *Guardian Society*, 20 November, pp. 2–3.

Pieda Plc (1996) *An Evaluation of the Disabled Facilities Grant System* (London: HMSO).

Pierson, C. (1991) *Beyond the Welfare State?* (Cambridge: Polity Press).

Plant, R. (1992) 'Citizenship, rights and welfare', pp. 15–30 in A. Coote (ed.), *The Welfare of Citizens: Developing New Social Rights* (London: Institution for Public Policy Research/Rivers Oram Press).

Plowden, B. (1997) 'Walking back to happiness', *Guardian Society*, 30 April, pp. 2–3.

Potter, P. and Zill, G. (1992) 'Older households and their housing situation', pp. 109–31 in L. Davies (ed.), *The Coming of Age in Europe: Older People in the European Community* (London: Age Concern England (ACE) Books).

Powell, R. (1996) 'Can the face of new labour deliver on social work?', *Professional Social Work*, June, pp. 10–11.

Pressman, J. and Wildavsky, A. (1973) *Implementation* (Berkeley: University of California Press).

Price Waterhouse/Department of Health (1991) *Implementing Community Care: Purchaser, Commissioner and Provider Roles* (London: HMSO).

Pynos, J. and Liebig, P. (eds) (1995) *Housing Frail Elders: International Policies, Perspectives and Prospects* (Baltimore: Johns Hopkins University Press).

Race, D. (1987) 'Normalisation: theory and practice', pp. 62–79 in N. Malin (ed.), *Reassessing Community Care* (London: Croom Helm).

Ramon, S. (1991) 'Principles and conceptual knowledge', pp. 6–34 in S. Ramon (ed.), *Beyond Community Care: Normalisation and Integration Work* (London: Macmillan).

Ramon, S. and Giannichedda, M.G. (eds) (1991) *Psychiatry in Transition: The British and Italian Experience*, second edition (London: Pluto Press).

Randolph, B. (1993) 'The re-privatisation of housing associations', pp. 39–58 in P. Malpass and R. Means (eds), *Implementing Housing Policy* (Milton Keynes: Open University Press).

Rapoport, A. (1995) 'A critical look at the concept of "home"', pp. 25–52 in D. Benjamin and D. Stea (eds), *The Home: Words, Interpretations, Meanings and Environments* (Aldershot: Avebury).

Reeves, D. and McCaskie, K. (1995) 'A slippery slope', *Inside Housing*, 28 July, pp. 14–15.

Report of the Mental Deficiency Committee (1929) *Part III – The Adult Defective* (London: HMSO).

Richards, E., Wilsdon, T. and Lyons, S. (1996) *Paying for Long-Term Care* (London: Institute for Public Policy Research).

Richardson, J. (ed.) (1996) *European Union: Power and Policy-Making* (London: Routledge).

Riseborough, M. and Niner, P. (1994) *I Didn't Know You Cared: A Survey of Anchor's Sheltered Housing Tenants* (Oxford: Anchor Housing Trust).

Ritchie, J., Dick, D. and Lingham, R. (1994) *Report of the Inquiry into the Care and Treatment of Christopher Clunis* (London: HMSO).

Robb, B. (1967) *Sans Everything: A Case to Answer* (London: Nelson).

Roberts, G. (1992) 'Legal aspects of community care', paper delivered to the Law Society Conference 'Community Care: A Challenge to the Legal Profession', 20 November.

Roberts, N. (1970) *Our Future Selves* (London: Allen & Unwin).

Roebuck, J. (1979) 'When does old age begin? The evolution of the English definition', *Journal of Social History*, vol. 12, no. 3, pp. 416–28.

Room, G. (1991) 'Towards a European welfare state?', pp. 1–14 in G. Room (ed.), *Towards a European Welfare State?*, SAUS Study 6 (Bristol: School for Advanced Urban Studies).

Rose, D. (1996) *Living in the Community* (London: Sainsbury Centre for Mental Health).

Rose, N. and Cooke, P. (1997a) 'The Betts possible way', *Municipal Journal*, 11 April, pp. 14–15.

Rose, N. and Cooke, P. (1997b) 'One thing is uncertain', *Municipal Journal*, 2 May, pp. 14–15.

Rossell, T. and Rimbau, C. (1989) 'Spain – social services in the post-Franco democracy' pp. 105–23 in B. Munday (ed.), *The Crisis in Welfare: An*

International Perspective on Social Services and Social Work (Hemel Hempstead: Harvester Wheatsheaf).

Rowe Report (1992) *Housing – A Question of Influence* (London: Royal Association for Disability and Rehabilitation).

Rowlings, C. (1981) *Social Work with Elderly People* (London: Allen & Unwin).

Rowntree Report (1980 edition) *Old People: Report of a Survey Committee on the Problems of Ageing and the Care of Old People* (New York: Arno Press).

Royal Institution of Chartered Surveyors (1996) *The Real Cost of Poor Homes* (London: The Royal Institution of Chartered Surveyors).

Rudd, T. (1958) 'Basic problems in the social welfare of the elderly', *The Almoner*, vol. 10, no. 10, pp. 348–9.

Rugg, J. (1997) *Opening Doors: Helping People on Low Income Secure Private Rented Accommodation* (York: Centre for Housing Policy, University of York).

Russell, L., Scott, D. and Wilding, P. (1996) 'The funding of local voluntary organisations', *Policy and Politics*, vol. 24, no. 4, pp. 395–412.

Ryan, J. with Thomas, F. (1980) *The Politics of Mental Handicap* (Harmondsworth: Penguin).

St Helens Metropolitan Borough Council Personal Services Department (1992) *Community Care Plan* (St Helens: The Council)

Salvage, A. (1995) *Who Will Care? Future Prospects for Family Care of Older People in the European Union* (Dublin: European Foundation for the Improvement of Living and Working Conditions).

Samson, E. (1944) *Old Age in the New World* (London: Pilot Press).

Sapey, B. (1995) 'Disabling homes: a study of the housing needs of disabled people in Cornwall', *Disability and Society*, vol. 10, no. 1, pp. 71–86.

Saunders, P. (1990) *A Nation of Home Owners* (London: Unwin Hyman).

Scull, A. (1977) *Decarceration: Community Treatment and the Deviant: A Radical View* (Englewood Cliffs: Prentice Hall).

Scull, A. (1979) *Museums of Madness: The Social Organisation of Insanity in Nineteenth Century England* (London: Allen Lane).

Seebohm Report (1968) *Report of the Committee on Local Authority and Allied Personal Services* (London: HMSO).

Servian, R. (1996) *Theorising Empowerment: Individual Power and Community Care* (Bristol: Policy Press).

Shakespeare, T. (1996) 'Power and prejudice: issues of gender, sexuality and disability', pp. 191–214 in L. Barton (ed.), *Disability and Society: Emerging Issues and Insights* (Harlow: Longman).

Shanas, E., Townsend, P., Wedderburn, D., Friis, H., Milhof, P. and Stehouwer, J. (1968) *Old People in Three Industrialised Societies* (London: Routledge & Kegan Paul).

Sheldon, J. (1948) *The Social Medicine of Old Age* (London: Oxford University Press).

Simons, K. (1995) *My Home, My Life: Innovative Ideas in Housing and Support* (London: Values into Action).

Slack, K. (1960) *Councils, Committees and Concern for the Old* (London: Codicote Press).

Smale, G. (1996) *Mapping Change and Innovation* (London: HMSO).

Smale, G. and Tucson, G. with Biehal, N. and Marsh, P. (1993) *Empowerment, Assessment, Care Management and the Skilled Worker* (London: HMSO).

Smart, G. and Means, R. (1997) *Housing and Community Care: Exploring the Role of Home Improvement Agencies* (Oxford: Anchor and Nottingham: Care & Repair).

Smith, G. and Cantley, C. (1985) *Assessing Health Care: A Study in Organisational Understanding* (Milton Keynes: Open University Press).

Smith, R., Gaster, L., Harrison, L., Martin, L., Means R. and Thistlethwaite, P. (1993) *Working Together for Better Community Care*, SAUS Study No. 7 (Bristol: School for Advanced Urban Studies).

Social Services Committee (1985) *Second Report: Community Care*, House of Commons Paper 13-1, Session 1984–85 (London: HMSO).

Steinfield, E. (1981) 'The place of old age: the meaning of housing for old people', pp. 198–246 in J. Duncan (ed.), *Housing and Identity: Cross Cultural Perspectives* (London: Croom Helm).

Stewart, M. and Taylor, M. (1995) *Empowerment and Estate Regeneration: A Critical Review* (Bristol: Policy Press).

Stuart, O. (1996) 'Yes, we mean black disabled people too', pp. 89–104 in W. Ahmad and K. Atkin (eds), *'Race' and Community Care* (Buckingham: Open University Press).

Sullivan, M. (1994) *Modern Social Policy* (Hemel Hempstead: Harvester Wheatsheaf).

Sumner, G. and Smith, R. (1969) *Planning Local Authority Services for the Elderly* (London: Allen & Unwin).

Swithinbank, A. (1991) *Audit of the Implications of Greater European Integration for Kent Social Se*rvices (Maidstone: Social Services Department, Kent County Council).

Swithinbank, A. (1996) 'The European Union and social care', pp. 67–95 in B. Munday and P. Ely (eds), *Social Care in Europe* (Hemel Hempstead: Prentice Hall).

Taylor, M. (1992) 'The changing role of the non profit sector in Britain: moving towards the market', pp. 147–75 in B. Gidron, R. Kramer and L. Salamon (eds), *Government and the Non Profit Sector in Comparative Perspective* (San Francisco: Jossey Bass).

Taylor, M., Hoyes, L., Lart, R. and Means, R. (1992) *User Empowerment in Community Care: Unravelling the Issues*, DQM Paper No. 11 (Bristol: School for Advanced Urban Studies).

Taylor, M., Langan, J. and Hoggett, P. (1995) *Encouraging Diversity: Voluntary and Private Organisations in Community Care* (Aldershot: Arena).

Tester, S. (1994) 'Implications of subsidiarity for the care of older people in Germany', *Social Policy and Administration*, vol. 28, no. 3, September, pp. 251–62.

Tester, S. (1996) *Community Care for Older People: A Comparative Perspective* (Basingstoke: Macmillan).

Thistlethwaite, P. (1997) *Finding Common Cause?* (London: Association of County Councils and Birmingham: The NHS Confederation).

Thomas, F. (1980) 'Everyday life on the ward', pp. 30–46 in J. Ryan with E. Thomas (eds), *The Politics of Mental Handicap* (Harmondsworth: Penguin).

Thompson, A. (1949) 'Problems of ageing and chronic sickness', *British Medical Journal*, 30 July, pp. 250–1.

Thompson, A. (1997) 'Working to a new rule', *Community Care*, 10–16 July, pp. 20–1.

Thompson, S. and Hoggett, P. (1996) 'Universalism, selectivism and particularism: towards a postmodern social policy', *Critical Social Policy*, vol. 16, no. 1, pp. 21–44.

Thornton, P. and Tozer, R. (1994) *Involving Older People in Planning and Evaluating Community Care* (York: Social Policy Research Unit, University of York).

Timmins, N. (1996) 'The politicians take over the asylum', *The Independent*, 21 February, p. 17.

Tinker, A., Wright, F. and Zeilig, H. (1995) *Difficult to Let Sheltered Housing* (London: HMSO).

Titmuss, R. (1968) *Commitment to Welfare* (London: Allen & Unwin).

Titmuss, R. (1976 edition) *Problems of Social Policy* (London: HMSO).

Topliss, E. (1979) *Provision for the Disabled* (Oxford: Basil Blackwell).

Townsend, P. (1963 edition) *The Family Life of Old People* (Harmondsworth: Penguin).

Townsend, P. (1964 edition) *The Last Refuge: A Survey of Residential Institutions and Homes for the Aged in England and Wales* (London: Routledge & Kegan Paul).

Townsend, P. (1981) 'The structured dependency of the elderly: the creation of social policy in the twentieth century?', *Ageing and Society*, vol. 1, no. 1, pp. 5–28.

Townsend, P. (1986) 'Ageism and social policy', pp. 15–44 in C. Phillipson and A. Walker (eds), *Ageing and Social Policy: A Critical Assessment* (Aldershot: Gower).

Tredgold, A. (1952) *A Textbook on Mental Deficiency (Amentia)*, eighth edition (London: Baillière, Tindall & Cox).

Vincent, J. (1995) *Inequality and Old Age* (London: UCL Press).

Waddington, L. (1997) 'The European Community and disability discrimination: time to address the definition of powers?', *Disability and Society*, vol. 12, no. 3, June, pp. 465–79.

Wade, B., Sawyer, L. and Bell, J. (1983) *Dependency with Dignity: Different Care Provision for the Elderly* (London: Bedford Square Press).

Wagner Report (1988) *Residential Care: A Positive Choice* (London: HMSO).

Walker, A. (1989) 'Community care', pp. 203–24 in M. McCarthy (ed.), *The New Politics of Welfare: An Agenda for the 1990s* (Basingstoke: Macmillan).

Walker, A. (1992) 'Integration, social policy and elderly citizens: towards a European agenda on ageing?', *Generations Review*, vol. 2, no. 4, pp. 2–8.

Walker, A. (1993) 'Introduction', pp. 7–17 in A. Walker, J. Alber and A.M. Guillemard (eds), *Older People in Europe: Social and Economic Policies – the 1993 Report of the European Observatory* (Brussels: Commission of the European Communities).

Walker, A. and Maltby, T. (1997) *Ageing Europe* (Buckingham: Open University Press).

Walker, C., Ryan, T. and Walker, A. (1996) *Fair Shares for All?* (Brighton: Pavilion).

Wallace, H. and Wallace, W. (eds) (1996) *Policy-Making in the European Union*, third edition (Oxford: Oxford University Press).

Watson, L. (1996) *Housing Needs and Community Care: The Housing Pathways Pilot Programme* (London: National Federation of Housing Associations).

Watson, L. (1997) *High Hopes: Making Housing and Community Care Work* (York: Joseph Rowntree Foundation).

Watson, R. (1996) 'EU personnel policy aims for zero growth', *European Voice*, vol. 2, no. 38, 17–23 October, p. 18.

Webb, A. (1991) 'Coordination, a problem in public sector management', *Policy and Politics*, vol. 19, no. 4, pp. 29–42.

Willcocks, D., Peace, S. and Kellaher, L. (1987) *Private Lives in Public Places* (London: Tavistock).

Williams, A., King, R. and Warnes, T. (1997) 'A place in the sun: international retirement migration from northern to southern Europe', *European Urban and Regional Studies*, vol. 4, no. 2, April, pp. 115–34.

Williams, C. (1996) 'An appraisal of local exchange and trading systems in the United Kingdom', *Local Economy*, vol. 1, no. 3, pp. 259–66.

Williams, R. (1976) *Keywords* (Glasgow: Fontana).

Wilson, E. (1977) *Women and the Welfare State* (London: Tavistock).

Wilson, G. (1991) 'Models of ageing and their relation to policy formation and service provision', *Policy and Politics*, vol. 19, no. 1, pp. 37–47.

Wilson, G. (1993) 'The challenge of an ageing electorate: changes in the formation of social policy in Europe?', *Journal of European Social Policy*, vol. 3, no. 2, pp. 91–105.

Wilson, V. (1996) 'People with disabilities', pp. 162–94 in B. Munday and P. Ely (eds), *Social Care in Europe* (Hemel Hempstead: Prentice Hall).

Wistow, G. (1995) 'Aspirations and realities: community care at the crossroads', *Health and Social Care in the Community*, vol. 3, no. 4, pp. 227–40.

Wistow, G. (1996) 'The changing scene in Britain', pp. 61–79 in T. Harding, B. Meredith and G. Wistow (eds), *Options for Long-Term Care* (London: HMSO).

Wistow, G. and Lewis, H. (1996) *Preventive Services for Older People: Current Approaches and Future Opportunities* (Oxford: Anchor Trust).

Wistow, G., Knapp, M., Hardy, B. and Allen, C. (1992) 'From providing to enabling: local authorities and the mixed economy of social care', *Public Administration*, vol. 70, no. 1, pp. 25–46.

Wistow, G., Knapp, M., Hardy, B. and Allen, C. (1994) *Social Care in a Mixed Economy* (Buckingham: Open University Press).

Wistow, G., Knapp, M., Hardy, B., Forder, J., Kendall, J. and Manning, R. (1996) *Social Care Markets: Progress and Prospects* (Buckingham: Open University Press).

Wolfensberger, W. and Thomas, S. (1983) *Program Analysis of Service Systems' Implementations of Normalisation Goals (PASSING): A Method of Evaluating the Quality of Human Services according to the Principles of Normalisation, Normalisation Criteria and Ratings Manual*, second edition (Toronto: National Institute on Mental Retardation).

Working Group on Joint Planning (1985) *Progress in Partnership* (London: Department of Health and Social Security).

Wright, D. and Digby, A. (eds) (1996) *From Idiocy to Mental Deficiency: Historical Perspectives on People with Learning Disabilities* (London: Routledge).

Young, R. and Wistow, G. (1996) 'Development of independent home care in 1995 UKHCA survey', *The Mixed Economy of Care*, Bulletin No. 4, pp. 14–15 (Canterbury: Personal Social Services Research Unit, University of Kent and Leeds, Nuffield Institute for Health, University of Leeds).

Zarb, G. (1993) 'The dual experience of ageing with a disability', pp. 186–96 in J. Swain, V. Finkelstein, S. French and M. Oliver (eds), *Disabling Barriers – Enabling Environments* (London: Sage).

Ziomas, D. (1991) *The Elderly in Greece: A Review of their Current Situation with reference to Economic and Social Policies*, Athens, March (submission to the EC Observatory on Older People).

Index

'abandonment': to state care   45
Abberley, P.   10
Abbott, P.   29
Abel-Smith, B.   61–2
Abrahamson, P.   199, 208, 249
Abrams, P.   5
acquired rights directive   224–5, 227
Action in Favour of the
      Disabled   222
Age Concern   24, 126, 155
ageing: cultural stereotype   41–2
Ageing, Intergroup on   220–1
Ahmad, W.   77
Alber, J.   203, 204, 205, 206, 210,
      211, 212
Allen, I.   150
Alzheimer's disease   see dementia
Amira, A.   205, 212
Amsterdam Treaty (1997)   218, 221
Anderson, M.   226
Anderson, R.   201
Arber, S.   42, 77, 80
Arblaster, L.   195
Archer, C.   249
arts, participation in   243
Askham, J.   77
assessment
   financial   54, 107–8, 121–2
   of needs   54, 96–7, 119–21; in
         White Paper   56–7, 110,
         138–9
asylums   27–8, 31
Atkin, K.   77, 130
Atkinson, D.   32
Audit Commission   14
   (1985)   12
   (1986)   33, 51–2, 128, 143, 230,
         247
   (1992)   102–3, 113–14, 115, 235
   (1994)   156
   (1996)   121, 138
   (1997)   236, 237
Aves, G.   4
Avon, supported housing in   177

Bailey, R.   67
Baldock, J.   152, 207, 208, 209, 211,
      212, 213, 237
Baldwin, S.   55, 56, 59, 80, 179
Balniel, Lord
      (D.A.R. Lindsay)   147
Barclay Report   232
Barnes, C.   41
Barnes, M.   97, 100, 242, 249
Baron, S.   2, 3
Bartlett, W.   63–4, 86, 229, 230, 233,
      234, 247, 248
Barton, L.   78, 247
BASW   194
Baxter, C.   76
Becker, S.   104
Begum, N.   76
Bell, J.   149
Beresford, P.   90
Bernard, M.   42
Bertelsen, O.   214
Betty, C.   221
Beveridge Report (1942)   45, 61
Bewley, C.   90–1, 248
Biggs, S.   59, 61, 170
Bines, W.   157, 198
black/ethnic communities   91
   and disability   76–7, 99
block purchasing   134
Boateng, Paul   240–1
Boddy, M.   65
Bone, M.   9
Bongers, P.   221, 249
Bornat, J.   247
Bosanquet, N.   4, 55, 84
Boucher Report   148
Bovell, V.   123
Bowl, R.   24
Bradford, I.   185
Brake, M.   67
Brauns, H.-J.   205
Braye, S.   70, 90
Brenton, M.   179
Brewerton, J.   189

British Council of Organisations of
Disabled People 60, 75
British Medical Association 155
Brockington, R. 146
Brown, M. 147
Brown, R. 146
Buckinghamshire: and
assessment 120–1
Buckley, M. 226
Burrows, R. 67
Butler, F. 249

Caldock, K. 120
Cambridge, P. 113, 174
Campbell, J. 74, 76, 77, 78, 95, 99,
248
Cantley, C. 44
Care and Repair 185
care(rs), informal 6, 10–11, 38–40,
60, 79–80
and 1990 Act reforms 235–7
in EU 200–3
v. users 78–81, 237
care management 110–14, 122–3
approaches 114, 116–19
and assessment 119–22
and CPA 156–9
need for investment 211–12
care programme approach
(CPA) 156–9
Carers (Recognition and Services)
Act (1995) 7, 60, 96
Caring for People see White Paper
Carter, T. 78
'cascade of change' 103, 113–14,
115, 235
case management 211–12
central government
v. local government 13–14, 67–8,
103
see also Conservative; Labour
certification 27–8, 30
Cervi, B. 105
Challis, D. 111
Challis, L. 11
Chancellor of the Exchequer 232
Chapman, K. 221
Chappell, A. 73
Cheshire Homes 26
Chetwynd, M. 104

Children Act (1948) 23
Chronically Sick and Disabled
Persons Act (1970) 6–7, 26, 97,
185
Church: and social care 201
'Cinderella services' 16–17, 32, 238
reasons for neglect 34–44
Clapham, D. 194
Clark, H. 151, 248
Clarke, H. 238
Clarke, J. 247
Clarke, L. 150
Clegg, S. 74
Clough, R. 1, 12, 229, 249
Clunis, Christopher 157
Cobbold, C. 189, 190
Cohen, S. 74
collaboration *see* joint working
collective lifestyles 179
Collins, J. 175
Colwell, Maria 24
Comité des Sages: 1996 report 218
community, concept of 2–3
Community Care 104, 167, 248
Community Care (Direct Payments)
Act (1996) 7, 60, 85
complaints procedure: in 1990
Act 58, 97
computers: and care
management 122–3
Conservative policies
and 1990 Act reforms 230–1, 232
on benefits for disabled 35
on housing 179–80
on ILF 85
on joint commissioning 162–5
on mental health services 157–60
on social care 63, 64, 68, 83
see also White Paper; National
Health Service and
Community Care Act; New
Right; quasi-markets
consumer choice: and
empowerment 212
continuing care 152–5, 231–2
contracting-out of social care:
attitudes 130–2
Cooke, P. 227
co-operative living schemes 179
Coote, A. 64, 95–6

COREPER   215
Corrigan, P.   244
Coss, S.   218
cost: of care   *see* funding
Council of Ministers (EU)   215–16
counselling: in care
    management   122
Cox, C.   175
CPA: and care management   156–9
Craig, G.   106
Crane, M.   198
Cranston, M.   96
Crowther, M.   17
cruelty: in institutions   32–3, 45
'C Team' (pressure group)   214

Daatland, S.O.   202, 207
Dalley, G.   11, 40, 80, 179, 247
DANSOC (care agency)   221
Dant, T.   37
Darton, D.   189
Davey, J.   84
Davies, B.   111, 112
Davies Report   157
Davison, B.   171
Deakin, N.   62, 64, 129
decentralisation: of services   64–8
'defectiveness, mental/moral'   29
De Jasay, A.   94
dementia, people with   238
    and assessment   108–9, 121
Denmark: social care   208, 210
    of older people   207–8; and
    empowerment   213–14
Department of Health   14
    (1989)   63, 137, 150; *see also*
        White Paper
    (1990)   6, 90, 110, 119, 123, 247
    (1991)   1, 70, 109, 111, 124
    (1994)   195
    (1995)   154, 156, 157–9, 163, 164,
        248
    (1997)   103, 159, 195, 222, 231,
        235–6, 237, 249
Department of Health and Social
    Security   5, 24, 33, 48, 49, 140
Department of the
    Environment   180, 195, 249
dependency/risk model   119–21
Devon: care management   114, 116

Dieck, M.   202, 206, 209
Digby, A.   17, 38, 247
Dilnot, Andrew   239
direct payments: legislation   7, 60,
    85
disability   8–10
    cultural stereotypes   41, 42
    political economy approach   34–7
    social model   10, 36, 75–6, 77
disability movement   74–8, 95–6, 99
disabled facilities grant   189, 191,
    192–3
disabled people
    accommodation agencies   191
    care   144–5; postwar   25–7
    and EU policies   218, 222–4
Disabled People International   75
Disabled Persons (Services,
    Consultation and
    Representation) Act (1986)   7,
    96–7
discharge: from hospital   150–1
    and NHS changes   152, 154
district nurses   145, 146, 147, 150
Dobson, N.   227
doctors   224–5
    see also general practitioners
*Domesday Book of the Hospital
    Services*   20–1
domiciliary care   *see* home care
Dominelli, L.   1
Downey, R.   240, 241
Drake, R.   25
Dumfries and Galloway: joint
    working   166–7

Eaton, L.   163
'Ecoworks' project   242
Edelman, M.   44
Education Reform Act (1988)   63
Edwards, P.   133
elderly   *see* older people
eligibility criteria: for care   119–21,
    122
Elliott, D.   9
Ely, P.   207, 209, 212, 213
Emerson, E.   48, 72, 174–5, 249
empowerment   70–2, 82, 233, 236
    and disability movement   74–6,
    95–6, 99

in EU 212–14
local initiatives 242–5
and normalisation 72–3, 74
service requirements 100–1
strategies 82, 95; 'exit' 83–8,
100, 212, 213; rights 94–8,
100; struggle 98–100;
'voice' 83, 87–94, 100
of users: *v.* carers 78–81
equal opportunities: in EU 226
Esping-Andersen, G. 249
ethnic minorities 91
and disability 76–7, 99
Eurobarometer Surveys
(1992) 200, 214, 219, 221–2
(1993) 202, 204
Eurolink Age 220
European Commission 214–15,
216, 217, 220
European Disability Forum 223
European Disabled People's
Parliament 223
European Parliament 215, 220
European Senior Citizens
Charter 219–20
European Seniors Parliaments 219,
221
European Social Policy
Forum 218
European Union (EU)
care workers' mobility 224–7
and family in caring 200–3
institutional care 204–8
mixed care economy 208–9; and
empowerment 212–14; and
joint working 209–12
policy-making 214–16; in
community care 217–27
user empowerment 212–14
European Year Against Racism,
Xenophobia and
Anti-Semitism 221, 226
European Year of Older People and
Solidarity between the
Generations 220, 222
Evandrou, M. 155–6
Evers, A. 202, 208, 209, 211, 213
'exit' (empowerment strategy) 83–8,
100, 212, 213
Eyden, J. 25

Falkingham, J. 155–6
families: in caring 10–11, 38–40, 79,
80–1
in EU 200–3
'feeble-minded' people 29
feminists: on caring 11, 79–80
finances *see* funding
finance staff: *v.* social workers 108,
121
Finch, J. 10, 11
Finkelstein, V. 27
Firth Report 50
Fisher, M. 112
Fletcher, P. 244
floating support schemes 176, 178
Flynn, N. 63
Foord, M. 195
Forder, J. 128, 134, 248
Fordism: and post-Fordism 67
forms, assessment 108, 121
Forrest, R. 170
Foucault, M. 37, 71, 73
Fowles, A. 37–8
France: welfare state 200
Franklin, B. 194
Fraser, D. 247
Friend, J. 143
Fudge, Colin 65
Fulcher, G. 73
funding 46, 103–5
recommendations: Audit
Commission (1986) 51;
Griffiths Report 53–5;
1989 White Paper 57–8
for residential care 49–50, 54,
107–9, 231–2
of voluntary sector 128–9
see also quasi-markets
future of community care
under Labour
government 238–41
local initiatives 242–5

Gaster, L. 91
Gateshead: care management 111
Gavilan, H. 173
gender: and care *see* women
General Household Surveys 10,
80

general practitioners (GPs)   139
  as fundholders   138; and
      continuing care   154, 155
  and welfare services   54, 144,
      145–6
genetics: and learning
    difficulties   28, 29
George, V.   249
Germany
  empowerment of elderly   213
  and EU policy   217, 218
  institutional care   205–7
  mixed care economy   209; and
      joint working   210–11
Giannichedda, M.G.   204
Gibbins, J.   28
Gillie Report   145
Ginn, J.   42, 77, 80
Gladstone, D.   28
Glendinning, C.   90–1, 248
Glennerster, H.   118, 121, 122,
    155–6, 237, 247, 248, 249
Godlove, C.   148
Goffman, E.   37
Goldsmith, M.   249
Goodwin, S.   31–2, 38
Grant, G.   81
grants
  disabled facilities   189, 191, 192–3
  for home improvement   185,
      186–7
Greece: care of elderly   204–5, 212
Green, H.   10
Grey Panthers: in Denmark   213–14
Griffiths, S.   105, 183
Griffiths Report (1988)   47, 63, 152,
    247
  proposals   52–5, 83–4, 168; and
      reactions   55–6
Groves, D.   11, 84
Guardian   21–2, 45, 231, 239
Guardian Society   70, 231
Guillebaud Report   48, 145, 148
Guillemard, A.M.   204, 205, 210,
    212
Gurney, C.   170, 248
Gwynne, G.   26

Haber, C.   42
Hadley, R.   1, 64–5, 229, 249

Haldane, J.   2, 3
Ham, Christopher   43, 137, 248
Hambleton, Robin   66
Hammersmith and Fulham: care
    management   116–17
Hamnett, C.   84
HANDYNET   223
Hantrais, L.   203, 223, 249
Harding, T.   231–2, 249
Harris, A.   24
Harris, R.   225
Harrison, Lyn   50, 55, 56, 78, 138
Hasler, F.   240
Hatch, S.   64–5
Hatton, C.   174–5, 249
Hayward, D.   169, 170
Health Advisory Service   35
health services
  in Griffiths Report   54
  and social services   137–41,
      149–50; in continuing
      care   152–5; and hospital
      discharge   150–2; in
      institutional care   147–9;
      joint working   141–7;
      working relationships   142–3,
      165–6
Health Services and Public Health
    Act (1968)   24
health visitors   145, 146
health workers: in EU   224–5
HELIOS (action
    programme)   222–3
Henwood, M.   151, 153
Herbert, G.   244
Herbert Report   146
Heywood, F.   189, 191, 192–3,
    249
Higgins, J.   168, 169, 173–4, 175,
    249
Hill, M.   43–4, 76, 225, 247
Hirschman, A.   83
history of community care   16–46
Hoggett, Paul   64, 66–7, 67–8, 88–9,
    94, 247
Holmans, A.   180–1
Holstein, B.E.   210
'home'   168–70
  for older people   170–3, 242
  v. institutions   168, 169, 173–5

home care 6–7
  and health/social services 146,
    150
  independent provision 24, 39,
    126, 128, 133
  v. residential care 4–5, 43
  see also care(rs), informal
home improvement
  agencies (HIAs) 185, 191
  grants 185, 186–7
homelessness 157, 181
Hoogvelt, A. 1
Hooton, S. 180
HORIZON programme 218,
  223–4
Hospital Plan (1962) 4
hospitals
  discharge from 150–1; and NHS
    changes 152, 154
  mental 28, 31, 32–3; *v.*
    community care 38, 47–9,
    50, 51, 140
  PAIs 18–23
  v. residential care 4, 148–9
House of Lords Library 60
housing
  and access 188–91
  grants: for adaptation 189, 191,
    192–3; for repair 185, 186–7
  mainstream 179–80;
    affordability/rents 181–3;
    availability 180–1;
    conditions 184–91
  sheltered 172, 176–7
  supported/'special needs' 175–9
  workers: *v.* social workers 194
  see also 'home'
Housing Acts
  (1988) 179, 182, 188
  (1996) 179
housing associations 176, 180
  funding problems 182, 188
housing benefit 182, 183
Housing Corporation 176
Housing Grants, Construction and
    Regeneration Act (1996) 186,
    192
Hoyes, L.: publications
  (1987) 50
  (1993) 58, 87, 100, 130, 160, 233

  (1994) 92, 114, 116–18, 119, 122,
    123, 134–5, 173, 237, 248
  (1996) 175–6
  (1997) 235
Hudson, B. 59, 61, 111, 134, 141–2,
    143, 160, 163–4, 178–9, 248
Hugman, R. 212, 249
Hutchinson, J. 244
Huws Jones, R. 148, 153
Huxham, C. 141, 248

Idiots Act 1886, 28
'idiots/imbeciles' 27, 29
impairment: *v.* disability ́ 75
  see also disability: social model
implementation deficit 43–4, 55
Independent, 155, 157
Independent Living Fund
    (ILF) 84–5, 95
Industrial Revolution
  and disability 25, 36
information technology: and care
    management 122–3, 132, 234–5
Inside Housing, 105, 182
institutional care 37–8
  in EU 204–8
  in PAIs 18–23
  postwar policy 147–9
  and scandals 45
  v. home 168, 169, 173–5
  see also hospitals; residential care;
    workhouses
INTEGRA programme 218
Intergroup on Ageing 220–1
International Year of Disabled
    People 75, 222
International Year of Older Persons
    (UN 1999) 222
Irvine, E. 145
Italy: institutional care 204

Jack, R. 70, 248
Jamieson, A. 203, 207, 213
Jani-Le Bris, H. 203
Jarre, D. 206
Jenkins, G. 109
Johnson, M. 41, 235
Johnson, N. 65, 208
Johnson, P. 36
joint commissioning 135, 160–5

joint working
  in EU 209–12
  by health/social services 140–7,
    165–7; in care management/
    CPA 143–4, 156–9; and
    continuing care 152–5; and
    hospital discharge 150–2;
    and housing 195; and
    institutional care 147–50; in
    mental health 140, 155–60;
    in planning/
    commissioning 90–1, 134–5,
    160–5
  by housing/social services 191,
    194–8; and health
    services 195
Jones, C. 249
Jones, Kathleen 27, 32–3, 37–8, 46,
  247

Kellaher, L. 173
Kenny, D. 133
Kestenbaum, A. 85, 95
Keynes, John Maynard 61
King, R. 221
King's Fund Centre 48, 73
Klausen, K 249
Knapp, M. 129, 162
Kramer, D. 205

Labour policies
  (1997–): and future of care 64, 98,
    238–41; plans for NHS 138;
    and Social Chapter 219,
    226–7; on social housing 180
  projected (post-1992) 103
Laing, W.L. 50
Land, H. 11
Landewehr, R. 206
Langan, J. 107, 108–9, 121, 170–1,
  172, 194, 242, 244
Langan, M. 59, 61
Lart, R. 92, 157
Laurie, L. 177
Lavan, A. 225
Laverty, S. 19
Lavery, R. 109
learning difficulties, people with 8
  history of services 27–33
  hospital *v.* community care 47–9

and normalisation 48, 72–3
  resettlement 173–5
Leat, D. 243, 247, 249
Leather, P. 184, 185, 189
Le Grand, J. 63–4, 86, 229, 230,
  233, 234, 247, 248
Leibfried, S. 249
LETS schemes 245, 246
Lewis, H. 242
Lewis, J. 118, 121, 122, 134, 237,
  247, 248, 249
Liebig, P. 38
lifetime homes: standards 189, 190
Lipsky, M. 143
Loader, B. 67
local government
  and care reforms 58, 232–5;
    attitudes towards 130–2
  and future of care 242–5
  reorganisation (LGR) 105–6
  service decentralisation 65–8
  v. central government 13–14,
    67–8, 103
  see also specific departments
Local Government Act (1929) 18,
  19
Local Government and Housing Act
  · (1989) 179, 182–3, 188
Local Government Management
  Board (LGMB) 133
London Federation of Housing
  Associations 183
long-term (continuing) care 152–5,
  231–2
Lowe, R. 247
Lukes, S. 71, 248
'lunatics' 27
Lund, B. 195
Lundy, L. 109
Lunt, N. 103
Lyons, K. 225

Maastricht Treaty 219
McCafferty, P. 176, 181
McCaskie, K. 188–9
McEwan, P. 19
Macfarlane, A. 177
McGrath, M. 81
Mackintosh, S. 189
Maclennan, D. 183

Malin, N. 27, 29, 30, 31
Malpass, Peter 183, 248
Maltby, T. 200, 207, 214, 219–20, 222, 249
management *see* care management
Manchester Guardian, 21–2, 45
Mann, A. 148
Manthorpe, Jill 106, 160
Mares, P. 185
marketisation *see* quasi-markets
Marsh, A. 183
Martin, J. 9
Martin, L. 91
Martin, M. 17, 18, 21
Matarasso, F. 243
Matthews, O. 19
Meade, K. 42
Means, Robin: publications
    (1985) 19, 22, 24, 35, 43, 126, 145, 147, 248
    (1986) 38, 148, 149
    (1988) 55, 56
    (1990) 78
    (1993) 58, 130, 170, 248
    (1994) 83, 92, 134–5
    (1995) 108–9
    (1996) 8, 78, 107, 121, 134, 170–1, 177, 181
    (1997) 138, 142–3, 170, 172, 185, 186–7, 191, 192–3, 195–8, 242, 249
    (1998) 247
means-testing 107
medical officers of health 144–5, 146
Meehan, E. 226
Meltzer, H. 9
MENCAP 48, 128
Mental Deficiency Act (1913) 29–30
Mental Deficiency Committee: Report (1929) 30–1
Mental Health Acts
    (1959) 32
    (1983) 156, 158
Mental Health Foundation 10, 156, 160, 174
Mental Health (Patients in the Community) Act (1995) 157
mental health problems, people with 10
    and CPA 155–60

history of services 27–8, 31, 32–3
and homelessness 157, 181
hospitals *v.* community care 38, 47–9, 50, 51, 140
in Italy 204
mental hospitals 28, 31, 32–3
    v. community care 38, 47–9, 50, 51, 140
mentally handicapped *see* learning difficulties, people with
Meredith, B. 249
Midgley, G. 177, 178
migration, retirement 221–2
Milburn, Alan 241
Millar, J. 201, 212, 249
Milier, E. 26
MIND (organisation) 48, 128
Minister: of Community Care 53, 55, 57
Ministry of Health 24, 148–9, 154
Mishra, R. 61, 62, 64
mixed economy of care 100, 126–35, 231, 240–1
    in EU 208–14
    White Paper on 1, 6, 138–41, 150
    see also quasi-markets
mobility housing 188, 189
Moriarty, J. 238
Moroney, R. 40
Morris, Alf 25
Morris, C. 20
Morris, J.: publications
    (1990) 41, 42, 188
    (1991) 75, 80–1, 237
    (1993) 40, 80
    (1995) 101, 178
    (1996) 77, 78, 247
Morris, P. 32
Morrison, T. 184, 185
Munday, B. 203, 213, 220, 221
Murie, Alan 248
Murphy, E. 27, 28, 32

Nash, C. 78
National Assistance Act (1948) 6, 22, 23–4, 126, 145, 147–8
    on care of disabled 25, 26
National Assistance (Amendment) Act (1962) 24

National Federation of Housing
    Associations (NFHA)   176
National Health Service
    changes: and hospital
        discharge   152, 154
    and PAIs   21
    and people with learning
        difficulties   31–3
    Trusts   137–8
National Health Service Acts
    (1946)   23, 31, 145
    (1973)   146, 147
    (1977)   24
National Health Service and
    Community Care Act (1990)   1,
        6, 47, 58, 137
    and empowerment   88, 90, 97–8,
        233, 236, 237
    and quasi-markets   85, 229–30
    reforms: evaluation   229–38
National Health Service
    Reorganisation Act (1973)   49
neglect of services: reasons   34–44
Neill, J.   151
networks
    awareness   143, 165
    of local services   244–5
Newby, Jonathan   157
Newman, J.   247
New Right   62–3, 67–8, 83, 94
Newton, J.   160
NHS   *see* National Health Service
Niner, P.   172, 176
Nocon, A.   230
Nolan, M.   80, 81, 120, 248
normalisation   48, 72–3, 74
Norton, A.   243
NOW (New Opportunities for
    Women)   226
Nuffield Provincial Hospitals
    Trust   20, 21
nurses
    district   145, 146, 147, 150
    in EU   224–5
nursing homes   *see* residential care

'obligations': in caring   10–11
Observatories (EC)
    on Older People   205, 212, 219
    on Social Exclusion   203

Office for National Statistics   180
Office of Population Censuses and
    Surveys (OPCS)   8, 10
Official Journal: of EC   216
older people   41–2, 77–8
    care   4–5, 243; in
        Denmark   207–8;
        funding   231–2; in
        Germany   206; in
        Greece   204–5, 212; health *v.*
        social services   144–7; history
        of services   17–24, 45;
        hospital *v.* residential   148–9;
        planning process
        involvement   91
    with dementia   108–9, 121, 238
    in EU   212–14, 218–22
    housing   177–8; costs   183;
        owner-occupation   181, 185,
        188, 231–2
    and idea of home   170–3, 242
    and pensions/retirement   17–18,
        35, 36, 83–4, 219, 221–2
Oldman, C.   183
Old People's Welfare
    Committees   24, 126
Oliver, M.: publications
    (1990)   34, 36, 75, 247
    (1996)   35, 71, 74–5, 76, 77, 78, 95,
        99, 247, 248
Olk, T.   202, 208, 209, 213
Owens, P.   142
owner-occupation   180
    by older people   181, 185, 188;
        and sale of houses   231–2
Oxfordshire, care management
    in   117–18

Pahl, R.   170
PAIs   18–23
Parker, G.   55, 56, 59, 238
Parker, R.   16, 23–4, 27, 37, 49, 247
Parton, N.   24
Patient's Charter   151
pavements: and disabled   243
Peace, S.   173
Pearson, M.   175
pensions   17–18, 36, 83–4, 219
    and labour market   17, 35
Perri   6, 243, 249

Personal Social Services Research
Unit (PSSRU): study 111–13
Peters, T. 67
Phillips, J. 122
Phillipson, C. 18, 35, 247
physically impaired *see* disabled
people
Piachaud, D. 244
Pieda Plc 191
Pierson, P. 249
planning: for care 90–1
failures (1980s) 50–2
involving users/carers 91–3, 135
and joint commissioning 134–5,
160–5
Plant, R. 96
Platz, M. 214
Plowden, B. 243
Poor Law: in 20th century 17, 18
Poor Law Act (1930) 18
post-Fordism: and care
reforms 64–8
Potter, P. 201
Powell, Enoch 32
Powell, R. 241
power: and resistance 71–2, 73–4,
98–9
Pressman, J. 43
Preston-Shoot, M. 70, 90
Price Waterhouse: report 124–5
priority matrices: in care 119–21,
122
Propper, C. 55, 84
Psichiatria Democratica 204
public assistance institutions
(PAIs) 18–23
purchasing: by social services 133–4
and purchaser–provider
splits 123–6
Pynos, J. 38

qualifications: in EU 224–5
quasi-markets 1, 63–4, 83, 137,
229–30
and conditions for success 85–7,
233–5
criticised 59, 229
developing: examples 114,
116–19
Qureshi, H. 230

race: and disability 76–7, 99
Race, D. 48, 72
Ramon, S. 82, 204
Randolph, B. 182
Rapoport, A. 169–70
Red Cross 24, 126
Reeves, D. 188–9
Rehabilitation International 75
resettlement: and 'home' 173–5
residential care 37
assessment/payment 54, 107–9,
231–2
private sector growth 49–50
v. community care 4–5
v. hospital care 148–9
see also institutional care
retirement 18, 36, 221–2
Richards, E. 232
Richardson, J. 249
Rimbau, C. 211
Riseborough, M. 172, 176, 183
risk/dependency model 119–21
Ritchie, J. 157
Robb, B. 32, 48
Roberts, G. 97, 98
Roberts, N. 18–19
Roebuck, J. 17
Rolfe, S. 170–1
Room, G. 221
Rose, D. 160
Rose, N. 227
Rossell, T. 211
Rous, John 157
Rowe Report 188
Rowlings, C. 41–2
Rowntree, Joseph, Foundation 232
Rowntree Report 22
Royal Commissions
on the Care and Control of the
Feeble-Minded (1908) 29
on Local Government in Greater
London (1960) 145–6
on Mental Illness and Mental
Deficiency (1954–7) 32
Royal Institution of Chartered
Surveyors 181
Rudd, T. 39
Rugg, J. 182
Russell, L. 104
Ryan, J. 29, 30

St Helens   118, 161
Salvage, A.   203
Samson, E.   22
Sapey, B.   189
Sapsford, R.   29
Saunders, P.   170, 174
Sawyer, L.   149
scandals: over care   32–3, 45, 48
  in community   45–6, 157
Scull, A.   27
Second World War   61
  effects on care   19–20; of
       elderly   21, 45
'Seebohm factories'   67
Seebohm Report (1968)   67
Servian, R.   70, 71, 73, 248
Shakespeare, T.   42
Shanas, E.   39, 40
Sheldon, J.   38–9
sheltered housing   172, 176–7
shopping: and elderly/disabled   244
Simons, K.   175
Slack, K.   128
Smale, G.   90, 143–4
Smart, G.   185, 189, 191, 249
Smith, G.   44
Smith, R.   24
Smith, Randall: publications
  (1969)   24
  (1985)   19, 22, 24, 35, 43, 126, 145,
       147, 248
  (1993)   143
  (1998)   247
Social Chapter: implications   226–7
Social Charter: and older
       people   218–19
social services   11–13
  and care management   110–23
  and funding reforms   106–9
  and Griffiths Report   54, 55
  and health services   *see under*
       health services
  as lead agency   56–7, 102–36, 243
  and mixed care economy   126–35
  and purchasing   123–6, 133–4
Social Services Committee   50–1
Social Services Inspectorate   1, 14,
       70, 109, 111
social workers
  and EU policies   225, 226–7

and financial assessment   107,
       108, 121–2
  v. finance staff   108, 121
  v. housing workers   194
Spain, joint working in   211
'special needs' housing   175–9
spot contracts: *v.* block
       purchasing   133–4
Stanley, N.   160
Staying Put projects   185
Steinfield, E.   173
Stevens, A.   76
Stewart, M.   185
Stuart, O.   99
Sullivan, M.   63, 247
Sumner, G.   24
supported housing   175–9
Swithinbank, A.   217, 224, 226–7

Taylor, M.   81, 82, 83, 93, 104, 129,
       185
Taylor-Gooby, P.   249
tendering   127, 227
Tester, S.   199, 202, 205, 206, 208,
       210, 211, 249
Thanet: care management   111–12
Thatcherism: and social care   63, 64
Thistlethwaite, P.   165
Thomas, F.   29, 30
Thomas, Frank   33
Thomas, S.   72
Thompson, A.   39, 98, 227
Thompson, S.   64
Thornton, P.   91
TIDE projects   222
Timmins, N.   46
Tinker, A.   172, 176
Titmuss, K.   61–2
Titmuss, R.   2, 3–4, 19, 20, 144, 145
Topliss, E.   25
Townsend, P.   22–3, 26, 35, 37, 39,
       40, 43, 171
Tozer, R.   91
Transfer of Undertakings (Protection
       of Employment) Regulations
       (TUPE) (1981)   227
Tredgold, A.   30
Trevillion, S.   90
Twigg, J.   80, 179

UK Home Care Association
  (UKHCA): 1996 survey   133
Ungerson, C.   152, 237
users: of community care   7–10
  and 1990 Act reforms   235–8
  empowerment   70–101, 233, 236
  v. carers   78–81, 237
  see also subgroups, *e.g.* older
    people

Values into Action   175
Vincent, J.   84
'voice' (empowerment strategy)   83,
  87–94, 100
voluntary sector   24, 49
  funding   104–5, 128–9
  and home care   39, 126

Waddington, L.   223, 249
Wade, B.   149
Wagner Report (1988)   5, 198
Walker, A.: publications
  (1989)   55
  (1991)   204, 205, 210, 212
  (1992)   207
  (1996)   100
  (1997)   200, 214, 219–20, 222, 249
Walker, C.   7, 8
walking: and disabled   243
Wallace, H.   249
Wallace, W.   249
Walsh, Kieron   64
Warman, A.   201, 212, 249
Warnes, T.   221
wars   45
  see also Second World War
Waterman, R.   67
Watson, L.   181, 214, 249
Webb, A.   141, 144, 166
Webb, J.   244
Webb, S.   238
welfare   *see* social services
welfare pluralism   65
  v. welfare mix   208
  see also mixed economy
welfare state   61–3, 64
  institutional   199, 202, 205–7, 209,
    210–11, 213
  modern   199–200, 202–3, 207–8,
    208, 210, 213–14

residual   199, 212
rudimentary   199, 204–5, 205,
  208, 211, 212
wheelchair housing   188, 189
White Paper (1989)   47, 56–9, 63,
  168, 247
  on care management/
    planning   90, 110
  on informal care   60, 79
  on mixed economy   1, 6, 126, 128,
    138–41, 150
  on purchaser–provider
    splits   123–4
  on users/empowerment   7, 70
Whitting, G.   226
Wildavsky, A.   43
Wilkins, N.   185
Willcocks, D.   173
Williams, A.   221
Williams, C.   245
Williams, J.   151
Williams, Raymond   3
Wilson, E.   11
Wilson, G.   41, 214, 247
Wilson, V.   223, 249
Wistow, G.: publications
  (1992)   131–2
  (1994)   130
  (1995)   152, 247
  (1996)   125, 128, 129, 132, 133,
    160, 237, 242, 248, 249
Wolfensberger, W.   72
Wolff, R.   206
women
  as carers   10, 11, 38–9, 79–81, 226
  disabled   42, 77
workhouses   37, 38
  and elderly   17, 18
Working Group on Joint
  Planning   51
Wright, D.   247
W(R)VS   24, 126

Young, R.   133

Zarb, G.   7
Zill, G.   201
Ziomas, D.   204, 205, 212
Zito, Jonathan   157